MARK STEYN…

…on Bob Hope:
He was the first comedian to run himself as a business, and he succeeded brilliantly. *Time* magazine reported in 1967 that he was worth half a billion dollars. Asked about the figure, Hope said, "Anyone can do it. All you have to do is save a million dollars a year for 500 years."

…on Idi Amin:
His Excellency was borne aloft in a sedan chair balanced with some difficulty on the shoulders of four spindly Englishmen from Kampala's business community, while another humbled honky walked behind holding the parasol. When it came to the white man's burden, the British could talk the talk. But that night the 300lb Amin made them walk the walk.

…on Strom Thurmond:
Ol' Strom had just cast an appreciative bipartisan eye over the petite brunette liberal extremist. Senator Boxer gave an involuntary shudder. Glancing down, I was horrified to see an unusually large lizard slithering up and down my arm. On closer inspection, it proved to be Strom's hand. Presumably he'd mistaken my dainty elbow for Barbara's, but who knows? In how many other national legislatures can a guy just wander in off the street and find himself being petted by a 97-year-old Senator?

…on the Princess of Wales:
August is the "silly season" in the British press, and this year the Princess had done her bit for her media chums, embarking on a dizzying summer romance that brought an extravagant array of her lover's ex-girlfriends tumbling out of the cupboard. A good time was had by all. On the very last day of the silly season, when the Queen's subjects woke to the news that Diana was dead, it seemed in some strange way the best plot twist of all. "I didn't think it was real," a friend told me sadly.

MARK
STEYN

can be read regularly in *The Atlantic Monthly*, *The Chicago Sun-Times*, New Zealand's *Investigate* magazine, *The Jerusalem Post*, *Maclean's* in Canada, America's *National Review*, *The New Criterion*, *The New York Sun*, *The Orange County Register*, *The Washington Times*, *The Western Standard*, many other publications around the world, and at SteynOnline.com.

COLLECT THE SET!

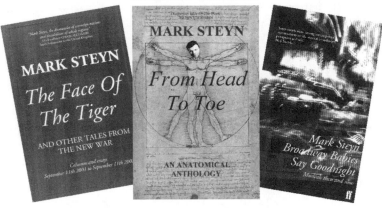

The Face Of The Tiger (2002)	Mark Steyn From Head To Toe (2004)	Broadway Babies Say Goodnight (1997)

www.SteynOnline.com

To Patrick,
Welcome to the club!

[signature]

MARK STEYN'S

Passing Parade

OBITUARIES & APPRECIATIONS

STOCKADE
BOOKS

Published in 2006 by
Stockade Books
PO Box 30
Woodsville, New Hampshire
03785

Printed and bound in the Province of Québec (Canada)

ISBN 0-9731570-1-1

First Edition

LIFE BRIEFS

I STARTED dabbling in obits when I was on the musical comedy beat at *The Independent* in London. It was mostly half-forgotten showbiz footnotes none of the cooler cats wanted to write about - Hazel Dawn, say, who introduced the famous "Pink Lady Waltz" on Broadway. Later, at *The Spectator*, I had a freer hand than most film critics and, in weeks when I couldn't face *Dude, Where's My Car? 7* or whatever other delights the release schedule held, I'd fall gratefully on the opportunity to memorialize a recently deceased screenwriter.

Later still, for an op-ed columnist at *The National Post* in Canada, it was a welcome break from the grind of war and politics to write about Lionel Bart or Princess Margaret. I don't have any great theories about column-writing except that you should vary the diet: jihad, jihad, jihad, jihad, elderly London literary queen, jihad, jihad, jihad, hard-living princess, jihad, jihad. It keeps readers from figuring they've got you completely pegged.

It was Cullen Murphy who made me an obituarist in the formal sense, when he asked me to start the "Post Mortem" column in *The Atlantic*. At the end of each month, he'd have a shortlist of potential subjects and so would I and we'd try and find someone on both lists. He'd propose, say, Judy Garland's ex-, Sid Luft, and I'd roll my eyes and say you don't really need a professional for that. And I'd counter with some sober heavyweight figure, and Cullen would react like the great pop guru Don Kirshner did when the Monkees told him they were sick of this bubblegum stuff and they needed to grow as serious artists. But then I'd forget the serious artist growth process and do Sid Luft and everyone would be happy. My rule with *The Atlantic* is never to do anyone I totally despise. It's easy from an East Coast media perspective to have a hoot and jeer at a Utah polygamist like Owen Allred, but it's insufficient.

The great thing about journalism is that whatever you do you're automatically an expert in. So within a month or three of starting in *The Atlantic* I was getting non-stop offers to do obituaries hither and yon. Most of them wanted advance obits – that's to say, fellows in the ruddy bloom of late middle-age who might collapse of a massive stroke tomorrow morning or might totter on for another 40 years. Eagle-eyed readers may have noticed that, at *The Guardian* and certain other publications, it's not uncommon to read obituaries of someone who died last week written by someone who died ten years ago. Sorry, but I've never been able to do it like that. With Sinatra and Irving Berlin and a couple of others, I was asked to do premature appreciations and just couldn't get a handle on it. One of the many disappointing characteristics of *The New York Times*, for example, is that the obits feel like modular furniture that's been shuffled around too often.

Anyway, here come a few of my favorites over the years. I would like to thank the editors at the respective publications: R Emmett Tyrrell Jr, Wladyslaw Pleszczynski and Marc Carnegie at *The American Spectator*; Cullen Murphy and Robert Messenger at *The Atlantic Monthly*; Charles Moore, Martin Newland, Dominic Lawson, Mark Law and Anna Murphy at Britain's *Daily Telegraph* and *Sunday Telegraph*; Jamie Fergusson, Louis Jebb and Diana Hinds at *The Independent*; Peter Murtagh at *The Irish Times*; Ken Whyte, Natasha Hassan and Ruth-Ann MacKinnon at Canada's *National Post*; John O'Sullivan at America's *National Review*; Hilton Kramer, Roger Kimball and James Panero at *The New Criterion*; Michael Kinsley, Judith Shulevitz and David Greenberg at *Slate*; and Boris Johnson and Stuart Reid at *The Spectator*. I would also like to thank my invaluable assistants, Chantal Benoît and Tiffany Cole.

As a rule, this collection retains the spellings of the originating publication, whether British, American or Canadian. So, if you dislike finding a "u" in the middle of "humorless" or an "e" on the end of "banal", don't worry: the humourless banality will likely recur with an entirely different spelling two or three pages farther on. Or further on.

New Hampshire, September 2006

CONTENTS

Introit
THIS OLE HOUSE: Stuart Hamblen   5

Stings & victories
SMILING THROUGH: HM Queen Elizabeth the Queen Mother   11
DUTCH COURAGE: Ronald Reagan   17
THE CHAP ON DUTY: James Callaghan   21
MISTER AVAILABLE: Eugene McCarthy   27
TURNING POINT: Leopoldo Galtieri   33

Blessedness & light
COMEDY, INC: Bob Hope   41
LAST POST: Alistair Cooke   49
WE MOSTLY HAD EYES FOR HIM: Aaron Spelling   56
THANK YOU AND GOODNIGHT: Jack Paar   62

August & royal
THE TRANSFIGURATION: Diana, Princess of Wales   69
A GENTLEMAN, OF A KIND: HSH Prince Rainier of Monaco   79
THE PROTOTYPICAL BICYCLING MONARCH:
      HRH Princess Juliana of the Netherlands   85
HINTING AT PLEASURE:
      HRH The Princess Margaret, Countess of Snowdon   90

Anthems & canticles
MINUTE MAN: Irving Caesar   97
EX-HUSBAND OF LOVE GODDESSES: Artie Shaw   102
THE LORD'S MUSIC, THE DEVIL'S WORDS: Ray Charles   108
BOZO IN THE HOOD: Tupac Shakur   113
BROADWAY'S LAST GOOD TIME: Cy Coleman   120
THE MAN WHO INVENTED ELVIS: Sam Phillips   126

Chains & sins
YES, WE HAVE NO BANANA: The Reverend Canaan Banana   133
THE IMPERFECT SPY: Michael Straight   137
THE PARIAH GUY: Edward von Kloberg   142
DOING THE DECENT THING: John Profumo   147

Heirs & relicts
HALF DRAGON QUEEN, HALF GEORGIA PEACH:
      Madame Chiang Kai-shek   155
POLITE AND CHEERFUL: The 11th Duke of Devonshire   160
BRIGHT YOUNG THING WITH A BLIND SPOT: Diana Mosley 165
SWINGIN' FASCIST: Romano Mussolini   171
THE KAY AGENDA: Katharine Graham   177
CRUISING ON AUTOPILOT: John F Kennedy Jr   182
GEORGE'S GIRL: Kay Swift   187
THE FIFTH NIXON: Rose Mary Woods   192

Body & spirit
MAN OF TASTE: William A Mitchell   201
BIG APPETITE: Idi Amin   207
THE SWEDES' SWINGINGEST SWINGER: Vilgot Sjoman   211
A FEEL FOR POLITICS: Strom Thurmond   217

Partings & sorrows
THE PALADIN OF PALIMONY: Marvin Mitchelson   225
THE MARRYING KIND: Owen Allred   230
WENDY'S HOUSE: Wendy Wasserstein   236
THE LEAST WORST MAN: Sid Luft   244
THE LOCAL ANGLE: Paula Yates   250

Whips & scorns
OLD-SCHOOL COPPER: Jack Slipper   257
DEATH OF A SALESMAN: Arthur Miller   263
THE LAST EDWARDIAN: Michael Wharton   268

Shatter'd & sunder'd
A DEATH IN IRAQ: Kenneth Bigley   277
A DEATH IN JORDAN: Moustapha Akkad   282

Sanctity & space
MOONSTRUCK: Bart Howard   291
BEAM MOVIE STAR: James Doohan   296
TRUTH AND CONSEQUENCES: Pope John Paul II   302
TWENTIETH CENTURY DARWIN: Francis Crick   308

Recessional
ONE FOR THE ROAD: Bill Miller   317

INTROIT

This ole house

STUART HAMBLEN

OCTOBER 20TH 1908 ~ MARCH 8TH 1989

This Ole House once knew my children
This Ole House once knew my wife
This Ole House was home and comfort
As we fought the storms of life...

MOVIE BUFFS will appreciate that moment in low-budget westerns when the leader of the bad guys, the brains of the outfit with the fancy suit and big cigars, swings open the saloon doors and says, "Saddle up, boys, we're ridin' out." In dozens of Republic and Monogram third features of the Thirties and Forties, the camera would then cut to the gang's heavy, chewing a stogie, downing a shot of red-eye, and playing poker in a menacing manner - Stuart Hamblen.

Most of his confrères in the gang were phonies - failed stage actors, effete Englishmen drifting through Hollywood - but Hamblen was the real thing: as a child in Kellyville, Texas, he'd learned to ride and rope and quickly graduated to the Texas rodeo circuit. When he moved to Los Angeles to sing on KFI Radio's "Covered Wagon Jubilee", it was inevitable that he'd mosey into cowboy pictures.

In the movies, his evil deeds were routinely foiled by Gene Autry or Roy Rogers and Trigger. Off-screen, it was the Los Angeles Police Department who regularly slung him into jail for barroom brawls or shooting out streetlights. "My Daddy was a Methodist minister," he said, "and I guess I was the original juvenile delinquent." To while away his prison stretches, he wrote songs like "Ridin' Ole Paint" (which he sang in the movie *The Savage Horde*) and "I Won't Go Huntin' With Ya, Jake, But I'll Go Chasin' Women".

In 1949, however, Hamblen was persuaded to attend a Billy Graham prayer meeting. Overnight, he abandoned the good ol' boy songs in favour of evangelical numbers like "When The Lord Picks Up The Phone". Even more impressively for one of the hardest drinkers in Hollywood, he also gave up booze, and in the 1952 Presidential election ran against Eisenhower and Adlai Stevenson on the Prohibition Party ticket, pledging to restore the outright ban on alcohol: he lost by 26 million votes. Marvelling at his old drinking buddy's newfound moral rectitude, John Wayne wanted to know how Stu was managing to stay off the bottle. "Well," said Hamblen, "it's no secret what God can do." "That sounds like a song," drawled the Duke. So Hamblen made it one – "It Is No Secret (What God Can Do)" – and he had a hit with it, and so did Red Foley and Jo Stafford, and later Elvis.

Until recently, Hamblen and his wife Susie hosted "The Cowboy Church Of The Air", one of the most popular programmes on the West Coast, broadcast on KLAC every Sunday morning from Hamblen's home, the California estate once owned by another hell-raiser, Errol Flynn. Although few of his religious numbers crossed over into the wider market, one of his songs, "This Ole House", did have the distinction of reaching Number One in Britain on two separate occasions, with Rosemary Clooney in 1954 and Shakin' Stevens in 1981.

"I always wanted to write music and for me it could be anywhere," he said. "This time, I was wandering way up in the mountains and came across this dilapidated cabin." He was hunting in the high Sierras and had noticed a mangy, starving old hound dog hanging around an otherwise abandoned cabin. "Inside, I found an old prospector lying dead. I saw curtains, so that meant a woman had been there. I saw kids' things lyin' around. And they were all gone now. The old man was alone." Most of us would just get out, some perhaps would go to the cops, but Hamblen sat down and, with the corpse lying next to him for inspiration, began to rough out a song. "It took about 30 minutes," he said. "I put it down on a brown paper bag the old fellow had left lying there:

> *Ain't a-gonna need this house no longer*
> *Ain't a-gonna need this house no more*
> *Ain't got time to fix the shingles*
> *Ain't got time to fix the floor*
> *Ain't got time to oil the hinges*
> *Or to mend no window pane*
> *Ain't-a-gonna need this house no longer*
> *I'm a-gettin' ready to meet the saints.*

Riding down the canyon, with the pooch on the pommel of his saddle, Hamblen firmed up the central idea of the lyric: There are two meanings to "this ole house" – first, the physical shelter, the wood frame and floor boards; second, the old prospector's body, the structure that houses his soul. Both houses end up as dust scattered to the winds. But the soul inside the "house" of the body is gathered up to meet the saints in the house of the Lord. Hamblen wasn't the first to put it like that. The apostle Paul, in his second epistle to the Corinthians, says:

> *For we know that, if our earthly house of* this *tabernacle were dissolved, we have a building of God, an house not made with hands, eternal in the heavens.*

But Stuart Hamblen was the first to get a hit song out of the idea:

> *My ole hound dog lies a-sleepin'*
> *He don't know I'm gonna leave*
> *Else he'd wake up by the fireplace*
> *An' jus' sit an' howl an' grieve…*

If Rosemary Clooney was aware of this deeper meditation, she didn't let it get in her way. Rosie's hit record treats Hamblen's reflections on the transience of corporeal reality as a jolly novelty number, a quintessential bouncy pop song from the Mitch Miller era.

But Hamlen was grateful enough to send her a bassinet with 125 yards of pink tulle for her baby: even on the Hit Parade, in the midst of death there was new life. The only Number One hit written in the presence of a dead body, "This Ole House" is the versatile Stuart Hamblen's most enduring legacy.

The Independent

STINGS & Victories

Smiling through

H.M. QUEEN ELIZABETH
THE QUEEN MOTHER
AUGUST 4TH 1900 ~ MARCH 30TH 2002

PREPARING King Edward VII's grand Durbar in Delhi in 1903, the Viceroy of India, Lord Curzon, thought it best to delete "Onward, Christian Soldiers" from the program. Not because of any lily-livered multicultural sensitivity (most of the soldiers present were Hindu or Muslim) but because of one offending stanza:

> *Crowns and thrones may perish*
> *Kingdoms rise and wane...*

Not a thought to plant with the natives.

Two years after the King's durbar, His Majesty's grandson, "Bertie", went to a children's birthday party and met a nice girl called Elizabeth, who gave him the cherries off the top of her cake. Born to an age of durbars, Queen-Empress of a quarter of the world's population, Her Majesty Queen Elizabeth The Queen Mother saw almost all the world's other crowns and thrones perish - those of her husband's cousins in Germany and Russia, plus Austria, Turkey, Italy, all the great empires – and the cherries tumble from almost every Royal cake. The nations dominating today's headlines - Israel and its enemies, Iraq, Syria, Saudi Arabia – didn't exist, nor, for that matter, did the provinces of Alberta and Saskatchewan. Kingdoms waned, but rarely rose. In a demotic age, Yankee Doodle came to London in the form of a peanut farmer who, on being presented to Her Majesty, kissed her smack on the lips. Long after the rest of the world had forgotten Jimmy Carter, the Queen Mum included him in her list of post-prandial "anti-toasts" to various *bêtes noires* - Idi Amin, Robert

Mugabe and the former US President, "the only man, since the death of my dear husband, to have had the effrontery to kiss me on the mouth."

Any long life is humbling, for it reminds us that all the great fixtures and features of our world are, in the course of one human span, no more than passing fancies. The Queen Mother was the last Empress of India, which means the last Empress - the last with an empire, as opposed to, say, the Empress of Japan or whoever the self-proclaimed Emperor (and cannibal) Bokassa was married to, back in Central Africa in the Eighties. If you're a real, live Empress, it must, if we're honest, be something of a comedown when the highlight of your centenary is receiving Adrienne Clarkson so she can induct you into the Order of Canada. But it also represents a kind of survival. The Kaiser, the Romanovs, the Soviet Politburo are gone, but the Queen Mum hung in there to bequeath her daughter the monarchies of Britain, Canada, Australia, New Zealand, the Bahamas, Papua New Guinea, Belize, Tuvalu... Today, over half the thrones in the world are the Queen's, which given the way things were looking in, say, 1919 isn't bad.

For the Queen Mother's generation, the impermanence of the world was defined by the Great War, which the British Empire entered on her 14th birthday, August 4th 1914. A year later, her brother Fergus was killed in action on the western front. By then, her family's Scottish home, the Macbeth-haunted Glamis Castle, was a military hospital for convalescing soldiers, and Lady Elizabeth an orderly. It's easy to mock the idea of rough Dundee Tommies being ministered to by some silly debutante, and no doubt, even as I write, some Fleet Street contrarian is gleefully putting the boot in. But it gets to the heart of how the Queen Mum lived her entire life: *noblesse oblige*. Toffs had it good, they got to live in the big house, that meant they had an obligation to give something back - or, as she put it, "The work you do is the rent you pay for the room you occupy on Earth." The Queen Mum occupied a swankier room than most and so worked hard, until the end.

She came from an illustrious line, a descendant of Sir John Lyon, Thane of Glamis, who married Jean, daughter of King Robert II of Scotland, in 1376, which I mention only because we columnists have very little opportunity to use the word "thane" these days. But her character was that of the late Victorian Imperial ruling class, whose devotion to duty was almost vaudevillian: for her, monarchy was a show, and the show must go on. At the racetrack, she'd pick up the binoculars and peer through them every few minutes, not because it helped her see any better but because it proved to the gawping crowds that she was paying attention: she was acting the part of a racegoer.

She was the first member of our Royal Family to smile in public: Queen Alexandra usually looked sad and distracted, as well she might; Queen Mary opted for severe, as if it were only Royal disapproval that held her subjects in check. But, as Duchess of York and then Queen Consort, the Queen Mum put on a happy face. She wore a smile, professionally, for nearly eight decades. She also invented the Royal "walkabout", in Ottawa in 1939, when she paused to chit-chat with some Scottish stonemasons. But that's where it stopped. In 1923, Lady Elizabeth gave a prototype Royal interview referring to her fiancé, HRH The Duke of York, as "Bertie". King George V was furious at this breach of protocol, and in the ensuing 79 years the Queen Mum never again gave another interview. If she was a performer, she was an old-fashioned one - the kind who does the show and lowers the curtain, rather than heading off to Diane Sawyer to talk about sex and battles with alcohol. She had the "common touch" - look at that splendid photo of her playing snooker on the cover of Mordecai Richler's recent book on the subject, or the picture of her pulling a pint behind the bar that you can still find hanging in East End pubs. But a touch was all you got. You never knew what she really thought, only what various intermediaries passed on. She disapproved of her grandchildren's divorces because she thought public dysfunctionalism broke the compact between rulers and subjects: the price of a life of privilege was that you never let the mask slip. Her brother-in-law, the Duke of Kent, was a bisexual drug addict and lover of Noel Coward, but he didn't give confessional interviews sobbing that he'd been living a lie and he and Noelie wanted to move in together. In the Queen Mum's view of monarchy, weakness delegitimized you. That's why she despised King Edward VIII: he was unprofessional. He couldn't do his job without the woman he loved? Get a grip, man! As Elizabeth was happy to concede, her marriage was arranged; love came afterwards.

She seemed, in that sense, even older than she was. Even as a gel about town in the early Twenties, she was never quite at home in bobbed hair and flapper dresses. If you look at those early photos - the moon-faced girl, barely five feet, but with that impressive bosom - she seems much more suited to those tight-waisted formal dresses with the plunging neckline, a post-war approximation of the Edwardian hourglass figure her grandfather-in-law so appreciated. Her nemesis, Mrs Simpson, was the modern woman, the Jazz Age fast liver who thought Buckingham Palace was just another stop on the cocktail circuit. Privately, the American divorcée called the Duchess of York "Cookie", after her soft, plump Scots cook. The Duchess proved a tougher cookie.

For that reason, she was the only Royal I ever really wanted to meet, just to see if I could discern a hint of the steel fist inside the pastel chiffon. The closest I got was being in a room with her, surrounded by her retinue of elderly queens and pursed-lip ladies-in-waiting. From the look of it, she travelled with more servants than the Queen. She had a four million pound overdraft at Coutts, the Royal bankers, who must sometimes have wondered what they'd done to deserve the honour. Unlike the downwardly-mobile Prince Edward ("Hi, Edward Windsor here") or Princess Anne (who travels up to London on a Cheap-Day Super-Saver rail ticket), the Queen Mum was queenly to the hilt. Not once in her 101 years did she have to draw her own curtains or run her own bath. The only reason I know she could answer the phone is because, in the early days of their marriage, Andy and Fergie liked to amuse their friends at late-night parties by dialing her private number and saying, "Hello, is Dick Head there? Dick? Dick Head?"

There were, to be frank, a lot of dickheads in the Queen Mum's class. But, for most of the modern age, they were the class that ruled much of the world. Mouldering old castles like Glamis sent forth the chaps who manned not just the British political establishment but their Imperial branch offices. The master plan, if there was one, was to have enough social mobility to co-opt anyone promising. That was the point of that 1903 durbar: to bring the Indian princes and middle classes within the British system. They did it in Canada, too. Wander into the Mount Royal Club in Montreal, past the gallery of portraits and marvel at the way fellows with quite ordinary names like Smith wound up as "Lord Strathcona" or "Lord Mount Stephen". It's a world that endures only in Fleet Street obituaries, such as that last month for the widow of Sir Ewan Forbes, who spent his first 40 years as Miss Elizabeth Forbes-Semphill and whose sex became a matter for the Scottish Court of Session when he attempted to inherit a Nova Scotia baronetcy created in 1630. Perhaps if Conrad Black had been willing to change his sex, M Chrétien might have looked more kindly on his peerage.

Lots of people are changing their sex these days. The surgeon who performed the Queen Mum's hip surgery, William Muirhead-Allwood, is now Sarah Muirhead-Allwood. I expect Her Majesty took it in her stride, literally. The British upper class had a good innings, from James II to the Second World War, but it ran up against forces it couldn't co-opt, submerge, assimilate. The Queen Mum exemplified these changes personally: an impossibly grand woman, during the war she succeeded in reinventing herself, her husband and their daughters as the apotheosis of the modest, decent, unassuming middle-class Home Counties family. The Duke of Edinburgh, being Greek and not quite so attuned to these things, took the whole business too far and modernized the Royals into the quintessential dysfunctional family. But by then the Queen Mum was no longer in charge, and could only rail in private as one fad after another chipped away at her world. She was instinctively conservative. She thought decolonization had come too soon, that the European Union was absurd, that Philip's uncle, Lord Mountbatten, had made a complete pig's ear shepherding India to independence, and that Tony Blair was a modish twerp. On all of these matters, I agree with Her Majesty. She would have made an excellent *National Post* columnist.

The Queen Mum summed it up well in a phrase that came back to me a couple of weeks after September 11th, in those panicky days when a trace of confectioner's sugar from some janitor's Danish was enough to send Senators and Congressmen stampeding from the Capitol. Buckingham Palace received nine direct hits during the Blitz, including one occasion when a single German bomber flew low up the Mall and dropped its load directly above the living quarters. The King and Queen were in their drawing room and showered with shards of glass. The first bomb fell on the Palace 61 years almost to the day before the attacks of 9/11, on September 13th 1940. Afterwards, Queen Elizabeth said, "I'm almost glad we've been bombed. Now I can look the East End in the face."

The Queen Mother's remark captures precisely the unspoken pact between the rulers and the ruled: they should be able to look us in the face. For 79 years, when it came to the things that matter, she could.

The National Post

Dutch courage

RONALD REAGAN

FEBRUARY 6TH 1911 ~ JUNE 5TH 2004

ALL WEEKEND long, across the networks, media grandees who'd voted for Carter and Mondale, just like all their friends did, tried to explain the appeal of Ronald Reagan. He was "the Great Communicator", he had a wonderful sense of humour, he had a charming smile… self-deprecating… the tilt of his head…

All true, but not what matters. Even politics attracts its share of optimistic, likeable men, and most of them leave no trace – like Britain's "Sunny Jim" Callaghan, a perfect example of the defeatism of western leadership in the 1970s. It was the era of "détente", a word barely remembered now, which is just as well, as it reflects poorly on us: the Presidents and Prime Ministers of the free world had decided that the unfree world was not a prison ruled by a murderous ideology that had to be defeated but merely an alternative lifestyle that had to be accommodated. Under cover of "détente", the Soviets gobbled up more and more real estate across the planet, from Ethiopia to Grenada. Nonetheless, it wasn't just the usual suspects who subscribed to this feeble evasion – Helmut Schmidt, Pierre Trudeau, François Mitterand – but most of the so-called "conservatives", too – Ted Heath, Giscard d'Estaing, Gerald Ford.

Unlike these men, unlike most other senior Republicans, Ronald Reagan saw Soviet Communism for what it was: a great evil. Millions of Europeans across half a continent from Poland to Bulgaria, Slovenia to Latvia live in freedom today because he acknowledged that simple truth when the rest of the political class was tying itself in knots trying to pretend otherwise. That's what counts. He brought down the "evil empire", and all the rest is details.

At the time, the charm and the smile got less credit from the intelligentsia, confirming their belief that he was a dunce who'd plunge us into Armageddon. Everything you need to know about the establishment's view of Ronald Reagan can be found on page 624 of *Dutch*, Edmund Morris' weird post-modern biography. The place is Berlin, the time June 12th 1987:

> *'Mr. Gorbachev, tear down this wall!' declaims Dutch, trying hard to look infuriated, but succeeding only in an expression of mild petulance ... One braces for a flash of prompt lights to either side of him: APPLAUSE.*
>
> *What a rhetorical opportunity missed. He could have read Robert Frost's poem on the subject, 'Something there is that doesn't love a wall,' to simple and shattering effect. Or even Edna St. Vincent Millay's lines, which he surely holds in memory...*
>
>> *'Only now for the first time I see*
>> *This wall is actually a wall, a thing*
>> *Come up between us, shutting me away*
>> *From you ... I do not know you any more.'*

Poor old Morris, the plodding, conventional, scholarly writer driven mad by 14 years spent trying to get a grip on Ronald Reagan. Most world leaders would have taken his advice: you're at the Berlin Wall, so you have to say something about it, something profound but oblique, maybe there's a poem on the subject ... Who cares if Frost's is over-quoted, and a tad hard to follow for a crowd of foreigners? Who cares that it is, to the casual (never mind English-as-a-second-language) hearer, largely pro-wall, save for a few tentative questions toward the end?

Edmund Morris has described his subject as an "airhead" and concluded that it's "like dropping a pebble in a well and hearing no splash." Morris may not have heard the splash, but he's still all wet: the elites were stupid about Reagan in a way that only clever people can be. Take that cheap crack: if you drop a pebble in a well and you don't hear a splash, it may be because the well is dry but it's just as likely it's because the well is of surprising depth. I went out to my own well and dropped a pebble: I heard no splash, yet the well supplies exquisite translucent water to my home.

But then I suspect it's a long while since Morris dropped an actual pebble in an actual well: As with walls, his taste runs instinctively to the metaphorical. Reagan looked at the Berlin Wall and saw not a poem-quoting opportunity but prison bars.

I once discussed Irving Berlin, composer of "God Bless America", with his friend and fellow songwriter Jule Styne, and Jule put it best: "It's easy to be clever. But the really clever thing is to be simple." At the Berlin Wall that day, it would have been easy to be clever, as all those Seventies détente sophisticates would have been. And who would have remembered a word they said? Like Irving Berlin with "God Bless America", only Reagan could have stood there and declared without embarrassment:

Tear down this wall!

- and two years later the wall was, indeed, torn down. Ronald Reagan was straightforward and true and said it for everybody - which is why his "rhetorical opportunity missed" is remembered by millions of grateful Eastern Europeans. The really clever thing is to have the confidence to say it in four monosyllables.

Ronald Reagan was an American archetype, and just the bare bones of his curriculum vitae capture the possibilities of his country: in the Twenties, a lifeguard at a local swimming hole who saved over 70 lives; in the Thirties, a radio sports announcer; in the Forties, a Warner Brothers leading man ...and finally one of the two most significant presidents of the American century. Unusually for the commander in chief, Reagan's was a full, varied American life, of which the presidency was the mere culmination.

"The Great Communicator" was effective because what he was communicating was self-evident to all but our decayed elites: "We are a nation that has a government - not the other way around," he said in his inaugural address. And at the end of a grim, grey decade - Vietnam, Watergate, energy crises, Iranian hostages – Americans decided they wanted a President who looked like the nation, not like its failed government. Thanks to his clarity, around the world governments that had nations have been replaced by nations that have governments. Most of the Warsaw Pact countries are now members of Nato, with free markets and freely elected parliaments.

One man who understood was Yakob Ravin, a Ukrainian émigré who in the summer of 1997 happened to be strolling with his grandson in Armand Hammer Park near Reagan's California home. They chanced to see the former President, out taking a walk. Mr Ravin went over and asked if he could take a picture of the boy and the President. When they got back home to Ohio, it appeared in the local newspaper, *The Toledo Blade*.

Ronald Reagan was three years into the decade-long twilight of his illness, and unable to recognize most of his colleagues from the Washington days. But Mr Ravin wanted to express his appreciation. "Mr President," he said, "thank you for everything you did for the Jewish people, for Soviet people, to destroy the Communist empire."

And somewhere deep within there was a flicker of recognition. "Yes," said the old man, "that is my job."

Yes, that was his job.

The Irish Times

The chap on duty

JAMES CALLAGHAN
MARCH 27TH 1912 ~ MARCH 26TH 2005

THE PAST MAY be, as L P Hartley wrote, another country, but it's rarely as foreign as Britain in the Seventies. Viewed from the United Kingdom of 2005, the day before yesterday is a banana republic without the weather. Inflation was up over 25 per cent, marginal tax rates were up over 90 per cent, and the only thing heading in the other direction was the pound, which nosedived so suddenly in 1976 that the Chancellor of the Exchequer, en route to an International Monetary Fund meeting, was summoned back from the departure lounge at Heathrow to try and talk his currency back up to sub-basement level. Her Majesty's Government had itself applied for a $4 billion loan from the IMF. Were the Britain of 30 years ago to re-emerge Brigadoon-like from the mists, it would be one of those basket-cases Bono would be hectoring Bush about debt forgiveness for.

Such great Britons as the era could muster – Roger Moore, Michael Caine – had decamped to Switzerland and Beverly Hills. As if to underline the national decline, every flailing industry flew the moth-eaten flag – British Steel, British Coal, British Leyland. They were all owned by the state, even the last, which was the national automobile manufacturer. The government had taken all the famous British car marques – Austin, Morris, Rover, Jaguar, Triumph – and merged them into one, named after the "lorry" – ie, 18-wheeler – division. That's right: the government made your car. Or rather a man called Red Robbo did, when he was in the mood, which wasn't terribly often. He was the local union man at the Leyland plant in Birmingham, though he seemed to spend more time outside the gate picketing. In Britain, the union leaders were household names, mainly because they were responsible for everything your household lacked. In the Seventies, if you opened *The Times* – when the print unions weren't on strike – or watched the BBC news – when the miners weren't on strike and the government hadn't ordered the TV to close down mid-evening to conserve electricity – it was a parade of potentates from strange unlovely acronyms like ASLEF and SOGAT and NATSOPA and NACODS being received by the Prime Minister as if they were heads of state, which in a sense they were. Britain's system of government in the Seventies was summed up in the phrase "beer and sandwiches at Number Ten", which meant the union leaders showing up at Downing Street to discuss what it would take to persuade them not to go on strike and being plied with the aforementioned refreshments by a Prime Minister reduced to the proprietor of a seedy pub, with the cabinet as his barmaids. The beer and sandwiches only went so far, and they'd usually be followed a day or two later by chaotic mob scenes on the evening news of big burly blokes striking for their right to continue enjoying the soft pampering working week of the more effete Ottoman sultans.

The man who presided over the death throes of this ramshackle realm was James Callaghan, Prime Minister from 1976 to 1979, and an instructive study for all those obituarists of President Reagan so anxious last June to attribute his success to a genial disposition, charming smile, tilt of the head, etc. If you want to know what Reaganite affability boils down to without political will or philosophy, look at Callaghan. He was famously avuncular, he was known as Sunny Jim. But by the time he and his Labour government left office in 1979 the sunniness had decayed into torpid complacency. His most famous words were "Crisis? What Crisis?", which he never actually said but were put in his mouth by an enterprising headline writer from Rupert Murdoch's *Sun* and they fit so well they stuck.

The non-crisis of the regime began in an attempt to control the endless ping-pong of runaway inflation and runaway pay increases to keep up with it. The government proposed a five per cent limit in pay rises, with penalties for companies that flouted the limit. This sounded a bit low to the Labour Party's union allies, and the car workers decided the very proposal was worth striking over. When Ford's UK subsidiary settled with a 15 per cent pay award, Callaghan attempted to impose penalties on the company, but Parliament declined to support him and the unions set out to teach him a lesson. The municipal manual workers demanded a 40 per cent wage increase and then struck. The truck drivers went on strike for a more modest 30 per cent. The garbage collectors followed, and in parts of the country the gravediggers.

In January 1979, the Prime Minister left for a G7 summit in Guadeloupe, and on the news bulletins the scenes from the coldest British winter in 16 years with the streets full of trash and the dead unburied alternated with footage from the Caribbean of a relaxed Callaghan in open-necked shirt working on his tan with the other colossi of the age, Jimmy Carter, Valéry Giscard d'Estaing and Helmut Schmidt. After the summit, he went to Barbados for a well-earned break his shivering citizenry felt he hadn't earned: Sunny Jim was spending too much time sunning himself. When he landed at Heathrow, he was besieged by the press and grumbled back, "I don't think that other people in the world would share the view that there is mounting chaos" – which *The Sun*'s man so lethally distilled. Callaghan had a point: the "mounting chaos" of the so-called "Winter of Discontent" was, in truth, only a slightly more extreme version of business-as-usual.

Four months later, the Labour government fell and the country turned to a Conservative Party led by Mrs Thatcher, whose impatience for the long delayed election had been mocked by Callaghan the previous year at his party conference, when he delivered a rendition of Fred Leigh's Edwardian music-hall song about a bride who never makes it to the altar: "(There was I) Waiting At The Church." Instead, it was Callaghan who faded into history as a unique footnote: the only British politician to hold all four of the kingdom's great offices of state – Prime Minister, Chancellor of the Exchequer, Home Secretary and Foreign Secretary.

In any other circumstances, it would be hard for the bare bones of the resumé to add up to anything other than a great success story. Leonard James Callaghan was born in 1912 in Portsmouth and raised in poverty. When he was nine, his father died. His mother struggled until the Labour government of 1924 belatedly gave her a widow's pension of ten shillings a week and helped cement her son's political loyalties. The ten bob was enough to let her keep the boy in school till he was old enough to take the Civil Service exam. When he did, at the age of 16, all her ambitions for him were fulfilled. Taken on as a clerk by the Inland Revenue for a pound a week, he was soon dissatisfied with conditions, joined the union and worked his way up to National Assistant Secretary.

He was never exactly a socialist firebrand – not compared to the fellows who brought him down decades later – but he was capable of righteous working-class indignation. When the Conservatives denounced big government as a denial of individual freedom, Prime Minister Callaghan snapped back, "I was brought up after my father died in a family which lived in two furnished rooms. That was a denial of freedom." Away from the public eye, among his party's swollen ranks of alleged "thinkers", Sunny Jim could be rather chippy about the furnished rooms and leaving school at 16.

He had nothing to be ashamed of: time has proved most of the thinkers hopelessly wrong on everything. But, on the other hand, Jim Callaghan's safe-pair-of-hands steady-as-she-goes don't-frighten-the-horses approach doesn't have much to show for it either. When he died, *The Guardian*'s headline writer billed him as a man "whose consensus politics were washed away in the late 1970s." But it's hard to have any meaningful "consensus" between public-sector closed-shop jobs-for-life workers demanding a 40 per cent pay raise and rational human beings. Jim Callaghan once confided to a friend of mine that he thought Britain's decline was irreversible and that the government's job was to manage it as gracefully as possible. He wasn't alone in this: an entire generation of Britain's political class, on both sides of the aisle, felt much the same way. So Callaghan rose onward and upward, "managing" problems rather than solving them. As Home Secretary in 1969, he sent troops to quell the civil unrest in Northern Ireland, and pessimistic colleagues fretted that they might be there for six months. They stayed there three decades, not to defeat the IRA but to manage an eternal stalemate. As Foreign and Commonwealth Secretary in 1974, he chose not to send troops to Cyprus after the Turks invaded – actually, he didn't even need to send them: there are already British military bases on the island. So, even though Britain was a guarantor of Cypriot sovereignty, he opted instead to "manage" the problem ineffectually, and the island is divided to this day, with the inevitable UN peacekeepers. In the spring of 1979, the electors decided that the ship was so full of leaks the old steady-hand-at-the-tiller routine was no longer enough: graceful decline was one thing, but Britain in the Seventies was becoming ungovernable. Lack of consensus was what was needed.

Eleven years later, shortly after the Fall of Thatcher, I was in the pub enjoying a beer with her daughter Carol when a fellow drinker, the punk poet Seething Wells, decided to have a go at her. After reciting a lengthy catalogue of the Iron Lady's crimes against humanity, Seething leant into Carol, and, stabbing his finger into her face, summed it all up: "Basically, your mum just totally smashed the working classes."

It has to be said this indictment loses a lot of its force when you replace "Thatcher" – or "Vatcha", as the tribunes of the masses used to snarl it – with "your mum". But Seething wasn't wrong. Basically, Carol's mum did just totally smash the working classes. Today, if one hears the term in Britain, it's usually from a polytechnic Marxist or socialist rock star. But 25 years ago there was a real "working class", even if it seemed less and less interested in working. Jim Callaghan was a product of that authentic working class and so was his party. He was the last "old Labour" Prime Minister and, when he fell, his comrades lurched left and into the wilderness for two decades. The Queen, who preferred Sunny Jim to Thatcher, elevated him to the peerage as Lord Callaghan of Cardiff, though Lord Winter of Discontent would have been a droller jest. By then, he was far more of an anachronistic hangover of a classbound society than Her Majesty. Whatever one thinks of Tony Blair, he is a quintessential post-Thatcher politician: The country is in the longest period of economic growth since records began in 1701. No-one now thinks that the government should run airlines and car plants and that the workers should live their entire lives in state housing - though what seems obvious to all in 2005 required extraordinary political will by a handful a quarter-century ago.

Jim Callaghan was not bitter in defeat, tending his farm and a beloved wife who died 11 days before him, and understanding that he was merely the chap on duty when the big geopolitical tide of history swept in and washed everything away. Another year or two and Washington might have been asking "Who lost Britain?" – that is, if America's less sunny Jim, President Carter, hadn't been peddling his own version of Callaghanite "malaise". The past is another country, but the Seventies is another planet.

The Atlantic Monthly

Mister Available

EUGENE McCARTHY
MARCH 29TH 1916 ~ DECEMBER 10TH 2005

I F YOU STRIKE at the king, you have to kill him. And, amazingly, Eugene McCarthy did. On March 12th 1968, the not exactly barnstorming Senator got 42.4 per cent of Democratic votes in the New Hampshire primary and denied the sitting President even a majority of his own party's supporters: Lyndon Johnson secured just 49.5 per cent. Within three weeks, he was gone: the President announced he would not seek re-election and effectively ended his political career. The king was dead, long live …well, not Senator McCarthy: the man who plunged the dagger in did not take the crown. But his few short weeks stumping the Granite State changed his party, with consequences it lives with to this day. The LBJ diehards who dismissed him as a mere "footnote in history" failed to understand how much damage one footnote can do when he doesn't mind whose toes he steps on and all the bigfeet turn out to have feet of clay. Thus, the paradox of Gene McCarthy: the revered liberal icon who destroyed the last successful liberal presidency. His act of insouciant regicide was the defining moment in the Democrats' modern history.

A few months earlier, a group of anti-war activists had formed something called the Alternative Candidate Task Force. It would have been easy to find some purer-than-thou leftist to run a doomed third-party campaign in the '68 election, but ACT calculated that it should surely be possible to talk a heavyweight establishment Democrat into opposing Johnson's re-nomination. They called on a score of Senators and Representatives, including their preferred choice, Robert Kennedy. But, presidency-wise, RFK was in the middle of his long Hyannis Hamlet routine, and ACT wound up settling instead for a fellow from a Minnesota hamlet. Senator McCarthy was nobody's idea of a dream candidate, least of all his: most of what passed for creative energy in his campaigning was devoted to the self-deprecating gags. But, with the big fish declining to nibble, ACT decided to go with Mister Available rather than Mister Right. He was a poet "mired in complexity", as one of his verses put it, and an unlikely man of action. Four days after the New Hampshire primary shocker, Bobby Kennedy entered the race himself, and nobody really needed McCarthy after that. But they needed him in those crucial months beforehand, when the party's princes were all prowling the battlements doing the old to-run-or-not-to-run-that-is-the-question soliloquizing. Gene McCarthy called himself an "accidental instrument", but he acted when nobody else would, and so LBJ's '64 landslide was overturned by 28,791 New Hampshire voters, some student campaign workers, and a non-barnstorming prematurely sidelined Senator.

In a profession abundantly endowed with cardboard heroes, glib opportunists and principled kooks, McCarthy was an unlikely standard bearer. A tall courtly figure who'd been a high-school teacher and a novice at a Benedictine seminary, he was what Denis Healey, Britain's former Chancellor, likes to call a politician with a "hinterland" – interests beyond politics. He loved Minnesota's flora and fauna and seemed ill-suited as either a fawner or floorer, a creep or a bruiser, into which categories most ambitious politicians fall. Elected to the House in 1948 and the Senate a decade later, he lent his name to a bloc of congressional liberals ("McCarthy's Marauders"), and floated upwards into the inner sanctum of Democratic power without ever seeming particularly engaged by the nuts and bolts of policy and legislation. From today's perspective, he had a parliamentary eloquence all but vanished from Washington. His colleague George McGovern hailed him for "a wit equal to Shaw's", though, like most political wit, it shrivels on citation. McGovern commends the riposte McCarthy made to Congressman Hill of Colorado, who in a debate on agricultural subsidies had brought up "some French girl" who'd been burnt at the stake. The gentleman from Minnesota replied, "I don't think Joan of Arc went to her death in defense of flexible farm price supports!"

Hmm. If one regards political wit as Samuel Johnson did women's preaching, that's good enough, and better than most of the other examples of McCarthy's nimble tongue. To a voter bemoaning an election-day choice of Johnson or Nixon, the Senator said, "That's like choosing between vulgarity and obscenity, isn't it?" – which has a certain blunt truth to it but seems a little heavy-handed to be dignified as Shavian. Watching Bill Bradley's somnolent campaign style enervate and empty a New Hampshire diner in 2000, a friend whispered to me, "He's trying to do a Gene McCarthy. But it's harder than it looks." And even the original couldn't keep it up past New Hampshire, when the laconic-maverick-vs-imperial-president dynamic got muddied by the entry of RFK and McCarthy's own complicated relationship with the Kennedy clan. The Minnesotan said he was "willing" to serve as President, which was a nice line in the snows of the north country but, six months later, after two assassinations and riots at the convention, didn't seem to have quite the command of events that the times demanded.

Yet, four decades on, though King and Kennedy may still be household names, it's McCarthy who left his party utterly changed. If his moniker weren't already a political adjective, one might describe today's Democrats as a wholly McCarthyite party: among the younger Congressional bigwigs, Barbara Boxer was a campaign worker for the Senator in '68 and later founded an imitative anti-war group of her own (the Marin Alternative); of the old lions, Ted Kennedy's reflexive hostility to the Iraq campaign is far closer to McCarthy's position than to either of his brothers'; and the Minnesotan's Senate contemporary, the octogenarian porkmeister Robert C Byrd, was pictured last year pumping his fist at a MoveOn.org rally in a scene that looks like a deranged burlesque of McCarthy's alliance with the anti-war youth of 1968.

After the 2004 election, Democrats took refuge in the conventional wisdom that "the American people don't change commanders-in-chief in the middle of a war". This conventional wisdom dates all the way back to, oh, nine-forty-three Eastern time on election night. Recent historical precedent suggests, au contraire, that wartime presidencies tend to end before hostilities do – or, at any rate, Democrat presidencies do. In Senator McCarthy's case, he regarded Vietnam as a "costly exercise in futility", but justified a break with his own President on the narrower constitutional principle of whether the Johnson Administration had the right to wage full-blown war without paying any heed to him.

Given that he'd voted for the Gulf of Tonkin resolution authorizing more or less whatever escalation took the President's fancy, the principle at stake was not so easy to discern. At one level, it seems not unreasonable that, in a country with growing opposition to a war, one of the two parties should represent that opposition at an electoral level. On the other hand, had the mostly young and not terribly representative anti-war movement failed to find their "accidental instrument" in McCarthy, today's political map would look very different. There's something to be said for taking the view that, regardless of the merits of this or that foreign war, once you're in it you might as well win it. Alternatively, there's something to be said for the position that, if you're going to cut and run, do it quick and get over it, as the British did when they abandoned Aden, on the Arabian coast, the day before McCarthy launched his Presidential campaign. On November 29th 1967, the Union Jack was lowered over the city, and the High Commissioner, his staff and all Her Majesty's forces left. On November 30th, the People's Republic of South Yemen was proclaimed – the only avowedly Marxist state in Araby. Yet the British shrugged off 130 years of colonial rule in Aden with nary a thought. Just one of those things, old bean. No sense making a fuss about it.

But to cut your losses and then mire yourself in an interminable psychological quagmire of your own has little to recommend it. "Vietnam casts long shadows", we're told, but not so much across the nation at large as over the Democratic Party. Forty years after McCarthy's swift brutal destruction of the most powerful

Democrat in the second half of the 20th century, it remains unclear whether his party will ever again support a political figure committed to waging serious war, any war: Carter confined himself to a disastrously botched helicopter rescue mission in Iran; Clinton bombed more countries in a little over six months than the supposed warmonger Bush has hit in six years, but, unless you happened to be in that Sudanese aspirin factory or Belgrade embassy, it was always desultory and uncommitted. Even though the first Gulf War was everything they now claim to support – UN-sanctioned, massive French contribution, etc - John Kerry and most of his colleagues voted against it. Joe Lieberman is the lonesomest gal in town as an unashamedly pro-war Democrat, and even Hillary Clinton's finding there are parts of the Democratic body politic which are immune to the restorative marvels of triangulation. Gene McCarthy's brief moment in the spotlight redefined the party's relationship with the projection of military force. That's quite an accomplishment. Whether it was in the long-term strategic interests of either the party or American liberalism is another question. Yet those few months in the snows of New Hampshire linger over the Democratic landscape like an eternal winter.

As for the Senator himself, he all but vanished except as an idea – a gentle giant, an inspiration, the conscience of the movement, etc. The way they talked about him you'd think he'd been assassinated in 1968, too. In fact, he remained politically active, at least in the sense that he became a perpetual Presidential candidate, the most reliable quadrennial flopperoo since Harold Stassen. He ran most recently against Bush Sr, Clinton and Perot in 1992. Were you aware of that? Don't be embarrassed. The 42.4 per cent "Clean for Gene" vote had dwindled down to a 0.2 per cent largely Unseen for Gene vote by the time he ran against Ford and Carter in '76. In 1968, he was the indispensable man whose charm was that he didn't regard himself as such. Having been dispensed with by his party, he spent the next quarter-century insisting on his relevance. In New Hampshire, he quoted Whitman's call to man's better nature: "Arouse! for you must justify me." In '72 and '76 and thereafter, McCarthy's self-aroused campaign philosophy seemed to be that "I must justify me".

Shortly after the 1968 campaign, his wife Abigail left him, although, as devout Catholics, they never divorced. And so it was with his party: They left the man but without ever being quite able to divorce themselves from the McCarthyite spirit of '68. Bliss was it in that dawn to be alive but to be young and Clean for Gene was very heaven.

The Atlantic Monthly

Turning point

LEOPOLDO GALTIERI

JULY 15TH 1926 ~ JANUARY 12TH 2003

GENERAL LEOPOLDO Galtieri was never one of your big-time dictators, just a run-of-the-mill generalissimo of the kind who once had a hammerlock on Latin America's presidential palaces. He died on Sunday in Buenos Aires, under house arrest or, more accurately, under one-bedroom apartment arrest. But boy, you should've seen him in the old days, back at the Casa Rosada. Everything was going swell until he made one tiny slip-up: He decided that the answer to Argentina's impending financial collapse was to invade the Falklands.

Hitherto, the regime hadn't put a foot wrong: some 30,000 Argentine dissidents are thought to have been "disappeared", many of them - in accordance with long-held judicial practice - tossed from aircraft into the sea. General Galtieri himself was said to have cooked up the 1981-82 program whereby the junta cut back on kidnapping and killing its enemies and instead kidnapped and killed its enemies' children.

On April 2nd 1982, the General brought the benefits of this administration to a couple of thousand British subjects in the South Atlantic. By April 8th, he had installed a new military governor on the islands, General Mario Menendez. The conquered Falkland Islanders, now citizens of Argentina's restored "Malvinas", were expected to "adjust" to the new arrangements. To be sure, there'd be one or two glitches in switching from English Common Law to Latin-American military dictatorship, but these could soon be ironed out.

That was more or less the line not just of the Argies but also of the British left, and of the defeatist wing of the Tory Party, and of Britain's sanctions-breaking "partners" in the European Community, and of the UN, and of the American media, and even of a substantial chunk of the Reagan Administration. They didn't all put it that way, but that was the upshot. Chances of restoring the status quo: zero per cent.

General Galtieri spent the last 20 years telling his dwindling circle of acquaintances that it never occurred to him the British would fight back. Who can blame him? In the Seventies, the map looked very different. The Soviets held half of Europe, had neutered most of the rest, and were advancing in every corner of the globe, from Afghanistan to Ethiopia to Grenada. The west never roused itself, except occasionally to co-operate: Cuban troops were in Africa, and Pierre Trudeau's contribution to the Cold War was to allow Castro's military aircraft to refuel in Canada. America had been humbled in Vietnam and humiliated in Iran, where the smiling eunuch Carter had allowed a superpower to be turned into a laughingstock, with cocky mullahs poking the corpses of US servicemen on TV.

So why would General Galtieri have had any qualms about seizing the Falklands? Yes, it was British "sovereign territory", but the American Embassy in Teheran was US "sovereign territory", and all the Peanut Peacenik had done was dither helplessly and then botch an ill-thought-out rescue mission. Why would the toothless, arthritic British lion be any different?

The Falklands War is the decisive war of the last quarter-century, if only because it's the one the world - like Galtieri - never expected. It marks the dividing line between the free world's territorial losses of the Sixties and Seventies and its gains in the Eighties and Nineties. Galtieri wasn't an ideological enemy: He was, in the shorthand of the time, a "right-wing" general and he had plenty of pals in Washington. But, when you're perceived, as the west was, as weak and paralyzed by self-doubt, you're anybody's fool. The Commies were swallowing acreage all over the globe, so were the Ayatollahs; why shouldn't some bargain-basement *caudillos* get a piece of the action?

That's my worry about the last year - that, whatever's going on behind the scenes, the perception among the world's loonies and losers is that America isn't serious. As General Galtieri came to appreciate, there are plenty of lessons in Mrs Thatcher's Falklands War, a model of fierce good sense in the face of all the usual insanity:

TIME IS OF THE ESSENCE

The first thing the British Government did was assemble and dispatch a vast task force as quickly as possible. From Mrs Thatcher's point of view, this put a clock on events: It would take a couple of weeks for the ships to reach the area. At that point, they'd start firing. So, if General Galtieri was seriously interested in avoiding war, that was the schedule, and Maggie intended to stick to it.

For its part, Argentina calculated that the longer the situation went on without being reversed the less likely it was that it would ever be reversed. World opinion gets used to things very quickly - the Argies have the Falklands, North Korea has nukes - and such will to rollback as there is dissipates quickly.

In the war on terror, it's easy to get the impression the clock has stopped.

THE U.N. IS FOR SHOW ONLY

To recall what the striped-pants set were advocating after the Argentine invasion is to understand why the world should never be left to the experts. The peace plan being promoted by Javier Pérez de Cuéllar, the United Nations Secretary-General, involved the UN taking over administration of the islands. This "solution" would have been seen, correctly, as a massive defeat for the British.

The Prime Minister understood the UN was institutionally inimical to the west. The Falklands, for example, came under the organization's absurdly anachronistic "Decolonization Committee", even though the islanders had no interest in being decolonized. Mrs Thatcher went through the motions of UN diplomacy, but she never ceded control of the agenda or the timetable.

TO THE EXPERTS, IT'S ALWAYS A QUAGMIRE

From *The New York Times* of May 8th 1982:

In Argentina, Junta's Confidence Grows
News Analysis by James M. Markham
> *One of the central premises of the strategy of Prime Minister Margaret Thatcher of Britain in the South Atlantic conflict - that gradually increasing military pressure will generate concessions from the Argentine junta - does not appear to be working...*

If it seems incredible that *The New York Times* would pay good money for Mr Markham's "analysis", look at all the Afghan quagmire guys still making a good living. Dictatorships are always unbeatable until that moment when they suddenly collapse and implode.

DICTATORS ARE NEVER RATIONAL

Why would anybody think, faced with economic catastrophe, that invading a string of distant islands is the answer? Never bet on a dictator's rationality. Indeed, one reason they become dictators is precisely to escape the tiresome constraints of rationality.

STABILITY IS A FETISH

From *The Washington Post* of May 26th 1982:

British Move to Seek A Definitive Victory Said to Unsettle U.S.
By Leonard Downie Jr
> *Prime Minister Margaret Thatcher is creating an uncomfortable dilemma for the Reagan administration in her determination to win a complete military victory in the Falkland Islands and restore them to full British colonial administration ...*
> *Reagan administration officials fear that a humiliating defeat for Argentina will sour American as well as British and*

*European relations with much of Latin America for a long time
to come, according to the sources...*

Well, the sources were wrong. Mrs Thatcher liberated not just the
Falklands, but also Argentina, at least from the military. Galtieri fell
and democracy returned. The "humiliating defeat" of the junta tainted
all the other puffed-up bemedalled tinpots by implication. And,
whatever the problems of Latin America today, no one's pining for the
return of the generals. Twenty years ago, the realpolitik crowd thought
a democratic South America was a fantasy and that we had to cosy up
to the strutting little El Presidentes-for-Life. Today, the same stability
junkies tell us we have to do the same with Boy Assad and co. They're
wrong again. They always are.

That great thinker Sheryl Crow declared the other day:

*War is based in greed and there are huge karmic retributions
that will follow. I think war is never the answer to solving any
problems. The best way to solve problems is to not have enemies.*

In the Falklands, war solved a lot of problems. For 20 years, the
islanders have lived in peace and freedom. So, in their own chaotic
Latin fashion, have the liberated peoples of Argentina and most of the
rest of the continent. If the best way to solve problems is not to have
enemies, then the best way not to have enemies is to get rid of them.
Thank you, Mrs Thatcher. Rest in peace, General Galtieri, wherever
you are.

BLESSEDNESS & Light

Comedy, Inc.

BOB HOPE

MAY 29TH 1903 ~ JULY 27TH 2003

I F YOU REMEMBER only one thing about him, make it this: Bob Hope made more people laugh than anyone in history. He's the only comedian to have been, over the years, the Number One star in radio, in film, and then television, at a time when each of those media was at its highpoint. The series of *Road* pictures with Bing Crosby was the highest-grossing in movie history until James Bond came along; his six decades with NBC hold the record for the longest contract in showbusiness; and his TV specials for the network remain among the most-watched programmes of all time. Plus he logged some ten million miles playing up to 200 live performances a year until he was into his nineties.

Success on that scale breeds a particular kind of contempt. Younger comics, who for 30 years have despised Hope as a pro-war establishment suck-up, forget that he more or less invented the form they work in: the relaxed guy who strolls on and does topical observational gags about the world in which we live. When Hope started eight decades ago, there were no "stand-ups". It was an age of clowns: weird-looking guys in goofy costumes taking frenzied pratfalls and telling ethnic gags in stage dialects - German, Irish, Negro. In the 1920s in Cleveland, Hope did as he was told and played in blackface wearing an undersized derby and an oversized red bow tie. But even then he knew enough, unlike most of the fellows he worked with, not to get trapped by the conventions.

How old was Bob Hope? Old enough to have been given his first big break by Fatty Arbuckle, who got him into a small-town tour of *Hurley's Jolly Follies* in 1925. Within a year, he and his partner George Byrne had formed the Dancemedians and graduated to hoofing with another British-born stage act, the Hilton Sisters. Daisy and Violet Hilton were Siamese twins joined at the hip and lower back and they specialised in three-legged tap routines. Not the easiest gals to dance with. "They're too much of a woman for me," said Hope.

Daisy and Violet's career peaked with an appearance in Tod Browning's 1932 film *Freaks*. In the early 1920s, Fatty Arbuckle was already on the skids and the Hilton Sisters had nowhere to go, and thus Hope's career began with two cautionary tales: if you get a break, don't blow it, as Arbuckle did, and don't get stuck in a self-limiting act, as Daisy and Violet were perforce. Over the decades, vaudeville died, and so did Broadway revue, radio comedy, Hollywood musicals and TV variety, but Hope never died with them. By the time NBC let him go in 1997, the world's only 94-year-old stand-up act could barely see the cue cards and hardly hear his co-stars. But he could hear the laughter.

The centenary he celebrated two months ago - quietly at home with just the family - is not the one he'd have chosen for himself. His strategy all his life was to get bigger and bigger and richer and richer: he never thought there'd be a peak and then the gentle downward incline of a late, enforced retirement. Mortality offended him not so much personally as in its long-term commercial implications. He was the first comedian to run himself as a business, and he succeeded brilliantly. *Time* magazine reported in 1967 that he was worth half a billion dollars. Asked about the figure, Hope said, "Anyone can do it. All you have to do is save a million dollars a year for 500 years."

When you're that big - when you're as mass as mass media can get - you don't have hardcore followers, you're not a cult or a genius like Buster Keaton or Monty Python. The old Broadway saw — "Nobody likes it but the public" - could have been made for Hope. He'll never be intellectualised or taught in college, which is as it should be: he worked hard at being breezy, and it paid off.

He was born poor, and had it rough, and took 15 years to slog his way to overnight stardom, but he never bought into the tears-of-a-clown, pain-of-comedy clichés. He started out in Eltham, Kent, on

May 29th 1903 as Leslie Townes Hope, the second youngest of seven brothers. His only sister died before he was born. "They ate her," he said. When he was four the family emigrated to America: "My youth was spent in a very tough neighbourhood. If you didn't get in three fights a day, you weren't trying." A sibling followed him into the business as "Bob Hope's Brother Jim". "Sure I helped him out," said Hope. "I helped him out of showbusiness."

Not all interviewers want to play the straight man. The more Hope blithely tossed off cheesy gag-writers' lines about his impoverished childhood, the more some journalists pressed him for psychoanalytical insights into the pain beneath the surface. So, just to get them off his case and back to the jokes, Hope would put on a straight face and tell them that his comedy sprang from a hunger for his mother's attention and approval as a young child in a large family. But with Hope the real depth is in the shallows, the real feeling is in the glib gags; if there is an "authentic" Bob Hope, you glimpse him in those "sure I helped him out" cracks.

As a boy in Cleveland, he would dress as Chaplin and waddle down Euclid Street. But, as soon as he could, he dispensed with the pathos of the little tramp, the sentimentality of the ethnic comics, and embraced instead the dapper assurance of a newer American archetype: the wise-guy, the kind of rat-a-tat quipster you could find in the sports columns and the gossip pages of the Jazz Age - but not in its comedy routines, in their way as convention-bound as grand opera. Much of what we now take for granted as the modern comedy monologue - the delivery, the structure, the subjects - comes from the template created by Hope. Larry Gelbart, who developed "M*A*S*H" for television and wrote for the comedian in the early 1950s, remembers being on tour with him in England and standing in the wings in Blackpool with a local girl he'd picked up. Hope told a joke about motels and the girl fell about.

"Do you have motels around here?" Gelbart asked.

"No," she said.

"Do you know what a motel is?" he asked.

"No," she said.

"So why are you laughing?"

"He's just so funny."

She had a point: by a certain stage, audiences were so attuned to the confident rhythm of Hope's act that they laughed at the right spots without knowing quite what the joke was. If Hope started out as the first modern comic, he quickly became the first post-modern one. Other comedians had writers, but they didn't talk about them. Radio gobbled up your material so you needed fellows on hand to provide more. But Hope not only used writers, he made his dependence on them part of the act:

> *I have an earthquake emergency kit at my house. It's got food, water and half-a-dozen writers.*

In vaudeville, a performer would have a comic persona – he'd be a yokel, say, and he'd tell jokes about rustics and city folk - but Hope's comic persona was the persona of a comic: he played a guy who told jokes for a living, and the conceit (in every sense) worked; by advertising the fact that he had a team who did all the tedious chores like providing the gags, he underlined his extraordinary preeminence. When he got too busy even to learn the material - and the TV sketches were played with a permanent sideways glance off-camera as he and the guests read everything off cue cards - that too became just another running joke.

"Bob's got the cue cards at home now," said Frank Sinatra. "He comes down in the morning and Dolores is sitting at the breakfast table and a guy behind her holds them up and Hope reads: 'How. Are. You. Darling? Did. You. Sleep. Well?'"

For the movies, his writers cheerfully acknowledge that they built a screen character around his own worst traits: the vain, cowardly, cheapskate skirt-chaser. The only difference was that on screen he chased skirt to little effect and played his liveliest bed scenes with animals (a bear in *The Road To Utopia*, a gorilla in *The Road To Bali*). Off screen, he was the animal, claiming Marilyn Monroe, Gloria De

Haven and countless others among his conquests. On the one occasion I met Hope he paid no attention to anything I said, his eyes looking over my shoulder as if we were doing a sketch and he was trying to find the boy with the cards. It turned out there was a well-stacked blonde 60 years his junior padding back and forth behind me. "Ain't that something?" he mumbled appreciatively, as she wiggled past us. He was a great connoisseur of women. He still called Doris Day "JB" - for "Jut Butt", because she had "an ass you could play cards on", though I don't believe he ever did.

Dolores Reade was a nightclub singer at the Vogue in Manhattan when Hope walked in one night in 1933. They got married, adopted four children, and Dolores figured if she waited long enough Bob the skirt-chaser would exhaust himself. It took the best part of seven decades before Mr and Mrs Hope finally enjoyed for real the contented, tranquil domesticity they promoted for years on TV, in that obligatory moment on the Christmas special when, after dancing with Ann-Margret and bantering with Brooke Shields, Bob would bring on Dolores for a duet of "Silver Bells". About a decade back, I made a documentary on a certain showbiz veteran, and asked his wife if she'd like to sing a number on the show. "Ah, the Dolores Hope moment," she said. "I don't think so."

Bob Hope understood the business of show better than anyone. He and Crosby joined a third partner to invest their *Road* movie profits in a new oil well. Almost immediately it was gushing a hundred barrels a day. Hope put his oil profits in real estate, buying up strategic chunks of Beverly Hills when it was still hills. The way he tells it, even the creative decisions were principally about money. He became the first big movie star to cross over to television because Paramount wouldn't match NBC's offer. When he needed a theme song for his new radio show in 1938, the plan was to use "Wintergreen For President" from the Gershwin hit musical *Of Thee I Sing* and re-write it to plug his sponsor: "Hope Is Here For Pepsodent". But the publishers wanted to charge him 250 bucks per show. "Nuts to that," he said. "I know a song we can get much cheaper: 'Thanks For The Memory.'"

He only put his foot wrong once. He was the American everyman and he wanted to be every man's American, fun for young and old alike. But Vietnam placed huge strains on that notion of a universal popular culture. For the first time in his career, Hope had to choose sides, and it wasn't so much that he chose wrong but the way that he chose. "Students are revolting all over the world," he said. "I don't know what they're revolting about, I just know they're revolting."

The limitations of his technique - of being a frontman for a factory of joke generators - were suddenly exposed. The reliable formulae, the old portable puns, sounded sour and small-minded. Unimaginably, the guy who'd always been one step ahead of the times was suddenly behind them. In a late 1960s poll of American high schools' favourite entertainers, he came second to the Beatles. By the time the war ended, he'd lost that generation forever.

In the Depression, Herbert Hoover ran for re-election on the slogan "Prosperity's Just Around The Corner". On stage, Hope said he'd run into a lady in the lobby. "She said, 'Young man, could you tell me where I could find the rest room?' And I said, 'It's just around the corner.' 'Don't give me that Hoover talk,' she said. 'I gotta go.'"

That's a perfect Hope gag: genially pointed - exactly where he wanted to be. But after Vietnam, he never quite recovered his timing. In the 1988 Presidential election, he thought Dukakis sounded "like something you step in". HIV? "Did you hear the Statue of Liberty has Aids? She's not sure whether she caught it from the mouth of the Hudson or the Staten Island ferry [pronounced 'fairy']." Hope wasn't "homophobic" - his closest professional confidante in later life was his lesbian daughter - but he couldn't seem to get his groove back. In transforming himself into a one-man laugh corporation, he'd blunted his own comic instincts.

So today there are two standard lines on Hope's transformation into a comedy brand. The first is the official one: he's a beloved American figure, the GIs' Number One entertainer for 60 years, Comic Laureate to the Republic.

The counter version, just as stale, is that he's a bland sell-out, Mister Squaresville, flattering third-rate politicians with golf gags so that they'll show up for his tournament. ("After you play with Gerald Ford, he pardons you.") When he first sauntered on stage with a club, it underlined his radicalism: the ease, the confidence, the naturalism. To his detractors, it symbolised laziness, conservatism, pandering.

I prefer a third version. When I saw Hope live in Toronto years ago, the best couple of minutes was when he did a soft-shoe to "Tie A Yellow Ribbon"; he didn't need the cards for that. Look at him trading steps with Jimmy Cagney in *The Seven Little Foys*, one of his best pictures. There are a zillion stand-ups today, but they can't do what Hope did in the late 1930s. He introduced "Thanks For The Memory" in his first feature, *The Big Broadcast Of 1938*. Everything else about the film - Martha Raye being loud, WC Fields doing routines involving a misplaced hat on the top of his cane - might as well come from the Stone Age: the only real thing in the picture is Hope and Shirley Ross as a married couple now parted. "Thanks For The Memory" is a beautifully grown-up song, sung by the pair sipping cocktails at the bar, their regret expressed through an accumulation of reminiscence, both scenic ("castles on the Rhine") and intimate ("stockings in a basin when a feller needs a shave"). Hope and Ross were told they'd be singing it live, and it's an extraordinary moment, two people, neither with any great reputation in acting, communicating everything they're not quite saying:

We said goodbye with a highball
Then I got as high as a steeple
But we were intelligent people
No tears, no fuss
Hooray for us...

At the end of the take, there were plenty of tears, from everyone on set.

No one matches that Hope today. Much of Woody Allen's persona - the cowardly schnook who gets the girl - is an extended homage to Hope's own screen identity in *The Paleface, Cat And The*

Canary et al. But Allen can't do that earlier Hope, the leading man brimming with sexy charm, teasing jokes and rueful romance.

Within a few years, Bob himself had put that guy in mothballs in the interests of greater profits. Shirley Ross retired from Hollywood in 1945 and you can measure Hope's career just from the orchestral transformation of "Thanks For The Memory", from a bittersweet ballad into a walk-on theme that got swankier and swankier and statelier and statelier, until it became the showbiz version of a national anthem. Bob Hope cast his lot and it worked out mighty lucrative, but in his last years as he padded around his second-floor quarters at the fancy spread at Toluca Lake, California, his children said it was the old songs that run through his head. And for many of us that's what we'll always hear, too:

> *And strictly entre nous*
> *Darling, how are you?*
> *And how are all those funny dreams that never did come true?*
> *Awf'lly glad I met you*
> *Cheerio and toodle-oo…*

And thank you so much.

The Sunday Telegraph

Last post

<u>ALISTAIR COOKE</u>

NOVEMBER 20TH 1908 ~ MARCH 30TH 2004

FOR BRITISH broadcasters visiting New York, it was the BBC equivalent of whale-watching off Cape Cod: After days of hanging around the corporation's Rockefeller Center studios, you'd be rewarded by a glimpse of a dapper figure in trilby and camel-hair coat. He'd glide past reception and into the studio, place a typed script on a wooden, straw-latticed lectern and begin to …talk.

Alistair Cooke had been at Rock Center a long time, since the days when the telephone number was CIRCLE 7-0656. There's a memo from Lindsay Wellington, the BBC's North American Director, bearing the Fifth Avenue letterhead and dated October 5th 1942 that the young reporter (in fact, already thirtysomething) used as a letter of introduction:

> *This is Mr. Alistair Cooke, who has been travelling around the United States on an official commission from the British Broadcasting Corporation in London to collect material for and write a series of programmes on the adaptation of American life to the war, for use in the Home and Empire Services of the B.B.C.*

The war ended, the Home and Empire Services became Radio 4 and the World Service, and over six decades later Mr Alistair Cooke wasn't doing quite so much traveling around. But he was still on his official commission from the BBC to report on the ongoing, unceasing adaptation of American life. Like Rockefeller Center itself, Cooke had a kind of sparely elegant modernity, offering commanding views of uptown swells and the more raucous types downtown, of lowdown jazzy hangouts in Greenwich Village and high-toned salons on the

49

Upper East Side. Most Americans, who knew him mainly as the host of "Masterpiece Theatre" on PBS, probably thought he retired a decade ago. But he carried on on radio, his true home, until a couple of weeks before his death at the age of 96.

In the early Nineties, I used to share the BBC's New York studio with him. The Corporation had decided to create a sort of chattier version of his "Letter From America" called "Postcard From Gotham", and hired me to host it. As to how they compared, let me quote the headlines of two reviews: "Treasured Letters And Garish Cards" (*The Observer*) and "All I Got Was A Lousy Postcard: Robert Hanks Browses Through Two Oh-So-Breezy Postscripts To Letter From America" (*The Independent*). Alistair was more indulgent, rightly recognizing that he'd see off this upstart as he'd seen off so many other variants of his indestructible franchise. But I enjoyed our weekly off-air chats, mainly about Dorothy Fields, Bunny Berigan, John O'Hara and other mid-century names he seemed relieved anyone in the office had still heard of.

Then in 1994, under a Birtian efficiency scheme, the BBC moved out of Rock Center to a low-rent, low-rise office above a disused abortion clinic. (My own show was terminated in the first trimester.) The framed poster of Cooke in his wing chair no longer hung in reception, mainly because, in the poky open-plan lay-out, there was no longer a reception to hang it in. They spared his weathered lectern, but it now sat incongruously amid the grey plastic studio fittings that looked as if they were bought second-hand from Radio Clwyd or East Midlands FM. It's a good thing he was a master of the "magic of radio" because by the end there wasn't a lot of magic at the Beeb.

Cooke had some 35 million listeners around the world. And, though at the BBC his huge popularity did not make him rich, it was enough to give him a rich address. A beneficiary of rent control, he lived on a stretch of Fifth Avenue lined with apartments worth millions, a long way from the stolid, grimy Lancashire of his childhood. The first Americans young Alistair met were the seven doughboys billeted on his family in Blackpool during the Great War: with his own father away at an aircraft factory in Manchester, they served as a septet of surrogates to the eight-year old boy.

After the war, when his parents and neighbours resumed their visceral anti-Americanism towards every innovation of the great Republic - jazz, gangsters, canned beef, movie stars, shirts with collars attached - Cooke declined to join in, and did so until the end. The youngsters at BBC New York served up an endless drivel of "Wow! Those crazy Yanks!" stories for Radio 5 Live and "Newsbeat". But Cooke remembered, after years of listening to visiting Britons bemoan the hugging and kissing in which American football jocks indulge, going in the Seventies to see his first English soccer match in decades:

> *Sure enough, the players had followed the usual English procedure of first ridiculing an American fashion and than adopting and exaggerating it.*

He anticipated the world's imperfect Americanization long before the world made it routine. Here he is in a glum part of Louisville, Kentucky, already suffused in war-weariness on a Saturday night in February 1942:

> *There seems to be, in the young people at least, only the tired motions of living and a glazed animal indifference to ideas, humor, the sight of new faces, even the presence of the roving soldiers. This is an atmosphere that no European need feel strange in. For it is the seeping seediness of English provincial towns. Yet this is an American town, and it has all the American fixtures, but it looks like a town in the English north or midlands trying to go American. In Texas, in Illinois, in Connecticut, in California, a drugstore, for instance, means the image of a complete American community - a shining fountain, the taste of lush syrups, an orgy of casual friendships and smart advertising, a halfway house between brisk comings and goings, the wayside first-aid station of American cleanliness and quick health. It*

should, and very often does, 'baffle the foreigner like an idiom'.
But here it is what a drugstore might be in Bulgaria or Leeds - a
sad imitation by a storekeeper who once read an American novel
and was filled with immortal longings.

That's a very sharp insight. At that time, there were, obviously, no drugstores in Bulgaria. But I went to one in Sofia just after the fall of the Commies and it was exactly as Cooke foresaw: "a sad imitation". Many provincial towns in England and elsewhere have superficially "gone American" in the years since - filled with pseudo-diners and burger joints - while retaining and, indeed, accelerating their "seeping seediness". Cooke predicted the limitations of the cheeseburger imperium: the more the world mimicked the superficial surface of American life, the less it understood the deeper cultural dynamic of the country.

He went to the United States in 1932 as a Cambridge graduate with a fellowship to study American theatre and, apart from a brief stint back in London as BBC film critic, spent his entire professional life there. But from all his years of commentary on the American scene it's not the political prescience or socioeconomic analysis one cherishes, so much as his eye for the telling detail – or even the detail that doesn't tell anything. Radio is a landscape of the imagination. And, just as Woody Allen says he spends his time searching for Cole Porter's New York:, I think I'd like to play in Alistair Cooke's America. Like a leaner Wodehouse or less fanciful Ira Gershwin, he combined New World vernacular with Old World erudition: after reviewing a golfing memoir by Bobby Jones, Cooke received a letter from the author, flattered but startled to have been compared, in a few short paragraphs, to Aristotle, Flaubert, John Donne and Walter Lippman.

He was so good at talking I stopped thinking of him as a writer - or, at any rate, a writer you could read on the page, without the aid of that clipped mid-Atlantic inflection that sounded, to Americans, like the perfect English gentleman and, to Britons, like a chap who'd been in the colonies too long. In fact, away from the radio microphone,

Cooke was a wonderful writer. At his best, he understood the power of words as sounds and rhythms: he found the music in America, even in its bleakest moments. Here's his opening sentence on George Gershwin's funeral:

> *I remember it as one of those midsummer mornings in New York when the skies can take no more of the rising heat and dump in the city a cataclysm of warm rain.*

What a marvellous evocation. Does it tell you anything about Gershwin? No. But, as much as "Summertime" does at the opening of *Porgy And Bess*, it draws you irresistibly into the piece.

So, to Britons, Cooke became the embodiment of the urbane (or, at any rate, acceptable) American, and, to Americans, he remained the quintessential English gentleman - a neat double-trick for a grammar-school boy from Lancashire. He was the kind of Englishman you meet only in America: like Cary Grant, too charming, too silvery-blue-haired, too permatanned for domestic consumption. Yet he managed to spend a good three-score-and-ten as a working reporter without falling prey to the self-regarding pomposity that afflicts "the media", not least in the US. He was a much sounder analyst of his own profession than the ethics bores who infest American journalism schools:

> *Most roving reporters, and indeed all foreign correspondents whenever they desert statistics for judgments of opinion and 'morale', become models of self-deception. They may call themselves, with proper gravity, 'reporters'. But any time after the youth of Sigmund Freud, they are nothing but quack psychiatrists who do not even know that this is the field they practise.*

In a TV age, when Palestinian terrorists artfully stage fake funerals from a non-existent Jenin massacre, the quack psychiatry is ever more the default mode of the foreign correspondent's trade. But Cooke's only warming up:

We are a tribe of artful men who have learned over the years to stifle our doubts about our own capacity to observe. We soon renounce the human beings we deal and live with for a context of 'public affairs'. This means usually the society of other journalists, diplomats, businessmen, civil servants, and the minor functionaries of State Departments and governments recently dethroned. Within this convenient frame of reference, you can find an approximation to the 'truth' that will glibly describe any current crisis in the political life of any country you care to name... There has never been anything to prevent even a minor poet from stumbling on an emotional truth that is a daily truism of an analyst's parlour. The only difference is that the 'foreign correspondent' solemnly believes his 'conclusions' are 'reached'.

Splendid, and, as Richard Nixon liked to say, it has the additional merit of being true. For Cooke personally, the week's events increasingly became a mere peg on which to hang his reminiscences. Over the years, as his delivery slowed and slowed, so the old favourites seemed to come round faster and faster - the leaves turning in Vermont, Thanksgiving in Vermont, Christmas in Vermont, anything in Vermont. (As listeners well know, he had a daughter there. Displaying the same judicious, understated evenhandedness with which he surveyed American politics, he had a child apiece from each of his two marriages.)

He bashed the scripts out on an old manual typewriter, whose last supplier in New York went out of business and left him relying on devoted listeners in Papua and Belize for gifts of compatible ribbons. "They say the advantage of these word-processors is that you can move your paragraphs around," he once told me. "I've never had the slightest urge to move my paragraphs around."

At the BBC, whose multicultural, multisexual employment policies embrace women, blacks and gays but not the elderly or even middle-aged, Cooke was half-a-century older than virtually everyone in the New York office. They got rid of his long-time studio engineer,

Ken, and he learned to make do with whoever was around, courteously remembering their names and co-opting them into the programme's rituals. The producer's only task was to agree to a weekly bet on the length of the talk: "Twelve minutes fifteen," Cooke would reckon. "Twelve forty-five," the producer would wager. When he'd recorded the Letter, the engineer would edit out all the coughs and wheezes, and the production team would listen through to the finished job, with Cooke chuckling with endearing self-satisfaction at his *bons mots*. Finally, the talk was pushed off down the line to London: "'Letter From America' coming," New York would announce. "Wozzat, then?" a bored World Service duty engineer would sometimes reply. "Never 'eard of it." Cooke shrugged off such small slights, as he did on his rare visits to Broadcasting House when the surly receptionists didn't know who he was and demanded to see a security pass.

As the years wore on, there were moments when he felt that offhandedness extended to the top of the corporation. By the end, aside from "Letter From America", he automatically refused every other programme request: He was no longer a BBC man. But he was a survivor: like Rockefeller Center - which opened the year he arrived in New York - he presented a smooth facade that's tough to crack. A while back, a corporation apparatchik was sent out from London to break the news to the old boy it was time for him to go the way of "Family Favourites" and "Housewives' Choice". But, face to face with the genially inscrutable essayist, the assassin chickened out.

Some months later a mischievous Cooke, under no illusions as to the purpose of the man's mission, inquired of a colleague back at Broadcasting House about that awfully nice chap they'd sent out to see him. He'd taken early retirement.

The Sunday Telegraph

We mostly had eyes for him

AARON SPELLING
APRIL 22ND 1923 ~ JUNE 23RD 2006

I N HIS ESSAY "The Myth Of 'Classic' TV", Terry Teachout argues just that – that, while *The New York Times* may regard "The Sopranos" as "the greatest work of American popular culture of the last quarter-century" and *The Nation* may truly believe that its "underlying themes evoke George Eliot", in the end it will end, and go away. As Teachout points out, before "The Sopranos", there were "Twin Peaks" and "Northern Exposure" and "Hill Street Blues" – and when was the last time you heard anyone say a word about them?

Indeed, the more "classic" your show, the more ephemeral it is. Getting in to Ovid or Gregorian chant is a piece of cake next to getting in to "thirtysomething" 15 years on. Conceivably, one might find oneself in a motel room unable to sleep at four in the morning and surfing the channels come across "St Elsewhere". But they made 137 episodes of complex multiple interrelated plotlines all looping back to Episode One: if you've never seen it before and you stumble on Episode 43, who the hell are all these people and what are they on about? By comparison, if you happen to catch, say, an episode of "Naked City" from the late Fifties, you might not know who the detectives are or recognize Billy May's wailing theme tune and the whole monochrome thing might be a bit of a downer, but you could still pass a pleasant hour with a self-contained one-hour cop drama. The "better" TV got (in the critically-acclaimed best-thing-since-*Middlemarch* sense) the more transient it became. I doubt "The Sopranos" will be an exception to this rule. Ninety per cent of all the people who'll ever be into it are already into it. That's not true of *Lucia di Lammermoor* or "My Funny Valentine".

But in between all the classics came the stuff Aaron Spelling cranked out, year after year, decade after decade – "The Mod Squad", "The Love Boat", "Dynasty", "Beverly Hills 90210", "7th Heaven", the stuff nobody ever compared to Dickens or George Eliot. In a town where not so long ago Jerry Lewis demanded of some executive supremo, "What do you know? You're *twelve*", Aaron Spelling was a hundred and twelve, give or take, and still a power. He was like Afghanistan's King Zahir at the post-Taliban loya jirga: the only old man in a land where male life expectancy is 43. His career stretched back to the dawn of television: He'd appeared in an episode of "I Love Lucy", playing the pump jockey at the gas station in Bent Fork, Tennessee, to which Lucy, Ricky, Fred and Ethel repair in order to visit Lucy's country cousin, Tennessee Ernie Ford. He was given his entrée into writing and production by Dick Powell – the Dick Powell who introduced "Pettin' In The Park" in *Gold Diggers Of 1933*.

A quarter-century on, Powell was hosting "Dick Powell's Zane Grey Theater" on CBS and young Aaron overheard him on the lot telling the head of the William Morris Agency that he was sick of the yawneroo intros he had to read for each episode: "In tonight's story, Tom meets Jane, Jane turns out to be already married, and you'll find out how they resolve their problems..." So Spelling went home and wrote six little intros that sidled up to tonight's theme in a more whimsical way: Powell would be in a western graveyard reading tombstones heartfelt and less so ("Stole a cow that wasn't his'n/Was hung before he got to prison"). The star went for it, and for 125 bucks a pop Spelling wrote all the intros that season, and then graduated to writing episodes. If he liked a script, Powell would sing "I Only Have Eyes For You", which he'd introduced in *Dames* (1934). Spelling heard a lot of "I Only Have Eyes For You" in those early years, and in the four decades afterwards a lot of Americans mostly had eyes for him: one night in the late Seventies, over half the TV sets in the country were tuned to "Charlie's Angels" – the kind of audience share you'd need a national disaster to get these days.

What is it that makes real classic TV? Flippy hair ("Charlie's Angels")? Shoulder pads ("Dynasty")? A 1974 red Ford Torino ("Starsky & Hutch")? A hokey sub-lounge theme song ("The Love Boat")? An Anglo-French midget excitedly yelling "De plane! De plane!" ("Fantasy Island")? Or some subtle combination of these elements that that schmuck who wrote *Middlemarch* could never have cooked up in a hundred years?

Who knows? The networks didn't. "Get rid of the little guy," advised the NBC exec after the "Fantasy Island" pilot. Eventually Spelling did, but only after Hervé Villechaize demanded as much per episode as Ricardo Montalban and hung on his trailer door a sign saying "The Doctor of Sex" (on the reverse it read "The doctor is in"). Spelling was formulaic, but then so's Coke, and on the whole he had more success at varying the formula. From "The Mod Squad" on, he gradually figured it out: new young talent but with a presiding father-figure type to hook the older crowd and plenty of room for starry guest shots. "Charlie's Angels" was the apotheosis of the formula: three hot chicks at the beck and call of the boss, but you never saw him – ie, that could be you, Mister Average Couch Potato, those gals are running around for. We don't really have *popular* culture any more, so much as a fragmented market crowded with expertly segmented mutually hostile opposing camps of various forms of unpopular popular culture. But Spelling was one of the last masters of universal pop culture – shows offering fun for young and old. He discovered a ton of new stars – from Farrah Fawcett to Shannen Doherty – and gave a lot of older players a grand last hurrah – from John Forsythe to Joan Collins – and resurrected most of Hollywood's Golden Age for somewhat improbable guest shots on *The Love Boat*: Lana Turner, Douglas Fairbanks Jr, Ginger Rogers, Don Ameche, Lillian Gish… Not so long ago, I happened to catch the tail end of *Tales Of Manhattan* (1942), which I vaguely recalled having enjoyed on a wet rainy afternoon when I was nine or so. It's about a rental tuxedo that gets passed from Edward G Robinson to Charles Boyer to Henry Fonda, and so on. Apparently it was Aaron Spelling's favorite childhood movie, the one he never forgot, and the one whose principal elements – fancy clothes, star guests, multiple plots - stand for much of his oeuvre, as Spelling Enterprises rented out its tux from Gene Barry in "Burke's Law" to Robert Wagner in "Hart To Hart" to Charlton Heston in "The Colbys". "T J Hooker" and "Starsky & Hutch" varied the look a little, but those long woolly cardigans of Paul Michael Glaser started a fashion craze on both sides of the Atlantic. I was in a bar in London about 12 years ago when a predatory woman of a certain age said that even now what still turned her on the most were "men in Starsky cardies": I don't mind being manacled upside down and flayed with a cat o' nine tails, but some tastes are just too kinky.

Plots? Dialogue? Oh, to be sure, Spelling had those, too. Hitchcock liked to refer to the "MacGuffin" – the device, the missing papers, the secret formula that jump-starts the plot. But nobody ever put the guff in the MacGuffin like a Spelling show did: in "The Colbys", Charlton Heston was obsessed with something called the "Imos Project"; for years on "Dynasty", John Forsythe and Joan Collins feuded over a mysterious "pipeline" they and their various shadow companies exchanged gazillions of dollars' worth of stock options over. There was as much plot as "St Elsewhere" or "thirtysomething", but the show managed to signal none of it really mattered, which was just as well by the time we got to the late-season twists about Fallon being abducted by aliens. If you want an exchange that encapsulates the series' cheery insouciance to narrative continuity, it's Heather Locklear being re-introduced to Joan Collins: "Weren't you my mother-in-law at one time?" Late in the Clinton era, I came across the President telling Susan Estrich, "They have no idea what we went through to save this marriage… Or perhaps how important it was that we did - not just for the country, but for the two of us." And I realized "The Clintons" was the show Spelling missed, the DC version of "Dynasty", in which occasional references to "the country" and "the government" and "Bob Dole" were merely the equivalent of "the pipeline" and the "Imos Project", just a pretext for the extramarital sex.

But by then Spelling had moved on – to the teens of "90210" and the twentysomethings of "Melrose Place". He was proudest of "Family", the semi-credible issue-drama with Meredith Baxter and Kristy McNicol. But of all Spelling's Seventies shows it's the one that resonates least today – and I'll bet he understood that. He changed with the times. For example, "Charlie's Angels" was said to have ushered in the era of "jiggle TV", an industry term deriving from the way Kate Jackson, Farrah Fawcett, and Jaclyn Smith spent most of their time running about while their finer points bounced around the screen like a primitive computer game. Jiggle has been in short supply in Hollywood since the hardbody look came in. When the gals on "90210" or "Melrose" run around, heads, arms, legs all move, but the breasts stay fixed on course with the precision of a Cruise missile.

The "90210" life was a long way from his own childhood. Growing up as a child of Jewish immigrants in Texas, he'd always wanted a rocking horse, but his folks couldn't afford one. And then one day his mom told him to look outside – and there it was! And he went out in the street and climbed up on it, and a photographer snapped a picture – and then they took the rocking horse away. Mom and dad had paid a nickel for the photographer and another nickel to rent the horse for the pic. Little Aaron cried the rest of the day. When his daughter Tori was born, he bought her a rocking horse the following morning.

Asked to recount his rags-to-mega-riches rise from Jewish schnook on the wrong side of the tracks in Dallas to Hollywood power broker living in the largest private residence in the state of California (56,000-plus square feet), Spelling had a string of anecdotes like that one: The *Variety* writer who came up with the headline "Stix Nix Hick Pix" hires him as the band boy for his wife's all-girl band, Preston Sturges comes to see his play, Vincente Minnelli casts him in *Kismet* as a dingy beggar and gives him only one line - "Alms for the love of Allah." And it was such an unrewarding experience that the hick nixed the pix and moved from acting into writing, producing and jiggling.

What a story. His life read like a script for one of his TV movies, adapted from Jackie Collins or Sidney Sheldon.

Or, anyway, it read like a treatment. Which he would have taken as a compliment.

The Atlantic Monthly

Thank you and goodnight

JACK PAAR
MAY 1ST 1918 ~ JANUARY 27TH 2004

I F ALL THE world's a stage, and all the men and women merely
players, with their exits and their entrances, then on the whole Jack
Paar preferred exits. The most famous line of his TV career
accompanied a walkout ("There must be a better way of making a
living than this"), and though NBC eventually coaxed him back ("I
have looked, and there isn't"), it wasn't for long. Paar enjoyed saying
goodbye, and put a lot of effort into it. For his final "Tonight Show" -
on March 29th 1962 - he assembled an audience of friends and
colleagues and announced that there'd never be another gathering like
it until his funeral. Three years later, for his final "Jack Paar Program",
he did the opposite: the studio was empty except for one lone audience
member, his German shepherd, and he ended by calling "Come on,
Leica!", picking up his stool, and leading her into the wings.

If the must-be-a-better-way flounce was the splashiest Paar exit,
the elegiac dog act is the insiders' exit, the one the pros love. In the last
episode of "The Larry Sanders Show", Garry Shandling's parody host,
seeking inspiration for his own sign-off, watches an old kinescope of
Paar's farewell and chokes up - either because Paar is genuinely moving
or because Shandling is mocking the reverence in which the hard-
nosed hosts of today hold the meanderings of a long-gone predecessor.

Johnny Carson signing off after 30 years made less of a
hullabaloo than Paar signing off after 30 months. Few fellows have
been so eager to get into showbusiness and then so eager to get out of
it. He quit school and, despite a stammer, was an announcer on a
Michigan radio station at the age of 16. After the war Jack Benny got
him a gig at NBC as his summer replacement, and RKO signed him as
an actor. Then both his radio and movie contracts lapsed, and Fred

Allen took to musing about "the young man who had that meteoric disappearance".

That's really Paar's entire career: a meteoric disappearance. Television is about showing up - night after night, decade after decade, like Johnny. Jay, Dave, and Conan have all been doing their respective shifts more than twice as long as Paar hosted "The Tonight Show", and in all three cases you'd be surprised if a farewell show was planned for this decade or the first half of the next, Likewise, it's hard to imagine anything unusual or surprising happening - with the exception of heart surgery and celebrity gubernatorial announcements - on any of those shows between now and the end. But so what?

Steve Allen, "Tonight"'s founding father, was a prodigious talent of the old school: composer, lyricist, pianist, singer, comic, actor. His "Tonight Show" was a show. Taking up the reins in 1957, Paar inaugurated the "talk show". Merv Griffin likes to call the format the only "art form" invented by TV; everything else - the quizzes, the soaps, the sitcoms - came from radio. We take it for granted now, but imagine trying to explain to the execs the logic of the furniture arrangements: a couch alongside a desk next to an orchestra. Until Paar did it, a talk show was at least potentially oxymoronic.

Paar's show was a transitional phase, and not just because guests still sort of did things (Cassius Clay recited a poem – "The Legend of Cassius Clay" - accompanied by Liberace at the piano). The talkers Paar favored were the likes of Oscar Levant, Bea Little, George S Kaufman, Hermione Gingold, Peter Ustinov, Elsa Maxwell, Robert Morley - theatricals, raconteurs, anecdotalists, British people. In my early days in broadcasting I was a bit player on a BBC show that valiantly upheld what was left of that tradition, featuring, indeed, many of the same guests - Miss Gingold, Sir Peter, and so forth. And at my tender age I found myself vaguely irked by the urbanity, the hard-polished parquet of the anecdote. As the host wrapped up an interview with one *grande dame* of the West End, she protested that he hadn't let her do her Laurence Olivier anecdote – or as she put it, in a phrase that encapsulates an entire school of reminiscence, "But dahling, I haven't told my Larry."

Such figures are conspicuous by their absence on the couches of Paar's successors. When, say, Peter O'Toole turns up on Letterman recounting David Lean camel stories, it doesn't seem quite right. Introducing Kenneth Branagh, Dave might as well have been ushering on a Bhutanese yak herdsman: "He's a *raconteur*, if you will." Dread word. Afterward a CBS big shot said to me, "I can't stand that guy. He tries too hard." You couldn't make the same damning criticism of Matt Dillon, slumped in denim, barely able to rouse himself to plug the movie.

Yet Paar's talkers drew as big an audience as Letterman and Leno and their tight list of inarticulate screen celebrities combined, and his was the classic water-cooler show. Paar and his guests were among the last beneficiaries of the great universal middlebrow culture of mid-century, in which operatic divas and slapstick comics were all part of the same landscape. Today's pop culture is not Marshall McLuhan's global village but a global housing project of warring ghettos. On the 21st century "Tonight Show" the musical guests are relegated to twenty-seven minutes past midnight, because the country fans hate the hip-hop, and the hip-hoppers hate the Lite FM stuff, and if you put 'em on any earlier, the audience tunes out. Even the big-time movie stars - the Leos and the Camerons - are pushed further and further past midnight. And the first half of Dave and Jay is closer to Steve Allen than to Jack Paar - skits with stagehands, man-in-the-street stuff, animal acts: ironic vaudeville. Less talk, more show. If the talk show really is TV's own art form, it's going the way of the Hollywood western and the Broadway musical.

Perhaps Paar instinctively understood this. Four decades back you'd get to the office and they'd say, "Hey, did you see what Jack Paar did last night?" But most of the did-you-see moments were subversions of his own format: he'd dismiss a guest for being drunk, he'd book a comic and refuse to laugh at the jokes, he'd switch cue cards and sabotage the duet, he'd get bored with the singer and cut the song off halfway through. You can do that sort of thing only so often, and certainly not for 30 years; "meteoric disappearance" seemed to be built into the show's identity. His opening theme was "Everything's Coming Up Roses" - which at one level is your basic showbiz anthem, but at another, as the Act One finale of *Gypsy*, is a kind of musical breakdown for a character going off the rails. "Mercurial" is the adjective Paar's friends settled on. He "took on" Walter Winchell - a sagging bully for a fading medium roughed up by the cocky young bully of a rising one. But he cried a lot, too.

If you wanted to come up with the perfect name for a parody TV host, you'd be hard put to improve on Jack Paar - Jack Norm, Jack Average, Jack Nightly, who's always reliable, always the same, always at par. But Jack couldn't do that. When he made way for his successor, Dick Cavett heard someone say, "If Carson's on that show ten years, he will never shed a single tear." To which someone replied, "For which I will be profoundly grateful."

One night a couple of decades on, Jack returned to the show, as a guest on Johnny's couch; if you freeze the frame, the two silver foxes could almost be brothers. But then you look closer - the rueful tilt of Jack's head, the angular snap of Johnny's. Carson's voice is brisk and assured; Paar's is wistful and oddly childlike. Johnny didn't do "mercurial". If the talk show is an oxymoron, Carson invented an identity to match: affable and remote, familiar and unknowable. Paar made an entertainment out of his own pathologies: as *Newsweek* put it, "Russian roulette with commercials". Letterman, some say, is his heir. But only up to a point. He'll permit himself to muse, apropos Matt Dillon's monosyllabic grunting, that perhaps it's the lead paint in the dressing room - but only after Dillon's wrapped up and left the set. Letterman is cranky but controlled - Paar for the course.

As for the original, after 1965 he finally achieved the meteoric disappearance he'd been racing for since his radio days. He bought a TV station in Maine, made some travel documentaries; if he ever missed his one brief shining moment, he was better than Steve Allen at concealing his need to get it back. He returned for the last time in

1997, for what proved to be the all-time highest-rated *American Masters* documentary on PBS. As often happens with so-called "public service" broadcasting, the bosses wanted everything shorter and snappier - the only way ignorant executives understand "pace" and "energy". They picked the wrong guy. "I will not have a clip show," Paar told them, putting his foot down. "Look, I've walked off three shows ..."

It was the last show, the last threatened walkout, the perfect Jack Paar epitaph.

The Atlantic Monthly

AUGUST & Royal

The transfiguration

DIANA, PRINCESS OF WALES

JULY 1ST 1961 ~ AUGUST 31ST 1997

O NE DAY, BACK in my disc-jockey youth, the program director called us all in and announced revisions to the Death of the Monarch procedure - a grand name for what was more or less just a dusty tape of solemn music sitting within easy reach in every radio and TV studio in the Commonwealth. It was felt that we needed to distinguish between core Royals - the Queen, the Queen Mother - who merited the full back-to-back-requiems treatment, and peripheral minor duchesses, for whom something melodious but respectful like "Greensleeves" or Pachelbel's Canon would suffice. Painstakingly, we worked our way down the list, until someone asked, "And what about the Princess of Wales?"

"Oh," said a voice from the back of the room, "just bung on the new Wham! album."

As things turned out, by the time she died, George Michael had left Wham!, citing artistic differences, and the Princess had left the Royal Family, for much the same reasons. But, otherwise, my friend had proved surprisingly prescient. There is no protocol covering the sudden, violent death of the beautiful ex-wife of the heir to the throne, but broadcasters throughout Her Majesty's realms reached a quick consensus.

In Quebec, where I happened to be that Sunday morning, radio stations lapsed, en masse, into the likes of Elton John's "Candle In The Wind" and Eric Clapton's "Tears In Heaven" - lachrymose ballads by Di's rock-star pals about others who had died far too young: in Clapper's case, the infant son who plunged to his death from the star's Manhattan apartment; in Elton's, Marilyn Monroe, that other tragic, doomed blonde "icon", whose cult seems likely to prove a mere warm-up to Diana's. In between songs, listeners called up, sobbing, to hail the people's princess as an "angel of mercy", a "saint", a "beacon of light in a dark world", and then to denounce the Prince and the rest of the heartless, dysfunctional, untouchy-unfeely family who had been so resentful of her healing powers.

The radio hosts, also tearful, heartily agreed and then invariably played Bryan Adams' "Everything I Do (I Do For You)". In taking her leave of us, the Princess of Wales had finally, triumphantly slipped free of the last restraints of Royal convention: in ways no Death of the Monarch procedure could ever devise, it was a fitting send-off - the same peculiar combination of intensity, sincerity, and tackiness as the Princess herself.

Somewhere in the attic, I still have my copy of the Death of the Monarch tape, even dustier now. But I don't suppose I or anybody else will get a chance to use it. Diana's death transformed her own image, but it also transformed her former in-laws. And, just as Elton and Sting so effortlessly supplanted Mozart and Beethoven, so, in the days that followed, protocol after protocol came tumbling down. On Britain's palaces, no flag is flown unless the Sovereign is in residence, and then only the Royal standard. So, as the Queen and her family were at Balmoral, the flagpole at Buckingham Palace was bare. But, day by day, the crowds milling around what they'd begun to call the "ice palace" grew more and more affronted by it, and on Thursday the Queen caved in, ordering an unprecedented Union Jack run up the pole of her empty residence just so that it could be lowered to half-mast to appease the mob.

Commonwealth governments around the world, equally uncertain what to do with their flags, phoned the Palace for advice, and were promptly abused by columnists and call-in shows for consulting the reviled House of Windsor rather than the people. By the end of the week, the Queen, the Duke of Edinburgh, and the Prince of Wales had been flushed out of their castle and forced to walk around outside the gates, inspecting the mounds of flowers and trying to look sufficiently distraught. For their pains, they were denounced by disaffected subjects back in London as "hypocrites… makes yer sick, dunnit?"

A revolution took place in Britain that first week of September. Unlike the ones in France and Russia, the masses did not rise up and kill the Royal Family. Instead, they have determined to subject them to a living death - in which everything they say, everything they do will be measured against Diana and found wanting; in which they will be stalked forever by those big, reproachful, kohl-ringed eyes. After the divorce, the Royal Family's strategy with the Princess of Wales was to sit her out, in the sure knowledge that, over time, her public would drift away, and she would come to seem a pathetic figure, as did the Duke of Windsor and, far more quickly, the Duchess of York — an object lesson for Royals in how to be too human.

From the Palace's point of view, it seemed a safe enough bet: in July, the Princess had been seen comforting a weeping Elton John and his lover at the grisly memorial service for Gianni Versace; in August, in between Mediterranean cruises, she had returned to Britain for what she hoped would be a quiet consultation with her favorite psychic — for which, in order to avoid drawing attention to herself, she landed by helicopter in the middle of her clairvoyant's small Derbyshire village accompanied by her millionaire playboy Arab lover, whereupon she was spotted by a little girl with a camera whom she told to go away.

Eventually, the Queen's courtiers reasoned, all but hardcore Diana groupies would weary of this sort of thing. At some point, all soap operas exhaust themselves, as their zigzagging plot twists come to seem increasingly arbitrary, implausible, and unmotivated. What none of those wily courtiers foresaw was that the erratic hairpin bends of the Princess's last months were careening toward one spectacular blowout of a series finale. A few days before her death, Earl Howe, a Conservative foreign affairs spokesman, attacked her as a "loose cannon". Well, she's a fixed cannon now - forever young, forever tragic, forever beautiful - and she's firmly targeted on Buckingham Palace.

The first battleground was the funeral. As "Entertainment Tonight" - these days a more reliable guide to Royal engagements than the Court Circular - put it, "From Elton John to George Michael, new details on who's been invited…" Traditionally, "who's been invited" to a Royal funeral is a list made up of His Royal Highness the Grand Duke of Luxembourg, His Royal Highness Prince Michael of Kent, the Earl of Ulster, His Excellency the Governor-General of Papua New Guinea, the High Commissioner for Tonga, the Lord Chamberlain, Silver Stick in Waiting, etc. But let's face it, compared to your favorite pop stars, they're just a bunch of yawneroos. So, instead, the Queen found herself having to invite Elton John. He announced that he'd be singing "Candle In The Wind", his ode to Marilyn rewritten as an ode to Diana. In place of "Goodbye, Norma Jean", it would now begin "Goodbye, England's rose…"

What happened in Paris that Saturday night is, for a society determined by precedent, bewilderingly unprecedented. Royals have been killed in accidents before - the Princess died a quarter-century almost to the day after poor forgotten Prince William of Gloucester's plane fell from the skies in an air race. But no Royal death has been so bizarrely attuned to the spirit of the age. August is the "silly season" in the British press, and this year, the Princess had done her bit for her chums in the media, embarking on a dizzying summer romance that sent Fleet Street into full-scale remarriage speculation and brought an extravagant array of her lover's ex-girlfriends tumbling out of the cupboard. A good time was had by all.

On the very last day of the silly season, when the Queen's subjects woke to the news that Diana was dead, it seemed in some strange way the best plot twist of all. "I didn't think it was real," a friend told me sadly. Most Diana stories aren't: the soft-porn video, allegedly taped by MI5, in which she and Major Hewitt enjoyed what Fleet Street calls a "romp", ran for days in the London tabloids and even on national TV news bulletins before it was revealed to be just a couple of look-alikes in a sketch for a comedy show. And, as the day dragged on, many TV viewers half expected a similar "retraction", or "clarification". Only gradually did people realize that their queen of hearts had, in fact, had only one, and its ruptured pulmonary vein could not be put together again. "I didn't feel sad at first," another woman told me on Tuesday. "But I can't stop crying now."

And so the grief intensified, and the bereavement-junkies multiplied, and Diana, Princess of Wales, gradually metamorphosed into what one tribute outside her home called "Our New Saint Diana, Canonized By The People If Not By The Pope". Before her death, Diana was a complicated figure, offering something for everyone: there was the slightly dim supermodel and the Royal rock groupie; the tireless super-mum and the vulnerable single mother; and, best of all, the manipulative suicidal bulimic neurotic with the highest staff turnover in London. Death streamlined her: now there was only the luminous angel who walked among her people bestowing love.

A man with Aids said he would have been dead two years ago had Diana not touched him; a three-year-old visited by Diana while in a coma had a miraculous recovery and has now left his best teddy outside Kensington Palace; a nine-year-old treated for heart disease said that Diana had visited her ten times and had offered to do the family's washing if they'd just drop it round at the Palace. For some, a world without the Saint was too much to bear: there were reports of at least two "Diana-related" suicides.

No one could doubt the sincerity of the people's reaction. But their sincerity did not make it any less repellent. The supposedly reserved, bloodless Brits had, like the Princess, swallowed wholesale the vocabulary of American Oprahfied psychobabble, a depressing enough prospect. But they had fused it with the brutish vulgarity of modern British mass culture to create a truly horrible mutant: aggressive empathy. Their message to their Sovereign was in essence: If you can't come out and feel our pain, we'll come in and give you some of your own to feel. Through a spokesman, the Queen protested to the British people that she was not indifferent to their grief.

Hang on: *She*'s not indifferent to *their* grief? The Queen, who had known Diana Spencer since she was a little girl, has to prove that she grieves as much as people who have never met her? On the one hand, the masses disdain the paparazzi for intruding into the privacy of their beloved Princess; on the other, the masses are quite happy metaphorically to storm Balmoral and intrude on the most private moments of all - the right of a family to grieve in their own way for someone close to them. In the week after Diana's death, the moral decay of the British people plumbed new depths. At least the paparazzi, in their own crazed fashion, were seeking something objective: a photograph of two lovers canoodling. The mournerazzi who flooded London were demanding only that those who knew the real Diana sign on to the approved myths: Diana was the queen of hearts, her mother-in-law is a Queen with no heart; Diana was a warm mother, Charles is a cold father. Were they? Who really knows?

Once upon a time, we were more mature: we knew enough to know we didn't know the Royal Family. You don't have to go back a century, just to that long-ago day before yesterday before Lady Diana came along. In the years immediately after the Queen's Silver Jubilee in 1977, the Royal Family were more popular than ever - and no one knew a thing about them. In popular mythology, they could muster a trait apiece - the Queen Mother was supposed to like to play the ponies, Princess Margaret was rumored to be a bit of a tippler - but even these had no reliable confirmation: in her 97 years, the Queen Mum has barely uttered three words in public; no one outside her circle knows what her voice sounds like.

But we all know Di. Like millions of others, I was a Close Intimate Personal Friend – that's to say, I met her briefly three and a half times. The "half" was a chance encounter at Launceston Place, a restaurant near our respective pads in Kensington: she was there to lunch with an old pal, I to lunch with my editor; obviously, we had both asked for discreet tables, so they had seated us back to back at the end of an otherwise empty room. We didn't say much apart from a quick "Hello" and her apologies when she put her chair on the back of my trailing coat and tugged my own seat out from under me. I enjoyed her girlish voice and orgasmic giggle.

I know it doesn't compare with the personal note she sent to Barbara Walters, which Barbara has been reluctantly revealing for the first time every hour on the hour on ABC. But I mention it because the Princess wasn't known for physical comedy, and you'd have thought that some of the diners in the adjoining room might have paused at least to note the incident. But they couldn't have cared less. We left at the same time: outside, the street was deserted; she got into her car and went home.

My point is a simple one: she wasn't always being hounded. It's not difficult for anyone to live a relatively undisturbed Royal existence. Almost everyone apart from Diana did. But a conventional Royal life wasn't enough for her. Elton John's rewritten "Candle In The Wind" spoke of how "your footsteps will always fall here/Along England's greenest hills". If so, it'll be the first time since her schooldays. She never showed the slightest interest in England's greenest hills - or, anyway, not when compared to Switzerland's whitest alps and the Caribbean's silveriest beaches and the Côte d'Azur's swankiest yachts. When her friend Versace was murdered, it was said that he had fused the worlds of fashion, rock, and movies. The Princess fused the worlds of fashion, rock, movies - and royalty. What mad self-destructive ambition.

When Tony Blair, with his usual brilliant opportunism, dubbed her "the people's princess", it was by implication a rebuke to those other, chillier, remoter princesses. I wonder whom he had in mind. The Princess Royal? She's worked for years for the Red Cross and Save the Children, earned herself a place on the British Olympic team, and yet never gets into *People* or *National Enquirer*. Or the Duchess of Gloucester? Princess Alexandra? These women preside over dozens of charities, many of them unfashionable ones without photogenic moppets or cadaverous young men; they serve as colonels-in-chief of regiments in boring places far from the paparazzi's lenses, like Saskatchewan; and in return receive nothing very much apart from the Solomon Islands Independence Medal (the Duchess of Gloucester) or the Canadian Forces Decoration (Princess Alexandra).

You can blame the photographers or the drunk driver or an irresponsible lover; you can even blame the French, under whose aegis Diana is not the only Royal (Aly Khan, Princess Grace) to die in a spectacular crash. But the Princess chose the life she led.

As a means of modernizing the monarchy, did it work? At the time of her death, the Princess of Wales was the most recognizable woman in the world and especially popular on this side of the Atlantic. One newspaper crowed that she was the "Queen of America", but, of course, she wasn't: America is a Republic. In the countries over which she had once hoped to reign as Queen - everywhere from Jamaica to New Zealand - the Diana years coincided with an astonishing rise in republican sentiment. The real story of her legacy is that the week before her death, support for the monarchy in Britain fell for the first time below 50 per cent; the week before that, Australia announced the start of a process to examine options to become a republic by the year 2000. A pin-up, even a saintly one, isn't enough. Indeed, Diana's tabloid popularity and tabloid life made serious discussion of the merits of monarchical government almost impossible. It will be the same in death.

"The English people need a light in their dark little tunnels," the Princess said, with exquisite condescension. "I'll be that light." But monarchy is not supposed to be a "Candle In The Wind". As the winds of change swirl all around, it's supposed to be a rock, not a rock song; it represents the deep, ancient roots of society - something all the more important in a present-tense media culture. Far from taking the monarchy into the 21st century, the Princess was on course to kill it in the 20th. If we must canonize her, make her Patron Saint of Republicanism.

National Review

I began to have second thoughts almost immediately after that assessment. And, as it turned out, I was too pessimistic about the Royal Family's post-Di prospects. The Queen is a wily old survivor. And by the time the Queen Mother died in 2002 and the people turned out to salute the last living symbol of the wartime leadership and their victory in that war, it was clear that Diana's stock had been somewhat overvalued, and that Her Majesty's subjects still heard what Lincoln called the "mystic chords of memory". Diana was a "celebrity", and celebrity depends on living presence: once you're gone, the people move on – to new pop stars, new supermodels, new lights in their dark little tunnels. A man like Ronald Reagan lives on because the ideas he promoted live on: he pushed against the grain of the age and changed it. Bill Clinton, by contrast, was America's Princess Di. Here's my reconsideration of Diana from almost a year later – July 1998:

THE OTHER day at Althorp, Earl Spencer's family estate, "Baywatch" hunk David Hasselhoff was delighting the crowds with "A Brand New Angel" - a song originally written for a deceased character on his TV show but, like a good Hallmark greeting card or those sweepstakes letters advising you that you've won $20 million, apparently of universal application. The hunk then prayed to the late Princess of Wales to stop the rain. "And she did," he said. "It was the most amazing thing."

In the last room of Lord Spencer's new Diana museum, visitors can watch one final video - of the Princess and her two sons on an amusement park ride. I'm glad the Earl has a video of his nephews, because he's not seeing much of them in real life. Despite his "serving notice" on the Queen at Westminster Abbey that the Spencers intended to continue Diana's "imaginative" approach to the princes' upbringing, the boys have managed to keep their distance from their maternal family. They missed, alas, Mr Hasselhoff's serenade to that brand new angel. Nor are they spending much time riding the rollercoaster. In the days after her death, that video was replayed endlessly. Along with the baseball caps and the trips to McDonald's, it was cited as conclusive proof of Diana the Good Mother. Had Diana been a suburban housewife in Jersey, the baseball caps, Big Macs and theme-park rides would not have been hailed as "imaginative" child-rearing, only as the dreariest compliance with the dictates of the age.

But here's the surprise: it turns out Wills and Harry don't much care for being shoved into baseball caps and schlepped around

McDonald's. Apparently, they prefer fishing in tweeds at Balmoral. No one would wish any child the loss of his mother, but ten months on you can almost sense the princes' relief that they're no longer swept along in the wake of their mum's heat-seeking glamour: no more Versace, no more Dodi, no more Hasselhoff, no more Tom Cruise and Nicole Kidman. Instead, just damp, drafty royal palaces where they can get on with dreary, traditional Windsor activities of no photographic value to the press. Last September's ululating mob, baying outside the gates for the heartless Queen to deliver up the young princes, may have seriously believed they had the boys' best interests at heart. In fact, they were just demanding that the princes abase themselves before their own narrow obsessions: celebrities and hamburgers. They owe the reviled Queen an apology: she knew her grandkids better than they did.

Let's take as read the official media line - that the Windsors are a bunch of stuffy, uptight, repressed, dysfunctional toff weirdos. Even so, it seems perverse in the extreme to hail the Princess for taking up with the one crowd even weirder than the Windsors - the Hollywood/rock star/Eurotrash celebrity circuit. The Prince of Wales may talk to his plants, but unlike Michael Jackson, he doesn't travel around with a 12-year-old boy in matching white gloves and surgical mask, the winner of a Michael Jackson look-alike contest in Norway.

The Queen can probably live with a celestial Diana with the power to stop the rain. On balance, that's preferable to the old earthbound Diana, who seemed more preoccupied in trying to stop the reign. Death has given the Royal Family the divorce they never quite pulled off in life. Monarchical democracy has traditionally distinguished between the "dignified" and "efficient" parts of the constitution; for the entertainment age, the deceased Princess provides a third wing - the undignified part of the constitution. So, if you want to light a candle in the windiness, then get on the bus to Althorp. Meanwhile, back at the palace, the greyer, wrinklier, duller royals will be getting on with business.

Southam News

A gentleman, of a kind

H.S.H. PRINCE RAINIER III OF MONACO
MAY 31ST 1923 ~ APRIL 6TH 2005

T HE GRIMALDIS had been intermittent rulers of their patch of the Côte d'Azur for three centuries before deciding, in 1612, to make themselves "princes". But, unlike other European rulers of that rank, Honoré II, Seigneur de Monaco, optcd to be styled not "His Royal Highness" but "His Serene Highness". For the last two decades of Prince Rainier's long reign over Monte Carlo, few highnesses had less to be serene about.

His American wife, who'd brought celluloid glamour to a realm where the real thing had been in short supply, died in a car crash in 1982.

His older "sensible" daughter married unsuitable Euro-playboys.

His younger, wilder daughter – now an older, wilder fortysomething - preferred consorting with butlers, gardeners, elephant trainers and (at the time of writing) a Portuguese trapeze artist. Her marriage to her bodyguard collapsed after he was captured on film guarding somewhat too closely somebody else's body – that of Miss Bare Breasts of Belgium. Princess Stephanie was herself no slouch in that department, as the most casual student of European photojournalism of the late 20th century would confirm. For a few months after using the high-speed Internet in a Paris hotel, I regularly woke up to spam e-mail containing extensive pictorials of Her Serene Highness giving us the full Monte, naked on a beach and engaged in the act of, ah, self-pleasuring. Possibly she was between circus acts at the time. At any rate, Prince Rainier's youngest grandchild has, for whatever reason, a father whose identity cannot be made public. It's presumably not the elephant trainer, or Princess Grace's old

Hollywood pals would have been round to serenade the kid with "Born In A Trunk".

If his daughter's life in middle-age appeared to be one unending audition for "Desperate Royal Housewives", Rainier's son by contrast declined to produce an heir or indeed any evidence that he was much interested in the principal activity likely to lead to that happy event. As *The New York Times* nudgingly reported, "Prince Albert, meanwhile, has been linked to a long list of high-profile women known for appearing on the arms of middle-aged bachelors. There have been no signs of anything like a romance." Hmm. But, just as you think the *Times* is trying to tell us something, His Serene Highness acknowledges that he's fathered a child in Paris by a Togolese woman. Oh, come off it, you cry. How many Euros did that scam cost? But it's the real thing: they've matched the DNA. It's his best career move in decades.

Easy lay the head that wore the crown, but underneath a profound sadness etched itself into Rainier's face. He aged a quarter-century in the couple of years after Princess Grace's death, and as the Eighties rolled into the Nineties it sometimes seemed as if the entire House of Grimaldi's sense of itself had careered round the hairpin bends on the Grande Corniche and plunged over the cliff with his beloved wife.

His was the worst-timed death since Aldous Huxley expired on the day of President Kennedy's assassination. Europe's longest-reigning monarch shuffled off a couple of days after the Pope and so, while his nuptials had been hailed as the wedding of the century, his passing wasn't even the funeral of the week. Nonetheless, in the half-century between the Duke of Windsor and the Princess of Wales, he was, briefly, the only member of a European dynasty to capture the imagination of the American public.

When Fred Astaire began his partnership with Ginger Rogers, Katharine Hepburn observed that he gave her class and she gave him sex. With Prince Rainier and Grace Kelly, she gave him sex and class, and it wasn't entirely obvious what a stiff mustachioed chap never exactly dashing even in his youth brought to the table. Monaco was, in Somerset Maugham's unimprovable summation, "a sunny place full of shady people", and exposed to the light they didn't bear too close scrutiny. Jack Kelly, Grace's father and a respectable self-made millionaire in the Philadelphia construction business, couldn't have been less impressed than if she'd come home with one of Princess Stephanie's circus acrobats: as he's reported to have said, "I don't want any damn broken-down prince who is head of a pinhead country that nobody knows anything about to marry my daughter." And who can blame him? If you'd married off Lana Turner, Betty Hutton, Mitzi Gaynor or most of the other livelier Hollywood cheesecake into a European royal house, you'd have had the premise for a lame B-comedy. But Grace Kelly was already more regal than most real princesses, speaking the Queen's English with an amused languid rarified over-articulateness the Queen couldn't get away with. As Frank Sinatra sang to her in *High Society*:

> *I don't care*
> *If you are called the fair*
> *Miss Frigidaire...*

She was certainly the most glacial of Hitchcock blondes, cooler with Jimmy Stewart than any leading lady before or after. In the last great group shot of Euro-royals before her death – at the Prince of Wales' (first) wedding in 1981 – she's carrying herself with far more sense of her royalness than, say, the Queens of Spain or the Netherlands, never mind Their Royal Highnesses the Duchess of Gloucester and Princess Michael of Kent.

By contrast, when Prince Rainier succeeded his grandfather in 1949, he was taking over an enterprise whose best days seemed well behind her. The pocket-principality had suffered from France's legalization of gambling in 1933, after a century of prohibition. It seemed unlikely ever to return to its 19th century heyday, when British music-hall songs hymned its raffish charms:

As I walk along the Bois Boolong
With an independent air
You can hear the girls declare
He must be a millionaire
You can hear them sigh and wish to die
You can see them wink the other eye
At The Man Who Broke The Bank At Monte Carlo.

The verse spells it out bluntly:

Dame Fortune smiled upon me as she'd never done before
And I've now such lots of money, I'm a gent.

That was the Grimaldis: lots of money made them gentlemen, of a kind. Rainier's mother, Princess Charlotte, was the result of a liaison between Prince Louis II and Marie-Juliette Louvet, the daughter of a laundrywoman at the Grimaldi palace who'd made her way to the nightclubs of Montmartre and become a "cabaret singer", after a fashion. Marie was for a while the husband of Achille Delmaet, one of those *belle époque* figures half-remembered for his nude photographs of the can-can dancers at the Moulin Rouge, but after taking up with Louis she gave birth to their daughter Charlotte in Algeria in 1898. The Grimaldis gave Charlotte the bum's rush for most of her childhood until, in the absence of any other heir and laboring mightily under a 13th century curse on the family, they passed a law recognizing her as Louis' daughter. This was struck down by the courts, so in 1918 they tried again, retrospectively legitimizing her and belatedly declaring the Montmartre nightclub act's Algerian love-child an hereditary princess, Duchess of Valentinois and first in line to succeed Louis II: as Charlotte's mother must have occasionally reflected, you came the long way to Prince Louis.

The following year, Princess Charlotte was married to the Comte de Polignac, and in 1923 they had a son: Rainier. His duty done, Charlotte had no further use for M le Comte. "To make love," she sneered, "he needs to put a crown on his head." Under the terms of their divorce, Polignac was forbidden to set foot in Monaco and the royal guard – the Prince's Company of Carabineers – were ordered to arrest him if he tried. Princess Charlotte eventually became a social worker and turned the Grimaldi estate outside Paris into a rehab facility for ex-cons. As for young Rainier, he was sent to enjoy the pleasures of boys' school in England, where the Comte attempted to reassert his parental authority. It was the British High Court who restored "Fat Little Monaco" (as he was known to his schoolmates) to his grandfather's custody.

By the time Fatty succeeded Prince Louis, the men who fancied breaking the bank at Monte Carlo had moved down the coast to Cannes and elsewhere, and the bank itself was near broke. The Société des Bains de Mer, which ran the casino and hotels, reported huge losses that year. Next, the Société Monégasque de Banques et de Métaux Précieux, which held 55 per cent of Monaco's reserves and much of the Grimaldi fortune, went bust. Aristotle Onassis, who served as the young Rainier's *éminence* Greece, thought a marriage into the upper strata of movie-stardom might restore the Principality's fortunes, and sounded out Marilyn Monroe, to no avail. Then, while in the neighborhood for the Cannes Film Festival, Grace Kelly was taken to the palace for a photo shoot and Rainier made his move.

It worked out well. His bride embarked on the usual charitable activities associated with Royal consorts but with the benefit of a much livelier Rolodex: throughout the Sixties and Seventies, old chums like Sinatra and Bob Hope turned Monegasque fundraising galas into the touring version of the starrier Friars' Club roasts. Tourism and development followed. Monaco is a small town of 30,000 people, mostly tax exiles but with about 6,000 Monegasques to play the role of Rainier's loyal subjects. As land was reclaimed and skyscrapers loomed over the fishing boats, Monaco's stellar princess gave her husband a cachet denied to the other mini-me Euro-royals like the Grand Dukes of Luxembourg and Liechtenstein.

Princess Grace missed movies and Rainier gave her permission to return to her old job for Hitchcock's *Marnie*. But his people found the idea vulgar and demeaning, and so *High Society* remained the House of Grimaldi's last on-camera performance until Princess Stephanie's husband made his film debut with Miss Bare Breasts of Belgium.

By then, Rainier was old, stooped and exhausted; his princess was dead; and his children seemed determined to return the family name to its seedy antecedents. He made his dilapidated casino kingdom briefly romantic and, when he couldn't maintain the romance, he had the satisfaction at least of knowing he'd made Monaco bankable again. But the 13th century family curse came along for the ride and in the end it broke the man at Monte Carlo.

The Atlantic Monthly

The prototypical bicycling monarch

H.R.H. THE PRINCESS JULIANA OF THE NETHERLANDS
APRIL 30TH 1909 ~ MARCH 20TH 2004

EVEN BEFORE the tireless efforts of Larry King, Kitty Kelley, and *People*, to most Americans outside Kansas City "the Royals" had always meant the House of Windsor. But there are other Royals too, and the collective term for the surviving Continental houses, at least in Britain, is "the bicycling Royals". Technically, not all Scandinavian or Low Country monarchs bicycle, but they do all affect a less obviously regal style than Queen Elizabeth, which British "reformers" (that is, republicans) say is more in keeping with an egalitarian age. This is a bit unfair to Elizabeth II, who does her best to keep up with the times - dancing Queen to queen with Sir Elton John to "Rock Around The Clock", and on another occasion taking tea with him in the Royal Enclosure at Ascot while the Duke of Edinburgh made somewhat strained conversation with Sir Elton's "partner". The Court of St James's, with its elaborate orders of precedence for widows of baronets and second sons of marquesses, has managed to adjust its rules of placement to accommodate the gay consorts of elderly rock stars.

But for its critics the House of Windsor is still impossibly snooty compared with the unstuffy bicycling monarchies. The lady who gave a name to this phenomenon was the prototypical bicycling monarch, Queen Juliana of the Netherlands. She had a bicycle, and she rode it around in public at a time when most monarchs stuck to their gold coaches. Sometimes she rode it to the supermarket. And although

85

she was 94 at the time of her passing (and, since her abdication, merely a princess), she died in the saddle, if only in newspaper shorthand: "Holland Mourns Bicycling Queen" (*The Observer*); "Informal Reign Of The Bicycling Queen" (*The Australian*).

"Imagine Prince Charles, whose highfalutin thoughts on the environment have bored us all, actually getting on a bike, as Queen Juliana did, and cycling to work among his subjects," Vanessa Feltz sneered in *The Express*. "Fat chance." I would have thought the chance was no fatter than that of seeing Ms Feltz, a decidedly queenly British telly personality, cycling to work among her viewers. Of course, were the Prince of Wales to do as he's told and mount his trusty, rusty Raleigh, Ms Feltz and the rest of the press would be the first to complain about the attendant security detail clogging up the bike path.

In truth, Juliana's homespun monarchy was the product of a particular combination of factors.

First, the House of Orange has leaned to the distaff side for more than a century: Queen Wilhelmina, Juliana's mother, succeeded to the throne in 1890, at the age of ten, with Juliana's grandmother as Regent until she was 18; Juliana's daughter, Beatrix, is Queen today. A bicycling queen fits easily into a "mother of the nation" tradition. Had King Zog of Albania tried it, it would have been further confirmation that he was a flake.

Second, Queen Wilhelmina was a devout woman who, among other expressions of her faith, forbade Juliana, a somewhat plain teenager, to wear makeup. When the Princess Margaret glamour-puss role is closed off to you, you might as well exploit the political advantages of homeliness. As Queen, Juliana bought her frocks off the peg.

Third, the German invasion forced Wilhelmina and her government into exile in England. For Juliana and her daughters (and eventually her husband, Prince Bernhard), it was merely an interim stop. King George VI's cousin Princess Alice was married to the Earl of Athlone, then the Governor-General of Canada, and it was decided that the Dutch princesses would live with them in Ottawa. Canada is a monarchy, but a minimalist one. The sovereign is, after all, several thousand miles away, and though the Canadian Crown mimics the mother country's in external appearances (royal officers in Ottawa share with London such appealingly obscure designations as Gentleman Usher of the Black Rod), the full works, the bowing and scraping would be ludicrous in a prairie kingdom. John Buchan, the thriller writer and Lord Athlone's predecessor as viceregal eminence, observed, "You have to know a man awfully well in Canada to know his surname." One of Juliana's first acts on her assumption of the throne was to abolish the requirement that ladies curtsy.

Fourth, in 1948 the central fact concerning the nation she'd become Queen of was that it had been under Nazi occupation. During the war virtually the entire Jewish population was murdered. There was a brave Dutch resistance, and there were others who reached accommodations with the new regime. But neither category was inclined to fawn before a Queen who'd sat out the war in Canada - and had a German husband. The postwar world diminished royal status in other ways: the Dutch lost control over their overseas possessions, from the East Indies to Indonesia, and Juliana became the first ruler of the Netherlands in almost half a millennium to be reduced to being ruler merely of the Netherlands. Even that modest territory seemed vulnerable. In 1953 tremendous floods killed thousands of people and put a sixth of her realm under water, like a disaster-movie remake of King Canute's seaside lesson to his courtiers in the limitations of regal power. The royal houses that had survived the calamities that befell the Continent were concerned for the most part not to catch their subjects' eye. After Third Reichs and October Revolutions, mothballing the carriages and biking to the palace was a way to avoid the cycle of violence. Juliana sent her children to public school, which in Holland isn't quite the sacrificial gesture it is in the District of Columbia but nevertheless had a symbolic power.

There was no coronation, no cheering throngs, no "The Queen is dead. Long live the Queen!" For one thing, the old Queen wasn't dead. Wilhelmina stepped down because 1948 marked her 50th anniversary, and like Johnny Carson, she thought it time to quit. Juliana, in her turn, retired in 1980, demoted herself from Queen to Princess, and made way for Beatrix. No fuss, no fanfare. Dutch monarchs aren't crowned but, rather, sworn in with less ceremony than a New Hampshire town clerk.

There are arguments to be made in favor of a monarchy or a republic, but Holland's rump monarchy of quasi-republican cheeseparers seems unsatisfying by any measure. In terms of private wealth Juliana was a much richer Queen than Elizabeth II. Her grandfather, King Willem III, was a founding shareholder of Royal Dutch Shell Petroleum (just as, 400 years ago, Prince Maurits of Orange started the colonial profits gushing by sponsoring the Dutch East India Company), the original Royal Dutch shell company, at least in the sense that the Oranges have been far more adroit than the Windsors in blurring the distinction between private income and the perks of colonial expansion. One could argue that in return for the life of ease deriving from this vast wealth, it's surely not too much to ask them to ride through the streets with a regiment of dashing hussars once or twice a reign. In 1980, when Juliana handed over to Beatrix, the induction prompted the biggest street riots in Dutch history. Mostly republicans, but it would be heartening to think that among the concrete-lobbers there were at least a few royalists who felt aesthetically cheated by this publicly dressed-down monarchy.

By then it was unclear whether the Dutch armed forces could have rustled up enough dress uniforms for a parade. In the course of her three-decade reign Juliana presided over a trickle-down informality that gave the Netherlands the first Nato soldiers with long hair, and legalized prostitution and pot and (eventually) euthanasia. The last would seem to be the logical answer to reconciling Elizabeth II's belief that monarchs should die in harness with Juliana's antipathy to reigning into advanced old age.

But perhaps the quirks of Dutch royalty will not be a problem much longer. Along with their relaxed attitude toward monarchy and marijuana, the Dutch seem to be relaxing themselves right out of business. Just over a year ago I had a conversation with a senior Dutch government minister apropos demographic trends in the kingdom (Mohammed is the most popular name for newborn boys in Amsterdam). In the wake of 9/11 he and his colleagues realized that something had gone wrong, that today's young Dutch Muslims are less assimilated than their grandparents; aware that I was Canadian, he told me his government wished to counter this with a citizenship ceremony modeled on Canada's, in which new citizens take an oath of allegiance to Queen Elizabeth. But he worried that the concept of an oath to the Queen might be a bit too overtly nationalistic for the Dutch. I suggested to him, as politely as I could, that when Canadian nationalism is too strong meat for you, you know you've got a problem.

Today the idea of an unaffected Queen bicycling among her subjects has a faintly comical innocence, like a restless soprano in a Silver Age operetta, or Princess Osra's secret visits to the miller of Hofbau in Anthony Hope's Ruritania. It was a transitional phase, and no one yet knows where the bike path ends. As he left America's Constitutional Convention, Benjamin Franklin, fearing an inevitable tendency toward monarchy, told an inquiring citizen that the country now had "a republic, if you can keep it". A bicycling monarchy is harder to keep.

The Atlantic Monthly

Hinting at pleasure

H.R.H. THE PRINCESS MARGARET, COUNTESS OF SNOWDON
AUGUST 21ST 1930 ~ FEBRUARY 9TH 2002

I HAVEN'T SEEN any official Canadian statements offering condolences to the Queen on the death of Princess Margaret. Perhaps the Bloc, as part of its heroic revolutionary struggle, has vetoed them. But I note that most reports begin with references to "years of heavy smoking" or, alternatively, "of heavy smoking and drinking". The great Australian wag Tim Blair contrasts this with the obituaries for Linda McCartney, who was respectfully styled as a "committed vegetarian": when a committed vegetarian dies of cancer at 56, it's just one of those things, could've happened to anyone; when a heavy smoker/drinker lives out her three score and ten, she's a victim of her addictions.

I can testify to her prodigious intake. A few years ago, I was on the judges' panel of some music prize and, come the awards ceremony, found myself sitting across the table from Her Royal Highness. This was way back in the mid-Nineties and even then the lunch had the vague feel of a parody Royal occasion. I'd been put next to Vera Lynn, Britain's famed "Forces' Sweetheart" of World War Two, celebrated songstress of "We'll Meet Again" and "(There'll Be Bluebirds Over) The White Cliffs Of Dover". She sent back the avocado, sniffing "This French food disagrees with me." That's the Dunkirk spirit.

Over the table, Princess Margaret seemed tetchy and irritable and, after some whispering with our host, the compère of the occasion stood up and announced that we would have the Loyal Toast a little early "thus enabling a certain personage among us to smoke". For any Bloquiste readers, I should explain that the Loyal Toast to Her Majesty comes at the end of the meal, after which guests are permitted to light up. But, for the first time in my experience, the Loyal Toast was being scheduled in the middle of the hors d'oeuvres. So, halfway through the avocado, we all shuffled to our feet, raised our glasses, toasted "The Queen!" and, before our bottoms had hit the upholstery, Princess Margaret had whipped out her ivory cigarette holder, loaded up, and was awaiting a light.

According to the obituaries, she was a 30-a-day gal. By my reckoning, she got through a good couple of dozen over lunch. By the time Vera Lynn sent back the fish and asked them to bring her some chicken, Her Highness had had at least three. By the time Dame Vera sent back the chicken, telling the waiter "This is inedible", Her Highness had had maybe six or seven. By the time Dame Vera remarked to me that "the colour of your jacket is making me nauseous", Her Highness was on her second pack. She smoked between mouthfuls, she smoked between gulps, she smoked between cigarettes.

The Princess' understanding of the deal was admirable in its simplicity. She had lent her Royal lustre to the occasion, and in return she expected to be entertained. I ventured an amusing anecdote - short, colourful, breezy set-up, zinger of a punch line. She seemed to be enjoying it, until, ten seconds before the end, she cut me off and demanded to know, "Has anyone seen *Jurassic Park*?" Someone had, and started to tell a Spielberg story, but again she cut him off and moved on to someone else. I'd got it figured out by now: When the cigarette burned down to approx. three-eighths of an inch from the filter, she'd kill your anecdote stone dead. If you could *raconte* quicker than she could smoke, you had a sporting chance.

She handed out the prizes with noticeable lack of enthusiasm – I'm comparing her not just to Di but to the Queen - and then tottered off, a tiny woman, barely five foot, atop huge chunky shoes, like Minnie Mouse with an attitude problem. "She was on good form today," an old Royal hand told me. "Doesn't always go as well." Someone said that the Princess had given the elderly lady-in-waiting accompanying her a toilet brush for Christmas because the Princess had had to use the bathroom at her house and discovered she hadn't got one.

The awards were supposed to honour up-and-coming young talent, but in my corner of the room, between Vera and Margaret, the whole thing seemed suffused in the grim monochrome austerity of post-war Britain. "Post-war Britain" is a term that covers not just a couple of years in the late Forties, but an entire era, constraints such as petrol rationing stretching languorously on to taint a generation, from VE Day to, well, somewhere "between the end of the *Chatterley* ban/And the Beatles' first LP", to quote Philip Larkin. In Britain's post-war baby boom, there were babies, but no boom. I have no first-hand experience of the time or place - I wasn't even a twinkle in my parents' eyes, they being barely twinkles themselves - but I always like the bit in pretty much any Mordecai Richler novel when the young Montreal protagonist arrives in 1950s London and is shocked by what the locals call the totty. "Where were the girls?" wonders Jake in *St Urbain's Horseman*. "Oh my God, the ones he saw in the pubs were so depressingly lumpy, all those years of bread-and-dripping and sweets and fishpaste sandwiches having entered their young bodies like a poison, coming out here as a moustache, there as a chilblain, and like lead through the teeth."

In a world where even the pin-ups were homely and/or beefy chantoozies like Dame Vera, Anne Shelton and Alma Cogan, Princess Margaret Rose was a rare bloom. If you look at the early portraits of the young princesses, Margaret and Elizabeth, they have the same features - same eyes, same lips, same nose, same curls, same impressive Windsor bosom - but there's a flash in Margaret's eyes, a tease in the lips. The Queen is all business, her sister hints at pleasure. Fifty years ago, on the death of her father, Princess Elizabeth returned from Kenya to London as Queen and was greeted at the airport by Churchill, who was so overcome by grief he could barely speak his words of condolence. The Queen is said to have replied, "A sad homecoming.

But a smooth flight." Yes, well, there we are. Mustn't grumble. All very English.

Margaret, on the other hand, ran with a raffish West End fast set. Unlike the rest of the family, she had no interest in the country, not the British kind anyway. When she left town, it was not for Sandringham or Balmoral, but Tuscany or Mustique. Her affair with Group Captain Peter Townsend, a dashing divorcé, became public on the very day of her sister's Coronation, when she was seen on the porch of Westminster Abbey familiarly brushing a piece of fluff from his uniform. When their love survived the machinations of courtiers, she was forced to make the classic Royal choice and announced she would not marry him, "mindful of the Church's teachings that Christian marriage is indissoluble, and conscious of my duty to the Commonwealth." That would be us.

How quaintly Ruritanian it seems. "Is love the only thing?" Princess Flavia asks her English adventurer in *The Prisoner Of Zenda*. "If love were the only thing, I would follow you - in rags, if need be - to the world's end; for you hold my heart in the hollow of your hand!.. But honour binds a woman too, Rudolf. My honour lies in being true to my country and my House."

The bright eyes dimmed. The dazzling smile soured. In some of the group shots for Charles and Di's wedding, Princess Margaret's the only one who doesn't seem to be under any illusions. She never found a role, only endless lunches like the one above, dinners and receptions, charities and openings, in London and Toronto, Belize and Botswana, the sum of whose parts never added up to any kind of coherent whole. She was a great booster of, for example, Aids charities but never flaunted her saintliness Diana-style. Meanwhile, after her Battle of Britain hero was deemed unsuitable, she ran around with Peter Sellers, Mick Jagger, and a Welsh gardener 17 years her junior, the emblem of duty decaying into an emblem of disappointment, and dissolution. I wouldn't have wanted to live her life and, if the price of its frustrations is that you smoke during the soup course and screw up showbiz anecdotes and give toilet brushes for Christmas, well, that's fine by me. But, as on Coronation Day, on the eve of the Golden Jubilee the Queen has been upstaged by her sister once again - for few people sum up so well how far English society's travelled from those drab, pinched British Fifties.

The National Post

ANTHEMS *&Canticles*

Minute man

IRVING CAESAR
JULY 4TH 1895 ~ DECEMBER 17TH 1996

I'D BEEN NERVOUSLY anticipating Irving Caesar's death, and not particularly because he was 101.

When I first met him, he was a mere whippersnapper of eightysomething, and took me through the genesis of some of his biggest hits. "'Swanee'? Wrote it in 11 minutes," he said proudly. "'Tea For Two'? Wrote it in ten minutes. I write fast. Sometimes lousy, but always fast."

In the years after, he was wont to reprise his favorite stories, as old folk are entitled to do: "'Swanee'? Wrote it in eight minutes. 'Tea For Two'? Wrote it in six minutes." At this rate of attrition, he'd soon be claiming less time to write the songs than it takes to sing them. When he insisted he'd written "Swanee" in one minute, I somehow knew it would be the last time I saw him.

He died a week before Christmas at the age of 101, and he took a large chunk of Tin Pan Alley and Broadway history with him: He was George Gershwin's last surviving lyricist. He wrote for the *Ziegfeld Follies* and the *Scandals*. He gave Al Jolson his signature song and Shirley Temple hers. Unlike George M Cohan, the Yankee Doodle Dandy, who claimed to be born on the Fourth of July but whose birth certificate said the fifth, Caesar's patriotic arrival is confirmed by the municipal records: he was born on the Fourth of July, 1895, on the Lower East Side. As with many of the immigrant kids in that teeming ghetto - Irving Berlin, the Gershwins - pop songs were his ticket uptown.

For half a century, he had his office in Broadway's famous Brill Building, a holdout against the marauding rockers. Eventually, he retreated a couple of blocks to more anonymous accommodations. But no matter how extensively the lobbies and elevators were remodeled in chrome or aluminum, behind Caesar's door everything stayed the same. You were back at Remick's or Mills Music, circa 1925: the sheet-music covers were quaintly dated, the faded photographs showed singers long dead, and each chair had its own spittoon. Caesar himself held court from his BarcaLounger, a protean recliner, puffing his cigar and singing obscure lyrics in a sort of lightweight Jolson, but with such animation that the BarcaLounger would rock back and forth until, by the 24th bar, he'd be fully reclined - a small, white-haired, bow-tied figure in a candy-striped jacket, prone, arms flailing, with only the cigar and rusty springs for accompaniment:

> *IIIIIIII'm* [puff, creak]
> *A little bit fonder of you* [creak]
> *Than of myself* [puff, creak]
> *It's true...*

In his pop songs, he was an old-school Tin Pan Alley opportunist, cashing in on bizarre novelties, with rhymes but no reason ("Lady, Play Your Mandolin" - why, of all things, a mandolin?). Yet, ever since Broadway's surprise hit revival of his 1925 musical *No, No Nanette* in the Seventies, Caesar's songs always seemed to be in the air. "I'm back in the Hit Parade," he barked down the phone to me a decade or so ago. "'Just a Gigolo.' Some black fellow out on the coast covered it." Actually it was a white fellow - David Lee Roth of Van Halen - and, if memory serves, he's from Indiana. But who cares? Singers come and go. Good songs endure.

Then there were those hits that were immune to fashion. Littering his office floor, stacked up against desk legs, were dozens of awards, mostly from Ascap (the American Society of Composers, Authors, and Publishers) and mostly for "Tea For Two" as Most Performed Song of the Decade - not in the 1920s, when it was written, but in 1984, '85, '86 – "They give it to me every year," he'd sigh. "I don't know what to do with 'em any more."

MINUTE MAN

It began when he was taking a nap, resting up for a party, when his composing partner Vincent Youmans shook Caesar's trouser leg and demanded he listen to the new tune. Caesar said no, he was tired, it could wait till the morning. Before cassette machines, lyricists used to write a "dummy lyric" - a bunch of meaningless words that would help them remember the musical stresses. Youmans insisted Caesar do a dummy - so, still half-asleep, he croaked:

Picture you
Upon my knee
Just Tea For Two
And two for tea...

At the end he told Youmans, "That stinks, but I'll do the real lyric in the morning."

It's one of those suspiciously neat showbiz anecdotes, but unusually plausible. For one thing, although the song's called "Tea For Two", there's no reference to the titular beverage after the first quatrain. Also, the middle section makes little sense except as a crude guide to where the rhymes should fall:

Day will break
And you'll awake
And start to bake
A sugar cake
For me to take
For all the boys to see...

"He blew it," Sammy Cahn, lyricist of "Come Fly With Me" and "My Kind Of Town", said to me a few years ago. "He should have capped it with:

For me to take
For Mike and Jake to see...

Well, maybe. But, at the party that night, with Gertie Lawrence and Bea Lillie, the meaningless doggerel was a smash. I wondered whether

99

Caesar still thought the lyric stunk. Nah, he said. "Now I think it's a great lyric."

Both his philosophy and lyric-writing style were summed up in "I Want To Be Happy":

> *Life's really worth living*
> *When you are mirth giving...*

Time magazine used to give pronunciation guides for proper names: Orwell (rhymes with "doorbell"), Longstreet (rhymes with "wrong beat"), etc. It would drive Ira Gershwin nuts. "These aren't being rhymed correctly," he declared, pointing out that Orwell rhymes with door-well, and Longstreet, with wrong street. They're straightforward feminine rhymes with the stress on the penultimate syllable. *Time*, he said, "is rhyming each syllable perpendicularly instead of double-rhyming the name horizontally." But no lyricist liked to rhyme perpendicularly as much as Caesar. Besides "worth living/mirth giving", he also gave us "my sentiment/never meant a cent". "Sentiment/meant a cent," he said, thumping his chest. "I wrote that - a kid from the Lower East Side."

Caesar was a sweet man, but you could detect a certain resentment of Ira Gershwin. When Ira established himself as a lyric-writer, Caesar lost his best composing partner. "Ira's funny with me," he told me once, furtively. "You know why? Because George told him on his deathbed that I'd written the music for 'Swanee'."

"Oh, yes?" I said politely, and wrote his comment off as the mild paranoia of a lyricist who'd been deprived of his source of tunes. Then I thought about it. "Swanee", George and Irving's first big hit (1919), sold more records and sheet music than anything George wrote with Ira. It's more a pop hit than one of the high-toned standards George typically wrote. But, more than that, musically it doesn't sound like George - not a note of it, except maybe the D natural in the ninth bar of the verse. Otherwise, its cornball resilience couldn't be less Gershwinesque. "Swanee" catapulted young George, not Caesar, to stardom but, on the evidence, I'd say there was a strong chance Gershwin's celebrity was kick-started by another man's tune.

We'll never know for sure. Caesar disliked the old question, Which comes first, the words or the music? He'd answer, "When everything's happening that fast, who knows who does what to whom when?" And in the five minutes they took to write "Swanee" at George's uncle's pad, things were certainly happening fast:

I'd give the world [peck]
To [peck]
Be
Among the folks
In
D-I-X-I-Even know my mammy's
Waiting for me...

When a guy's barking those lyrics at you, the tune practically writes itself.

In the late Eighties, I asked him if he had any new songs. "Sure," said the nonagenarian Caesar, who loathed rock and its ancillary activities. "I've written an anti-drug song called, 'Who Needs Marijuana, Baby, When All I Wanna Marry Is You'."

"Don't tell me," I said. "You wrote it in two minutes?"

I like to think of him up there on his celestial BarcaLounger, bugging all those dead rock stars with it.

Slate

Ex-husband
of love goddesses

ARTIE SHAW
MAY 23RD 1910 ~ DECEMBER 30TH 2004

ARTIE SHAW was the last of the big bandleaders of the Swing Era. We think of them as musicians now, and a few of them – very few, according to Shaw – were great artists. But for anyone under a certain age it's hard to comprehend the scale of their celebrity - instrumentalists in tuxes fronting orchestras, and yet they were as big as the biggest movie stars. Imagine Britney if she could play a clarinet. Brilliantly.

On the eve of World War Two, *Time* reported that to Germans America meant "skyscrapers, Clark Gable and Artie Shaw". And Shaw lived more like a movie star than Gable did. In the ranks of legendary heterosexuals, he's rivaled only by Sinatra when it comes to the number of A-list Hollywood babes he got to see in non-Hays Code situations. He was engaged to Betty Grable when he ran off with Lana Turner. He married Ava Gardner and had an affair with Rita Hayworth. Among his eight wives were Evelyn Keyes, who played Mrs Jolson in *The Jolson Story*, and Kathleen Winsor, bestselling naughty novelist of *Forever Amber*, and Betty Kern, daughter of Jerome.

And he loomed large with fictional gals, too. Most fans of P G Wodehouse regard his literary landscape as a timeless playground sealed off from reality: "Mr Wodehouse's world can never stale," wrote Evelyn Waugh. "He has made a world for us to live in and delight in." But Artie Shaw was so ubiquitous at the height of his fame that he has the distinction of being one of the few real, live, flesh-and-blood contemporaries to invade the Wodehouse canon. In *The Mating*

Season, a Hollywood starlet recounts to Bertie Wooster her encounter with an elderly English spinster, who turns out to be something of a movie fan:

> *She knows exactly how many times everybody's been divorced and why, how much every picture for the last twenty years has grossed, and how many Warner brothers there are. She even knows how many times Artie Shaw has been married, which I'll bet he couldn't tell you himself. She asked if I had ever married Artie Shaw, and when I said no, seemed to think I was pulling her leg or must have done it without noticing. I tried to explain that when a girl goes to Hollywood she doesn't* have *to marry Artie Shaw, it's optional, but I don't think I convinced her.*

When he stopped marrying, he started lecturing on it at colleges – "Consecutive Monogamy & Ideal Divorce" by an "ex-husband of love goddesses". "These love goddesses are not what they seem, especially if you're married to one," he explained. "They all think they want a traditional marriage, but they aren't made for that sort of thing. Somebody's got to get the coffee in the morning, and an Ava Gardner is not going to do that. So you get up and get it, and then you find you're doing everything. And why? Because she's the love goddess and that's all she has to be." He had children with a couple of 'em, but didn't care much for them either. "I didn't get along with the mothers," he said. "So why should I get along with the kids?"

Still, celebrity broads were a rare compensation in a world where everything else was a pain in the neck. He was a swing bandleader, but he hated the word "swing", and he was a jazz musician, but he hated the word "jazz". He resented singers, and despised dancers, and loathed fans; the audience were "morons", and the musicians were "prima donnas", and the ones who weren't were hacks who did that cheesy synchronized swaying with the saxes and the trombones that the morons were dumb enough to go crazy for. Glenn Miller? "It would have been better if he'd lived and his music had died." Well, okay, lots of jazz guys have a problem with Miller; how about Benny Goodman? "Musically, he had a limited vocabulary," sniffed Shaw.

Gene Lees has described the big bands of the late Thirties and early Forties as "the sound that will not go away". For Shaw – restless and obsessive – that was the problem. So he went away instead. He started quitting the music business "permanently" a few months after his first hit, and kept on quitting it. But every time he came back the fans were still there, demanding "Star Dust" and "Frenesi". He found out it was one thing to "Begin The Beguine", quite another to try and stop it. "Every time someone comes up to me and says, 'Oh, Mr Shaw, I love 'Begin The Beguine'," he told me, "I want to vomit."

"Sorry," I said, "but I *do* love 'Begin The Beguine'."

"Well, then, you make me want to vomit," he replied. "I did 'Beguine'. It's over. If you want it, get the record. People say, 'Why did you give up music?' I say, 'Have you got every record I ever made?' They say, 'Well, no.' Well, get 'em all and then come back and complain."

He made "Beguine" a hit, all 108 bars of it - the longest standard in the standard repertoire, thanks to Shaw. Cole Porter wrote it as a piece of faux exotica – "Down by the shore an orchestra's playing/And even the palms seem to be swaying…" – but Shaw threw out the lyric and made the tune jump. It may have made him vomit, but people love that record because, two-thirds of a century on, the double thwack of those opening bars is as wild and exciting and unmistakable as anything in American music. It's nothing to do with Porter, just a little figure Shaw and his arranger Jerry Gray cooked up, and then his clarinet comes in riding the rhythm section. You don't have to do it like that, you can play it a thousand different ways, but Shaw's recording opened the way for all the others. Cole Porter understood. On being introduced to the bandleader, he said, "Happy to meet my collaborator."

Three of the best bandleaders of the period were clarinetists – Shaw, Benny Goodman, Woody Herman – and it seems to me that's the core sound of the era, so seductive, so insinuating. Artie, naturally, had no time for that kind of talk. According to him, the executives liked the clarinet because, in those days of primitive recording, its higher pitch made it cut through the band more clearly than the sax. Whatever. Digitally remastered and cleaned up, the arrangements still sound good. On his smash 1940 recording of "Star Dust", Shaw's solo manages, in just 16 glorious bars, to sum up both the broad legato sweep of Hoagy Carmichael's tune and yet get giddily away from it in those lovely triplets. There's so much going on in those early hits – joyous explosive vamps that, for many listeners, became part of the song. You can find later recordings of "'SWonderful" and "My Blue Heaven" that aren't performances of the numbers so much as of the Shaw band's arrangements of them.

As much as he reviled the music biz, he had little time for the pomposity of post-big band jazz. "It doesn't have to sound like broken crockery to be jazz," he sighed. "It's solemn rather than serious. I told Clint Eastwood that *Dirty Harry* was the closest to art he ever got. That picture's America as it really is. Whereas a picture like *Bird*, which was meant to be a serious thing, was solemn and boring. If you're going to pick an artist who's at odds with his time you don't pick Charlie Parker. He was worshipped in his lifetime. He just screwed up."

He went into music just to make enough money to finish his education. He sold 100 million records and found out it wasn't about the money. For most of its practitioners, the point of jazz is that it's not fixed, it's never the same, it's improvisational. For Shaw, that's what made music frustrating. "The trouble with composing is that, when it's done, it doesn't exist. It's just notes on a piece of paper. Until it's performed. And each performer will stick his own thumb print on it and change it. Whereas in a book there it is, you can't change it. If you read Thomas Mann, you're reading Thomas Mann. Nobody improvises around his sentences. The two most honest and pure media are painting and literature. Van Gogh's Starry Night remains the same wherever you hang it. You can achieve your perfection. In music, you can only approximate it."

So he gave up the clarinet, and became a novelist, and a dairy farmer, and a film producer, and the fourth-ranked precision rifleman in America. A decade back, he made his only visit to Britain for a one-night stand, conducting Prokofiev, Mozart and some of his old hits at the Royal Festival Hall. He'd been a hero to a colleague of mine for decades and was supposed to be interviewed by him for the BBC. But my friend fell ill, and I got the call to come in at the last minute. Listening from his sick bed, my pal scribbled me a note saying he'd been "horrified" by Shaw, but I loved that interview. Cole Porter said of the Duchess of Windsor's conversational style that "she always returned the ball". Shaw couldn't wait that long. He leaned over your side of the net and whacked it down your throat while you were still serving. I mentioned his version of "These Foolish Things" because it was co-written by a BBC producer, Eric Maschwitz. "So what?" snapped Shaw. "The song doesn't mean anything. What I did had nothing to do with the tune. The last 11, 12 bars I did that cadenza – that's as close to perfection as I'll ever get." It was one of his last records. In 1954, he put his clarinet away, never got it out again and never wanted to. "I did all you can do with a clarinet. Any more would have been less."

As for Artie's fellow bandleaders, the sound may not have "gone away" but a lot of the business did, and Dorsey and Goodman found themselves like most celebrities, clinging to a moment, as it recedes into the past. When Shaw decided to pack it in, Duke Ellington told him, "Man, you got more guts than any of us."

"I can say truthfully what very few people can say - that I did something better than anyone else in the world." And he did: he was the best clarinetist, the one with the fullest tone and the slyest shadings. And then he stopped, and did other things, and outlived every other bandleader. "My life turned out the best, too."

To his "dimwit" wives, he was a deranged obsessive. To his estranged sons, he was a miserable lonely man. But he was chasing different priorities. "The Mozart Clarinet Concerto, we know that's a good piece of work. Here it is couple hundred years later. Here's some of my work 50 years later. I would say if a piece of popular music lasts 50 years it's got a good shot at what we laughingly call immortality. We're aiming to transcend this short lifetime. You hope to put a footprint where it will last a little while."

He certainly left his mark on Evelyn Keyes. If he went into a bathroom and saw the toilet roll hung up to unwind from the back rather than the front, it drove him nuts. Years after their divorce, she said, "Every time I change a toilet roll, I think of Artie Shaw."

The Atlantic Monthly

The Lord's music,
the Devil's words

RAY CHARLES
SEPTEMBER 23RD 1930 ~ JUNE 10TH 2004

S OMEWHERE along the way in his vast autobiography, in among all the namechecking, wonkery and self-exculpation, Bill Clinton remarks: "I had loved Ray Charles since I heard his great line from 'What'd I Say': 'Tell your mama, tell your pa, I'm gonna send you back to Arkansas.'"

It *is* a great line. Like Hoagy Carmichael, composer of "Georgia On My Mind", Ray Charles had a natural affinity for the lie of the land: his voice could embrace the purple-mountained uplift of "America The Beautiful" and ramble slyly through the backroads and shanty towns, too. At 16, he was singing with an all-white hillbilly band called the Florida Playboys. At 18, he'd decided he'd gone as far as he could in the Sunshine State, unrolled a map of the country, pinpointed the town that was kitty-corner to Tampa, and then got on a bus to Seattle, where he formed his own Nat Cole-style trio.

Likewise, wherever you are on the musical map, he's there, too. He was, said Frank Sinatra, "the only genius in our business", and Ray wasn't minded to disagree, putting it right up there in the LP title: *The Genius Of Ray Charles*. At the Stax Museum of American Soul Music in Memphis, he explains in the introductory video to the official tour that soul is what happens when church, blues and country are "all intertwined some kind of way". On the album covers, he spelt out the relevant formulae more mathematically: *Genius + Soul = Jazz*. Plus he was a little bit country, he was a little bit rock'n'roll. He was a rare literal rocker, rocking back and forth at the piano as he sang Lennon and McCartney. But he rocked to Jerome Kern and Oscar Hammerstein, too. From Stephen Foster to Stevie Wonder, he claimed a century of American commercial song as his personal archive, and then added hymns and spirituals. He did "Hee Haw" and *Porgy And Bess*, and acquitted himself well on both. And, in the ultimate act of boundary-breaking, he did jingles for both Coke and Pepsi.

There are many category enforcers in the complicated apartheid of popular music who don't care for the above: like the stock clerk at Coconuts, a lot of critics want to know which bin to file you in. And, when it's not that simple, they doubt your motives: Genius + Orchestra = Sell-out. But the doubters have a point. There's a name for this kind of behavior and Ray Charles used it when he started his own record label in the Seventies: Crossover. "Crossover" used to mean a fellow in a specialist genre ("race records") crossing over to the main Top 40, and then somehow got stood on its head to mean a great artist condescending to a vernacular genre: José Carreras strangulating the vowels and mangling the consonants of "As Time Goes By" – "de worl' weel ohlwez welcomm loafers", rendered with all the passion of a sales exec addressing a footwear convention.

But, even when it's not that bad, it's not that good. In the Fifties, on "If I Were A Bell" (from *Guys And Dolls*) and a hundred others, Dinah Washington manages to signal through all the orchestral bounce that she'd still rather be singing the blues. A decade later, when Columbia leaned on him to do an album called *Tony Bennett Sings The Great Songs Of Today*, the singer was so disgusted with himself at having to do a lot of lame soft-rock covers he was physically sick before the session: Tony Bennett pukes the great songs of today. Even if the stuff doesn't make you vomit, a guy who does everything comes over like an opportunist (Ray Charles' old buddy Quincy Jones) or a poseur (Elvis Costello, who, after avant-garde string quartets and Burt Bacharach, now seems to be doing to his wife Diana Krall's career what he did to his own).

In considering Ray Charles, Sinatra's advice to Tony Bennett seems more germane: "You can only be yourself. But you're good at that." Ray was 16 when he cut his first songs, on a friend's wire recorder, and he's already good at being himself. The trio's in conventional style for the late Forties, but the 16-year old voice is moaning the blues like a 60-year old.

By then, young Ray had gone through more in his brief life than most of us would want to bear in our three-score-and-ten. He was born in Albany, Georgia in 1930, the same year "Georgia On My Mind" was published. His father was gone, and his mother eventually moved her children across the state line to Florida. One day five-year old Ray was playing outside in the wash tub with his little brother, when the younger boy's clothes got waterlogged and he drowned. Instead of running inside immediately and getting his mom, Ray struggled to pull his brother out, and, by the time he realized he couldn't and went for help, it was too late. At seven, he went blind. At 14, his mother, barely 30 herself, died suddenly in her sleep. She had raised her children in poverty so extreme that, as Charles once told me, "even the blacks looked down on us. Going down the ladder, you had rich whites, poor blacks, then us. And there weren't nothing between us and the bottom."

On the other hand, even singing hillbilly with the Florida Players, the teenage Ray Charles already seemed liked a man who transcended the facts of his life. When he'd lost his sight, his mom sent him to the state school for the blind in St Augustine. It had a white section and a colored section, and even at the time Ray thought it "kinda weird" that white kids and colored kids who couldn't see which was which nevertheless had to be segregated on that basis. "Ain't that a bitch," he said.

You wonder what other segregations make less sense to those who can't see it. Almost as soon as he hit the big time, critics complained he'd sold out – when he left Atlantic Records, when he got a string section, sang country, went Hollywood, did showtunes. But isn't a lot of that prejudice to do with the externals – the orchestra's tuxedos, the Nashville cowboy get-ups, a suburban concert hall filled with middle-class white folks? If you can't see any of that, all you can hear, as Ray Charles heard growing up, is the music. "Take Artie Shaw," he said. "I didn't even know he was white."

In those early days with the trio in Seattle, he's trying to sound like Nat Cole, and it doesn't work. But, other than that, whatever he does sounds like Ray Charles. On "Makin' Whoopee", Dinah Washington's blues inflections and harmonic variations seem unconnected to the material; Charles drops it several socio-economic notches below Eddie Cantor, does it low-down and confessional, and wrings every last drop of rueful comic juice from it. On "Eleanor Rigby", the queasy Tony Bennett was so intimidated by the mournful formality of the Beatles original he declaims it like a poem he's been forced to learn for school; Charles' version is tough and personal, up closer to the characters than the Fab Four got. He understood how to find his sound in the most familiar song. The obvious example is "Georgia", which he'd sung for ages in the back of his car to and from gigs until his driver prevailed upon him to record it. Hoagy Carmichael and his college roommate, Stu Gorrell, had written it 30 years earlier, and Mildred Bailey did a lovely warm sweet record of it. But Charles changed the song. All that soul and all that ache – "The road leads back to yoooooo…" at the end of the bridge, and then that falsetto back into the final eight: after Ray Charles, you couldn't glide through it the way Thirties crooners used to.

He was cool in all genres, and funny in most of them, too. He appropriated the music of faith and deployed it in the service of romance: "Talkin' 'Bout Jesus" became "Talkin' 'Bout You"; "This Little Light Of Mine" became "This Little Girl Of Mine". "He took the Lord's music and the Devil's words and make this amalgam they call soul music," said Jerry Wexler, his producer at Atlantic Records. He added strings to soul, and then did a country album in it.

Was he a nice fellow? Well, you hear the usual stories about stars, and the only difference was Ray told some of them himself. For his girl group, he ran a well-worn casting couch. "You can't be a Raelette unless you let Ray," he'd say with a chuckle. For the first two decades of his career, he was a heroin addict, and, because he was blind, he required others to shoot him up, a small operational detail which somehow magnifies the self-degradation. For the last two decades, the genius coasted on way too many celebrity duets and synth-pop boilerplate. "I don't mind the women," a colleague of his said to me. "But he's cheating on the music."

He made two great jazz albums, one instrumental – Charles on Hammond organ with Basie sidemen – and one vocal – with Betty Carter. The last was an instant classic, and promptly went out of print. I had a Japanese LP of it I used to play all the time in my disc-jockey days. The engineer saw "Alone Together" on the running order late one night, and groaned, "God, I hate that song." I played Ray and Betty's version, two idiosyncratic voices matched perfectly, close-miked, slow and conversational, intense and intimate, the opposite of that raw abandon he has on most of his big hits. It's as if they're sprawled on the rug in the dark at the end of a long evening. "Wow," said the engineer at the end. "Now I get it."

Most of us get Ray Charles at some point in our lives. "'What'd I Say' didn't feel like a big deal at the time," said Tom Dowd, his engineer at Atlantic. "Ray, the gals and the band live in the small studio, no overdubs. Next!" In pop, there's always something next. You move on, and yesterday's hot groove is stone cold. But, 40 years on, the party-crowd call-and-response can still "make you feel so good right now". My favorite Ray Charles album cover is his obligatory Christmas record. It's a big snowbound field in the middle of the woods, with one horse and an open sleigh, and, standing on the sleigh holding the reins, a grinning blind man in a slick striped tux, blue shirt and big bow tie, ready to go dashing through the snow on the wildest ride of all. That's the man in a single image: stick him in the middle of anything and he still comes up Ray Charles.

The Atlantic Monthly

Bozo in the hood

TUPAC SHAKUR
JUNE 16TH 1971 ~ SEPTEMBER 13TH 1996

SO WHERE WERE you when you heard the news that Tupac had been shot? Statistically, there's a pretty good chance you were with him: there were 49 assorted boyz'n'hoods and hoes'n'bitches in his entourage, dozens more milling in the street. "But nobody saw anything," said Sergeant Kevin Manning of the Las Vegas Metropolitan Police Department. "Strange, huh?" Statistically, there's an even greater chance that you're one of the thousands who emerged to eulogize him in the press as "the James Dean of hip-hop" - both were talented young men, both died in automobiles (though Tupac was in the passenger seat). The media divided into those who were hip and those caught on the hop: *The Village Voice* was ready with rap insiders, men with one name ("Touré"), men with lower-case names ("dream hampton", which is not apparently a New York realtor's designation but a hiphopper who knew Tupac well enough to call him Pac); the squaresville publications were forced to go for the broader brush stroke, getting their middle-class boyz from the 'burbs to argue, as *The Washington Post* tried, that he was yet another victim of the Gingrich Terror. Bob Dole, who'd been handed speeches in which he attacked 2Pac, was puzzled by the news, having assumed 2Pac was like Gopac, only liberal and Democratic. (2Pac, incidentally, was Tupac's preferred appellation: like many gangsta rappers, he opted to spell his name like a vanity license plate; in 2Pac's case, his name was converted into a number, and ultimately into a statistic.)

As for the rest of us, thousands upon thousands of ordinary citizens, we gathered in vigil with friends and family to sing our favorite Tupac songs. And then we realized we didn't know any. And when they brought out the lyric sheets for the singalong we realized it was probably best to send auntie and gran'ma home first.

When Bing died, most Americans knew he was the guy who sang "White Christmas". Elvis? "Heartbreak Hotel". Lennon? "Imagine". But 2Pac is a model of contemporary shortcut celebrity: he became a household name without ever having had a household song. First, he was famous for sexual assault; next, he was famous for being shot; now, he's famous for being dead. His latest album, the prophetically titled *All Eyez On Me* shot (as we say) from 69 on the Billboard album chart to 18. Twenty years ago in Britain, a guy called Pete Wingfield had a hit single called "Eighteen With a Bullet" - a reference to Billboard's practice of highlighting fast-selling records with the aforementioned ammunition. Poor old Tupac is the first guy on the Hit Parade to be literally 18 with a bullet.

Le mort du 2Pac was full of distracting details like that. This guy, Suge Knight, for example - the 300-lb gangsta impresario of Death Row Records who seems to be taking a surprisingly relaxed view of the murder, in the adjoining seat, of his biggest-selling artiste. I was vaguely aware that in 1994 Suge had paid $1.4 million to spring Pac from jail, and that Suge was a member of the Bloods, or maybe it was the Crips - anyway, not the Elks; I dimly recalled that during contractual negotiations he'd threatened Eazy-E, since dead of Aids, with a baseball bat. But, until the aftermath of Tupac's death, I never knew that Suge's house in Vegas was next door to Wayne Newton's.

Wayne Newton! What did Wayne ever do to deserve that? It's like discovering Saddam Hussein lives next door to Angela Lansbury. What do they talk about over the fence?

We can only imagine how poor old Wayne feels. Friends of mine nominated for the wussier categories at the Grammies (classical, show album, best liner notes for a telephone-sales wartime compilation) told me that, where pop had once been merely metaphorically "dangerous", this year it was literally so, with warring rappers and their bodyguards, all armed to the hilt, taunting each other backstage. Wayne doesn't need that in his backyard. I hadn't thought of Mister Las Vegas in years, but, ever since he came up in connection with 2Pac's death, I can't get his maddeningly catchy "Danke Schoen" out of my head:

Danke Schoen
Darling, danke schoen
Thank you for all the joy and pain...
I recall Central Park in fall
Where you tore your dress
What a mess
I confess
That's not all...

I never have figured out what Wayne's going on about there: some sort of easy-listening wilding? With 2Pac, on the other hand, you always knew where you stood - ideally, on the other side of the street. In 1994, he was convicted for holding down a ho (or, as we used to say, young lady - indeed, a teenage girl) while his pals forcibly sodomized her.

Thank you for all the joy and pain. That was more or less the line of his eulogists: there are 2 sides to every Pac, and we must understand both of them. His, we're told, was a tragedy moving remorselessly towards its final act. Like Hamlet, any internal agonizing wasn't going to make any difference: "To pack or not to pack? That is the question," he may have mused as he was picking out firearms for the MTV Awards, but, ultimately, he had no choice but to embrace his fate.

Moved by these elegies, I went out and bought the album. It doesn't, alas, print the words, but, after several listens to, say, "2 Of Amerikaz Most Wanted" (a duet with Snoop Doggy Dogg), you get the gist of the lyric, which boils down to: "Don't motherf--- with me, you motherf----- , or you'll wind up like all them other motherf------ motherf-----s (Repeat until fade)..."

Oh, I'm sorry, I've made a frightful faux pas: "motherf-----s" should, of course, be "muthaf-----z".

As the CD plays, you see what his obituarists are getting at: more than the James Dean of hip-hop, the Kurt Cobain of hardcore, or even the Hamlet of the 'hood, his was an inexorable tragedy of Sophoclean proportions, coursing relentlessly to its final scene with ululating Greek choruses of raptivists and industry insiders explaining what's really going down. Like Oedipus, he was a real bad muthaf----.

Obviously, there are variations on the theme:

> *I won't deny it I'm a straight ridah*
> *You don't wanna f--- with me...*

And occasionally the young man's fancy turned to traditional Tin Pan Alley fare. You remember Ray Noble's lyric to "The Very Thought of You"?

> *I see your face in every flower*
> *Your eyes in stars above...*

Tupac has much the same problem:

> *No matter where I go*
> *I see the same ho...*

The lady in question turns up everywhere. As he observes later in the song:

> *I'm watchin' the Million Man March*
> *and I see the same bitch on the Million Man March!*

Possibly this is what *The New Republic*'s Michael Lewis had in mind when he hailed rap as "the nearest thing to a political voice of the poor. Tupac says he discovered his music and its themes 'when I was out there with nowhere to stay, no money,' and that theme runs right through his lyrics, along with an impressive indifference to mainstream politics." In fact, Tupac has an impressive indifference, running right through his lyrics, to almost anything except the ho or bitch he happens to be riding at the time, and even then he has a kind of amused detachment ("Wonda Why They Call U Bitch"). Even his contribution to the supposed East Coast/West Coast rap wars was admirably single-minded. Tupac, convinced that the New York rapper The Notorious B.I.G. had played a part in his 1994 shooting, boasted on "Hit 'Em Up" that he'd "slept with", as *Entertainment Weekly* coyly phrased it, Mrs B.I.G. - or, as 2Pac put it: "I f---ed your bitch, you fat muthaf---er."

As for more conventional politics, he calls, in his liner notes, for the freeing of "all Politikal Prisonerz", including his stepfather Mutula Shakur. Presumably, Mutula counts as a political prisoner because, when any black man is jailed by the racist white state, that act by definition is political. It would be interesting to know if, up in the celestial world, 2Pac now takes the same line on his own black murderer. Still, as surgeons cut open his "Thug Life" tattoo to get at the three bullets inside him, Jesse Jackson and the Nation of Islam were both in attendance at the hospital, laying claim to his legacy: Tupac, it seems, is not just the James Dean of hip-hop, the Hamlet of the 'hood, but also the Gandhi of gangsta rap.

As his life ebbed away, many commentators, evoking timeless songs like "Thug Passion" and "Run Tha Streetz" with their deathless deathful prose, rushed to discuss Tupac not as a gangsta rapper (which, sadly, has pejorative connotations) but as a poet. Lyrical forebears such as Oscar Hammerstein and Ira Gershwin disdained the term, but Tupac, it seems, was not just the James Dean of hiphop and the Gandhi of gangsta rap but also the Shelley of the shoot-outs. Traditionally, admired pop stars are hailed for being "dangerous", "on the edge", for "pushing the boundaries". Aware perhaps that, for most tastes, 2Pac had gone over the edge, obliging obituarists tried to pull him back inside the boundaries, to make him less dangerous. They pointed out that he was a graduate of "Baltimore's prestigious High School of the Performing Arts" - in other words, not a real revolutionary, just another in the long line of art-school poseurs inaugurated by Mick Jagger. In *The New York Times*, Jon Pareles' line seemed to be that, left to himself, 2Pac would have been a benign figure, the Andy Williams of gangsta rap. Instead, he'd been lured down the hardcore end and been consumed by stardom: the James Dean of hip hop, the Shelley of the shoot-outs, was also, tragically, the Karen Carpenter of Compton.

The day after Tupac expired, Juliet Prowse died. Years ago, when she and Sinatra and Shirley MacLaine were filming *Can-Can*, they were visited on the set by Khrushchev. He looked at the highkicking dancers and denounced the whole thing as "decadent". But we've defined decadence down since those days. Tupac's mom was a Black Panther charged with "conspiracy against the United States government"; his godfather was a convicted thief and murderer; his stepfather was on the FBI's "Ten Most Wanted" list and eventually imprisoned for his part in an armed robbery in which two cops and a guard died; his aunt was an escaped convict, incarcerated for killing two state troopers. In the old days, music was your ticket out of the ghetto. For Tupac, rap was a ticket into a kind of psychological ghetto. William Bennett supposedly shamed Time-Warner into selling their stake in Interscope, who control Death Row – one of those "maverick" "authentic" "independent" labels that are, in fact, operating units of the biggest corporations in the world. But, if you scan the fine print on the album, you'll see that 2Pac's songs were co-published by Warner-Tamerlane, Chappell, Polygram, EMI-Virgin, MCA, Ascap, BMI... The biggest, most respected names in the music business are all in there, profiting in some small way from 2Pac's brief thug life. It is, in the end, minstrelsy; black pain, even unto death, served up for the amusement of white audiences. He wasn't an "authentic voice of the black urban poor": 75 per cent of rap's sales are to white suburban youth; they're the ones sending off for the hooded sweatshirts you can order from the merchandising pullouts in Pac's album so they can play gangsta in residential cul de sacs.

There's nothing unAmerican about getting rich peddling attitude to impressionable teenagers. Black writers like Nelson George have described him as "self-aware" about the "ironies" of the gangsta life, but whatever self-awareness the dumb schmuck had, it wasn't enough. With exquisite timing, a few days after their star's murder Death Row Records couriered 2Pac's last video over to MTV, with the innocent suggestion that they might like to rush it into high rotation. Filmed a couple of months ago, it shows, by a remarkable coincidence, the vocal artiste dying in a drive-by shooting in a car not dissimilar from Suge's. All it lacks is a bullet-ridden 2Pac turning to Suge and gasping with his dying breath, "Et 2, Brute?"

Thus life imitates art, or at least the video. But Death Row has a product to push, and the respectable media are happy to string along, mythologizing the bozo in the 'hood mainly out of the insecure assumption that his half-baked hoodlum exhibitionism is way cooler than anything they'll ever do. Years ago, asked why songwriters wrote mainly love songs, Richard Rodgers replied that no-one had ever had a hit song about hate. What a chump. He wouldn't get past reception at Time-Warner.

The American Spectator

Broadway's last good time

CY COLEMAN
JUNE 14TH 1929 ~ NOVEMBER 18TH 2004

T HESE ARE glum times on Broadway if you're looking for a musical. Unless it's a revival, chances are you'll find yourself either facing a barrage of portentous overwrought over-orchestrated bombast that sounds like it made the lower end of the shortlist for Track 19 on Céline Dion's new CD or stuck in some semi-operatic twilight zone in which some tasteful Sondheim clone twiddles about with a lot of pseudo-recitative for a couple of hours without ever breaking into song: music that's neither one thing nor the other – it's not serious music so much as solemn; and it's certainly not popular.

In this barren soil, Cy Coleman was Broadway's last good time, a musical comedy man in an age when the American musical was no laughing matter. He liked funny scripts by Neil Simon and Larry Gelbart, with lotsa laffs. Example: In Coleman's *Little Me* (1962), the luxuriously endowed heroine is called Belle Poitrine. After she saves a Mitteleuropean duchy from bankruptcy, a grateful Prince Cherny raises her to the peerage as the Countess Zaftig.

Coleman could match the funny lines with funny songs, but he also knew when not to – when the job of the composer was to provide a respite from the non-stop gag-fest and provide something rueful or charming or romantic. He liked showstoppers, too - numbers you could whack to the back of the second balcony, like "Hey, Look Me Over!" for Lucille Ball, and "If My Friends Could See Me Now" for Gwen Verdon, and "It's Not Where You Start (It's Where You Finish)" for Tommy Tune; songs that come with built-in exclamation points:

It's Not Where You Start
It's Where You Finish
And you're gonna finish
On top!

Hard to make that work in *Les Misérables*. But Coleman knew what he liked: *Barnum* was about Barnum, *The Will Rogers Follies* was about Will Rogers, *City Of Angels* was about Los Angeles, and *The Life* was about showbiz at the horizontal level - 42nd Street hookers in the Seventies. *Sweet Charity* was adapted from Fellini's *Nights Of Cabiria* but it wasn't very Cabirian by the time Coleman, Simon, Verdon, and Bob Fosse were through with it.

Coleman started near enough the top: Nat "King" Cole picked up an early song, "I'm Gonna Laugh You Right Out Of My Life", and put him in the big leagues. Sinatra did "Witchcraft" and Peggy Lee "Hey, Big Spender!" And, even though they retired and died and there was no-one left to get the song to and, even if there were, no radio station would play it, Coleman always gave you the impression he still had an eye on the "take-home tune", the break-out number, the showtune everyone knows even if they've never seen the show. In the months before *The Will Rogers Follies* opened in 1991, he was working the big ballad, "Never Met A Man I Didn't Like", at benefit performances all over town. I ran into him a couple of days after he'd sung it at the Manhattan Eye, Ear and Throat Hospital. "You should have seen him," said his lyricist Adolph Green. "There wasn't a dry eye, ear and throat in the house."

"Musical comedy's difficult," Coleman told me once. "When I was doing movies, I used to say, 'Why don't I ever get a good melodrama?' Comedies are very hard, you never get the credit you should. But, in a good melodrama, you hold one note, change four chords and you're up for an Academy Award." In their productive periods, most distinctively American art forms – musicals, westerns, jazz – were blissfully unaware they were art forms at all. Then they wised up, and mostly with catastrophic consequences. In the Eighties, when the British through-composed pop-opera took up seemingly permanent residence on Broadway, Coleman regarded it as "a *Reader's Digest* version of opera. It seems to give people the feeling of culture."

You mean it gives them the feeling as opposed to the culture?

He snorted his distinctive sneezy-wheezy laughing-gas laugh. "A-hur-hur-hur. That's what I said."

I mentioned this to Cameron Mackintosh, producer of *Cats*, *Les Miz*, *Phantom Of The Opera*, etc. "What does Cy Coleman know about culture?" he scoffed.

In fact, he knew quite a lot. *Sweet Charity* has a soliloquy and "The Rhythm Of Life" is a funky fugue – or, at any rate, fugue-esque. Musicalizing *On The Twentieth Century*, about the famous train, Coleman was bored by the thought of doing 1920s Tin Pan Alley pastiche and so wrote a comic opera – Rossini off the rails.

The classical stuff came first. A tenant at his parents' Bronx apartment house moved out and left the piano behind and, even though his carpenter dad nailed the lid down, four-year old Seymour managed to pry it open. At seven, he played Carnegie Hall. His favorite composer in those days was Beethoven. How do you get to Carnegie Hall? Practise. How do you get away from it? Improvise. The child prodigy heard the call of jazz and his wandering fingers told him the whole classical thing was just hemming him in too much. So he skipped Juilliard, and at 15 began playing nightclubs. While still a teenager, he wrote a fiendishly complex sonata but, between his hectic club life and social life, misplaced it.

"Surely you can play it from memory?" I suggested a few years back.

"Sit down and order dinner," he said, and turned to the keyboard. If you asked him, he'd still tinkle a little Chopin or Beethoven, but after a few bars he'd segue into a party piece about the cocktail pianist trying to play *Clair de lune* or some such.

So the teenager got a trio and was sufficiently impressed by his dressing room at the Sherry-Netherland that he moved in. The problem with being musically sophisticated at an early age is that you're not always lyrically sophisticated. He wrote a Latin number and a pal put a lyric to it:

> *Oh, Castanetta*
> *Oh, lovely lovely Castanetta*
> *I can't forget the night I met 'er*
> *She cast a net round my heart*
>
> *Her heels were kicking*
> *Her castanets were gaily clicking*
> *With every click my heart was ticking*
> *She had me right from the start...*

Joe McCarthy, a more professional hand, rewrote it as:

> *The Riviera*
> *On every street a gay casino*
> *Where continentals sip their vino...*

Mabel Mercer and a few other upscale chanteuses began singing it. It would be hard not to improve on "Castanetta", and "The Riviera" certainly has its moments – "where matrons draped in Paris fashions/Prolong the twilight of their passions" – but its "sophistication" always seemed to me only marginally less unconvincing than the original. It was the mid-Fifties and Coleman was starting out as a writer of pop standards just as the entire field was about to get plowed over by rock'n'roll. His ballads in that period were lovely: "Why Try To Change Me Now?" was Sinatra's final record for Columbia, a flip of the finger to executive honcho Mitch Miller, who'd been trying to change Frank into Guy Mitchell or Patti Paige and saddle him with every witless novelty song of the day, from "Mama Will Bark", the canine duet on which he was accompanied by the small-voiced but big-breasted Swede Dagmar, to "Tennessee Newsboy", on which he was accompanied by a man who could make chicken noises with his guitar. "Why Try To Change Me Now?", a plangent conversational ballad, was Sinatra's way of saying no, thanks, I'll stick with the music, and in the end the music will win.

To be honest, I wasn't sure. It seemed to me the songs Coleman wrote for Sinatra and others had come along too late to secure a hold in the repertoire. But I was wrong. These days they're everywhere. I was in a hotel room the other week and caught some dreadful Sean Young non-stop-shagging female self-empowerment movie on Channel 139 and just as I was about to flip channels Nancy Wilson came on the soundtrack singing "The Best Is Yet To Come". Every time I watched CNN before the election, I got distracted by that hotel-chain commercial that uses Coleman's "The Rules Of The Road". I went to see Dorothée Berryman, who played the much put-upon wife in last year's Oscar-winning *Invasions Barbares*, in cabaret in Montreal and she opened with a wonderfully tender "Walk A Little Faster", a Coleman ballad about the anticipation of love.

All three of those songs were written with his best partner, Carolyn Leigh. Miss Leigh liked to rhyme and when she'd tired of masculine rhymes – moon/June – and feminine rhymes – fatter/matter – she liked to put the stress on the third or even fourth syllable before the end of the line – "rules of the road", for example, rhymes with "fools of the road". Noel Coward was partial to this, forever rhyming on the ante-penult:

> *Why Must The Show Go On?*
> *Why not announce the closing night of it?*
> *The public seem to hate the sight of it?*

In Coward's hands, it seems obtrusive and often points up the dreariness of the tune. But with Miss Leigh it sits so perfectly on top of Coleman's sensuous, sinuous jazzy melodies, you hardly notice it. Take the middle section of "Witchcraft":

> *When you arouse the need in me*
> *My heart says yes indeed in me*
> *Proceed with what you're leadin' me to...*

It doesn't look much in print, but, set to those notes, the rhymes slyly intensify the headiness of the music. It's harder than it looks. A lot of Coleman's tunes aren't obviously vocal. He wrote "The Best Is Yet To Come" to play with his jazz trio – it's a series of fun progressions to kick around late in the set – but Carolyn heard it and managed to fit words to it, and singers love it. The Coleman/Leigh songs from the Fifties and Sixties will endure as long as Gershwin or Porter.

The first time I interviewed Coleman I was a young slip of a lad and I wanted to know why his best lyricists were the ladies - Leigh, Dorothy Fields, Betty Comden, Peggy Lee. I put it rather awkwardly and it came out as "Do you write with women because there are certain qualities in what they do that you find attractive?" He howled with laughter and said, "No, I *date* women because there are certain qualities in what they do that I find attractive." He was for five decades a debonair man about town, a swinger musically and socially, the house pianist on the *Playboy* TV show and not a guy who had to make do with Hef's leavings from the grotto. But in 1997, to the amazement of Broadway, he got married, to Shelby Brown. Aged 70, he produced a daughter, Lily Cye, put her down for piano lessons and installed her baby grand next to his trusty full-size one.

He died a few hours after being taken ill at a first-night party for Michael Frayn's new play. One of the minor losses occasioned by his passing is that he's no longer around to sing at other people's funerals. He did "Here's To Us" at Judy Garland's, and at Irving Berlin's he sang a gorgeous, slowed-down version of "There's No Business Like Show Business". That's what he did at his best – he could take the most tired, trite, worn, familiar showbiz sentiment and somehow find the truth in it. Sinatra sang all the great songs but it was Coleman's he put on his tombstone: "The Best Is Yet To Come".

"Wouldn't it be nice," said Cy, "if it's true?"

The Atlantic Monthly

The man who invented Elvis

SAM PHILLIPS
JANUARY 5TH 1923 ~ JULY 30TH 2003

O N THE DAY Sam Phillips died, the crowd at the world's (alleged) all-time biggest rock concert, in Toronto, booed and threw bottles at teen heartthrob Justin Timberlake, of the boy band 'N Sync. Master Timberlake was said to be too "plastic" and "manufactured" for the taste of rock fans there to see Rush and AC/DC. This is the fellow to whom, as she revealed this summer, Britney Spears surrendered her much-advertised virginity, which suggests that letting the suits in the head office mold your identity is not without its compensations. But young Justin sportingly said he thought the bottle-hurling was "understandable".

And so it is. Rock'n'roll may be the most aggressively corporate branch of showbusiness ever invented but it's still obsessed with being "raw" and "authentic" and "countercultural". That's where Sam Phillips comes in: he represents rock's BC era - Before Corporate - before Elvis said goodbye to Sam's Sun Records, in Memphis, and headed for RCA and Hollywood and Vegas. But back in 1954 it was Sam who told Elvis to sing the country song ("Blue Moon Of Kentucky") kinda bluesy and the blues song ("That's All Right") kinda country, and, as Elvis was a polite 19-year old who obliged his elders, somewhere in the crisscross something clicked.

It's the Phillips tracks that redeem Elvis for everything that came afterward. It's "Mystery Train" and "That's All Right" that the pop-culture historians are thinking of when they write about the rock'n'roll "revolution". "The *Ancien Régime* fell in 1789 and once

126

again a century and a half later," declared Herbert London in *Closing The Circle: A Cultural History Of The Rock Revolution*. "Rock Around The Clock" is the most successful call to arms produced by the revolution, the one kids tore up movie seats over. But its composer, Jimmy DeKnight, wrote it as a fox trot, and its lyricist, Max Freedman, whose last hit had been for the Andrews Sisters, originally wanted to call it "Dance Around The Clock". And Freedman was born in 1890. When he was a rebellious teenager, the big hits were "The Merry Widow Waltz", Kipling's "Road To Mandalay", and "When A Fellow's On The Level With A Girl That's On The Square". He may not have been exactly *Ancien Régime*, but he was certainly pretty *ancien*. And the regime itself - in the shape of RCA, Columbia, etc - proved far wilier survivors than Louis XVI.

That's why Phillips' moment is central to rock's sense of itself, and why critics still insist that Elvis's *The Sun Sessions* is the all-time greatest album. As Robert Hilburn put it, on the Sun set "you hear rock being born" - not to Tin Pan Alley hacks and big-time corporations, but in a one-story brick studio where a kid walked in off the street. Just as real revolutionaries watch the Revolution Day tank parade from the presidential palace and reminisce about the days when they were peasants with pitchforks, so fellows who spend eight months in a studio remixing a couple of tracks fondly reminisce about the days when Ike Turner's amplifier fell off the car roof on the way to the studio and Sam Phillips stuffed the punctured speaker cone with paper and accidentally created a "wall of sound". The Sun motto was "We Record Anything, Anytime, Anywhere" - including the men's room, where the toilet served as the studio's echo chamber. The conventional line on Phillips is that he's the guy who encouraged Elvis, Jerry Lee Lewis, and Roy Orbison to "experiment". "I'd try things I knew I couldn't do," Carl Perkins remembered, "and then have to work my way out of it. I'd say, 'Mr Phillips, that's terrible.' He'd say, 'That's original.'"

I interviewed Phillips once for the BBC. Well, that's not exactly true. I pretended to be from the BBC. Unfortunately, a genuine

BBC chap had turned up the day before I did, which meant that, when I was ushered into his presence, Phillips seemed vaguely suspicious that I wasn't quite what I claimed to be. Desperate to reassure him that I was a legitimate rock interviewer, I somehow fell into a terrible rhythm of earnest cliché questions I couldn't get out of - about the "rawness", the "authenticity" - and, Elvised out as he was, he politely gave the standard answers for the umpteenth time. He had a laid-back cool that Elvis never quite managed, and he wore a little lightning-bolt pin with the Presley motto: "TCB." Taking Care of Business.

Here's what I would like to have discussed. He knew Elvis before he was Elvis, before he was a star and then a parody. He knew Elvis when he was an 18-year old who parked his Ford pick-up outside the studio on Union Avenue and said he wanted to record a song for his momma's birthday: "My Happiness", a big hit for the Ink Spots. The teenage Elvis liked the Ink Spots, and Eddie Fisher. He wanted to sing like Dean Martin.

Elvis's career after Phillips is regarded by rock critics as a ghastly sellout to commercialism and conformity, though there's nothing obviously commercial or conformist about a ragbag like "Old Shep", "Rock-A-Hula Baby", "Peace In The Valley", "No Room To Rhumba In A Sports Car", plus adaptations of "O Sole Mio" and "The Battle Hymn Of The Republic". Justin Timberlake's minders would be unlikely to recommend any of 'em. Elvis had an extraordinary range - two octaves and a third - but not a consistent voice. He was a chameleon but unfocused, and when he wasn't doing Dino he could sound like Al Jolson, Mahalia Jackson or an Irish tenor. The wacky eclecticism is the real Elvis. The "raw", "authentic" *Sun Sessions* Elvis is the manufactured product. "I encouraged him to be real raw," said Phillips, "because if he was artificial he wouldn't be able to keep it up." *Au contraire*: it was being raw he couldn't keep up.

Go back to that summer's day in 1953, when Phillips first heard that voice. He wanted Elvis, but he didn't want him singing "My Happiness". Nobody needed a one-man Ink Spots, or a hillbilly Eddie

Fisher. "I always said," Phillips told everybody, "that if I could find a white boy who could sing like a black man I'd make a million dollars."

So he steered Mister Eclectic away from everything but one particular corner, and Elvis, as always, said, "Yes, sir." Imagine if Phillips had said, sure, kid, how about a couple more Ink Spots covers, and that "Stranger In Paradise" from *Kismet*'s pretty nice, and you've got the pipes for it, and how about we round things out with a little Eddie Fisher. There would have been no rock'n'roll Elvis, and nothing for RCA to buy up. It would never have occurred either to them or him.

Phillips started in the Forties, recording dance bands from the roof garden of the Peabody Hotel. But that was just a job. What he really wanted to do was "race records". When he first heard Howlin' Wolf he howled, too: "This is where the soul of man never dies." To Phillips, black music was a passion. To Elvis, it was an option. And so the producer lent the singer his authenticity.

Phillips never made his million bucks, not from Elvis. RCA bought out the Sun contract for $35,000. He owned some radio stations, and he was one of the original investors in Holiday Inn. He was a businessman, and half a century ago he made a commercial decision. Would other white boys have come along at other studios? Sure. But none ever did who sang rockabilly-country-blues like Elvis. Sam Phillips invented Elvis, and thereby mainstream rock'n'roll, and rock. Not a revolution, just a smart move. Like the tiepin says, Taking Care of Business.

The Atlantic Monthly

CHAINS *& Sins*

Yes, we have no Banana

THE REVEREND CANAAN BANANA
MARCH 5TH 1936 ~ NOVEMBER 10TH 2003

IT WOULD BE remiss of me not to note the passing last week of the Reverend Canaan Banana, and not just because he has a funny name. It is, of course, deplorable to make cheap gags about a fellow because of his handle (I seem to remember a Monty Python line from years ago announcing that "Mr Arthur Penis is changing his name by deed poll to Mr Art Penis"). But, when the Reverend Banana became the first President of Zimbabwe in 1980, the citizenry seemed reluctant to accord His Excellency the dignity his office required and two years later a law was passed forbidding jokes about his name.

The Reverend Banana became President because, at the Lancaster House conference in London, the British forced a Westminster-style constitution on the new country, splitting the roles of head of government and head of state. Robert Mugabe became Prime Minister, and Mugabe's party put up Canaan Banana as its choice for President. It is said that Lord Carrington and his colleagues went along with the idea in part because it seemed an excellent jest on the recalcitrant white Rhodesians to transform their rebel colony into the first literal Banana republic. Until this sudden eminence, the Reverend Banana was an obscure underling in Mugabe's ZANU-PF movement and a conventional proponent of liberation theology: he rewrote the Lord's Prayer as a call to resist white supremacy, and declared that, "when I see a guerilla, I see Jesus Christ." Each to his own. Alas, when his guerillas saw fellow Christians, they didn't always recognize them as kindred spirits: In 1978, in the Vumba mountains, Mugabe and Banana's plucky "freedom fighters" slaughtered nine white missionaries, after raping the women and their four children -

one a month old, another found with a boot imprint on her shattered skull.

In 1987, Mr Mugabe revised Zimbabwe's constitution, eased the Reverend Banana out of his job, and became an executive President of dictatorial bent, setting the country on a course to its present state of economic ruin and mass starvation. The Reverend Banana, meanwhile, having earned a place in his nation's history books as a symbol of racial liberation, went on to earn himself a footnote as a somewhat more controversial symbol of sexual liberation. In 1997, Jefta Dube, a former bodyguard of Banana's, was on trial for murder and pleaded in mitigation that he'd only committed the crime after the victim repeatedly taunted Dube as "Banana's wife". He claimed that at State House one night the President had slipped a sleeping draught into his drink. Mr Dube came round to find himself on a duvet naked from the waist down, with a smiling President Banana hovering over him. "While you were sleeping," said the President, "we helped ourselves." Not the words a chap wants to wake up to. He forced his bodyguard into a sexual relationship that lasted three years.

The Reverend Banana denied the allegations, but within weeks several cooks, gardeners, policemen, air force officers, scores of students at the University of Zimbabwe, and most of the President's football team came forward with similar stories. You don't have to be Banana's to work here but it helps. It was impossible to keep count: "Come, Mister Tallyman, tally up Banana's" is easier said than done.

In Zimbabwe, homosexuality is punishable by ten years in gaol, and Mr Mugabe is famously antipathetic to the practice. You'll recall that he's denounced Tony Blair as a "gay gangster" leading "the gay government of the gay United gay Kingdom". This was at a time when its first openly gay Secretary of State was being received with his partner at Buckingham Palace and another less openly gay Secretary of State was in the papers for an ill-starred encounter with a young lad on Clapham Common, and the unbiased observer might well, like Mr Mugabe, have been struck by the British cabinet's lack of visible heterosexuals. But, eschewing the convention whereby former colonies are allowed to abuse the imperial power to their hearts' content, Mr Blair took umbrage.

In such a climate, it's hardly surprising President Banana found himself on trial for sodomy. Even the 1982 law forbidding jokes about the Presidential name couldn't help him: who needs gags when you've got headlines like "Man Raped By Banana" (*The Herald*), "Banana Forced Officer To Have Sex" (*The Guardian*), "Banana Appeals Against Sodomy Conviction" (the BBC) and (my personal favourite) "Hand Over Banana, Mandela Is Told" (*The Daily Telegraph*)?

Mr Mugabe has accused Britain of a plot to impose homosexuality throughout the Commonwealth. "We as chiefs should fight against western practices," he said. "British homosexuals are worse than dogs and pigs." The whole business was apparently hitherto unknown in Zimbabwe. His line on gayness is basically: yes, we have no Bananas. Yet it was assumed by almost everyone that Mr Mugabe, for all his visceral hostility to homosexuality, must have been aware of what President Banana was up to and there was much speculation as to why he turned a blind eye to it. Shortly before sentencing, the disgraced leader got wind of a rumour that Mugabe was about to have him killed and so Banana split: he fled to South Africa in a false beard. Nelson Mandela persuaded him to return home to gaol and disgrace. His wife went to live with her daughter in London, and by the time of his death last Monday the man who'd received his seals of office from the Prince of Wales at the birth of a new nation was recalled only as a pathetic joke figure.

In a poignant way, President Banana's reductio ad absurdum from black revolutionary to convicted sodomite mirrored his country's transformation in the eyes of the west's *biens pensants*. Though Mr Mugabe's views on *le vice anglais* are pretty standard among African leaders and granted that Tony Blair does have a vaguely camp air, it probably wasn't a good idea to draw attention to it at the Commonwealth Conference. Preoccupied with internal affairs, the Zimbabwean leader neglected to keep *au courant* with changing fashions in the preferred progressive causes in western drawing rooms, where today a homophobe is as unacceptable as a kaffir-bashing racist in the Seventies. *The Guardian*, which backed Mr Mugabe in the Zimbabwean elections that brought him to power and greeted his victory with the headline "The Clearest And Best Outcome", was mighty disillusioned to discover they'd been promoting Norman Tebbit in blackface: "From Freedom Fighter To Oppressor" ran a more recent headline in the paper.

In fact, Robert Mugabe is much as he's always been. While Britain and other former colonial powers turned a blind eye to Africa, the likes of Mugabe looted their governments' treasuries, their countries' resources, their peoples' wealth, and western taxpayers' bountiful "development" funds. To this day, you still hear African leaders demanding to know why America won't launch a "Marshall plan for Africa", which conveniently overlooks the fact that since 1960 the west has sunk the cost of the Marshall plan many times over into the Dark Continent with nothing to show for it other than a few extra zeroes on the Swiss bank balances of the dictators-for-life. While the west snoozed complacently, the Afro-Marxist kleptocrats ransacked a continent.

Or to borrow President Banana's post-coital catchphrase: "While you were sleeping, we helped ourselves."

The Irish Times

The imperfect spy

MICHAEL STRAIGHT
SEPTEMBER 1ST 1916 ~ JANUARY 4TH 2004

H E WOULD HAVE liked the *Washington Post* headline:

Michael Straight dies;
Magazine editor, NEA official

Yawn. On to the next page. Straight was a mediocre editor of the family mag, *The New Republic*, and it's doubtful whether anyone other than fellow arts bureaucrats wants to read of his service as Deputy Assistant Associate Whatever at the National Endowment for the Arts. Michael Whitney Straight led a long, comfortable, undistinguished life as the sort of chap who turns up in the index of other people's biographies as the third fellow on the left in the picture of the committee meeting or the wedding party or the mixed doubles. He was related by blood or marriage to everyone from the Vanderbilts to Jackie Onassis. When he returned to America from Cambridge University in 1937, he was in need of career advice and so looked up an old family friend, President Roosevelt.

But the only distinguishing feature of his lethargic progress through the American establishment is that Michael Straight was a Soviet spy.

At this point, wherever he is now, Mr Straight is no doubt objecting, as he did to *The London Review Of Books* in 1995:

I was not a spy in the accepted usage of that word.

Whatever gets you through the night. But he was a spy accepted and used by the Soviet NKVD, at the same time as he was a speechwriter for President Roosevelt. He lived with his secret for

137

almost half a century until outed by Britain's *Daily Mail* in 1981. And once his past was known it seemed at least partially to explain why a man born with all the right connections had made so little of them. Straight was the American end of Britain's "Cambridge Spies", to use the title of last year's very appreciative BBC drama about them. They were recruited by the Soviets at university in the 1930s and came close in the Fifties to gaining control of Her Majesty's Secret Service. When it all began to unravel, the first to defect were Guy Burgess and Donald Maclean, followed by the so-called "Third Man", Kim Philby, after which there was a Fourth Man, Sir Anthony Blunt, Surveyor of the Queen's Pictures, and possibly a Fifth, rumored for a while to be Sir Roger Hollis, Director of MI5. And then there was Michael Straight, who wasn't the Sixth, Seventh or Eighth Man so much as the Straight Man – not so much in the sense that the others were mostly homosexual, but in that he was a dull stick among a coterie of flamboyant, hard-living, hard-drinking, supremely confident clubby Englishmen. In 1935, Straight and Blunt were among a group of Cambridge "idealists" on pilgrimage to Moscow.

"Do I look like a proletarian?" he asked an acquaintance, anxious to fit in.

"No," came the reply. "You look like a millionaire pretending to be a proletarian."

And so he did. One day he'd be out on the street selling copies of *The Daily Worker*, the next off to ski at Klosters. His father had died in the Great War, and his mother was a goofy Whitney heiress who took him off to England to serve as an early guinea-pig in the "progressive" school she helped found: light on arithmetic and spelling, heavy on Freudian psychology and unisex showers. The Thirties was the heyday of the Stalinist toff, the languid upper-middle-class Englishman for whom, after public (ie, private) school, the rigors of Bolshevism were a breeze. Straight was the American aristocracy's contribution to the cause and frankly not a success. Blunt was a frightful snob who adored the Royal Family his entire life and saw no contradiction between fawning on his Sovereign and betraying her.

With Straight, it was all more tortured: Arnold Deutsch, who helped run the Cambridge spies for Moscow, despised the rich American. "He sometimes behaves like a child in his romanticism," he reported. "He thinks he is working for the Comintern" – ie, just doing a little freelance PR for the cause, not spying for hard men in the shadows. "He must be left in this delusion for a while."

Straight and Blunt sound awfully like a spoof spy team, and not just because Blunt wasn't straight and Straight wasn't blunt. He was an insecure man who wanted to be part of the gang, but never quite was. Almost three decades on, in 1963, offered a post at what would become the NEA and convinced he wouldn't withstand a background check, he finally went to the FBI and then MI5 and spilled the beans on Blunt. "We always wondered how long it would be before you turned us in," drawled Sir Anthony, bored by his least impressive protégé even in Straight's moment of "courage".

But it took a while. In 1937, Blunt gave Straight his "assignment": return to America, get an important job, and feed information to Moscow. Straight was "reluctant", but in the end agreed. Eleanor Roosevelt got him into the State Department, and he started supplying his Soviet contact with, he insisted, nothing more than copies of the briefing papers he wrote. No "hard information". Certainly nothing useful. The small lies we tell ourselves in our darkest moments shrivel in even the faintest light. His most plausible defense was that he was as half-hearted about spying as about everything else – as William Safire wrote, "no purpose or passion guided his double-life".

Meanwhile, Burgess, Maclean, Philby and Blunt advanced rapidly to the point where Philby was on the shortlist to succeed as "C", the head of the Secret Service, and Maclean could conceivably have become British Ambassador in Washington, and Burgess is said by some to have leaked the information that led to the slaughter of General Macarthur's men at the Yalu River in Korea in 1950. Had Straight come clean in, say, 1942, many lives would have been saved. "I needed one beckoning word or gesture to lead me on," wrote

Straight. "Without it I lacked the resolution to carry my impulse through." So he dithered for 26 years.

He was 66 when it all came out, and his response was a memoir, *After Long Silence*, that his old pals, guzzling Scotch at their retirement dachas in Moscow, must have roared their heads off at. As pitiful apologias go, it's in a class with the more recent book by Sarah, Duchess of York, attempting to explain how she ended up naked on the front page of *The Sun* having her toes sucked, but without the mitigating factor of being written by a child of the Age of Victimhood. Straight knew he was a weak man. One can forgive the metaphorical flourishes – "Caught up in the current of history and carried out of my depth" – more easily than what now reads like an early Oprah audition: his upbringing not only burdened him with a sense of guilt but left him with "a deep-seated need to love and to be loved."

When he was an infant, Joseph Conrad popped round to the family townhouse on Fifth Avenue. Young Michael was upstairs in the nursery, but looking back on that day he liked to think that downstairs Conrad was reading from *Under Western Eyes*, the story of Razumov, the young student whose loyalty and then betrayal of an older friend costs him his soul. If he has to go down in history as a double-agent, he'd prefer not to be a spy "in the accepted usage" but something a little more literary. The comparison is itself an act of self-flattery of the kind that got poor old Razumov into trouble when he's called in by the authorities:

> *Razumov smiled without bitterness. The renewed sense of his intellectual superiority sustained him in the hour of danger. He said a little disdainfully:*
>
> *'I know I am but a reed. But I beg you to allow me the superiority of the thinking reed over the unthinking forces that are about to crush him out of existence.'*

That's how the agonized prose of the memoir feels, like a Victorian ham actor laying it on with a trowel, sustained by a misguided sense of his intellectual superiority. In 1948, with a condescension some of his successors at *The New Republic* may find vaguely familiar, Straight had dismissed Truman as a man who had "a known difficulty in understanding the printed word". Not, I think, as much difficulty as Straight had for over a quarter-century in understanding the plain meaning of who he was and what he'd done. Underneath his carefully cultivated mask, Blunt was blunt. Straight was never straight, especially with himself.

In the end, most of his obituarists took him at his own estimation: the "reluctant" spy. What does "reluctant" mean? He did as he was ordered, but, unlike Philby and Blunt, he didn't have much fun? As Conrad wrote, "Let a fool be made serviceable according to his folly."

The Atlantic Monthly

The pariah guy

EDWARD VON KLOBERG III
JANUARY 9TH 1942 ~ MAY 1ST 2005

POLITICS, according to Christopher Hitchens, is showbusiness for ugly people. That being so, the ugly people need representation, and nobody built up an uglier clientele than Edward J von Kloberg III. He was the Washington lobbyist for the dictatorial A-list: Ceauşescu of Romania, Mobutu of Zaire, Saddam of Iraq, Samuel Doe of Liberia, Juvenal Habyarimana of Rwanda, the Myanmar military junta... If you had enough blood on your hands, chances are you were on his books. Anyone can have an axis of evil, but von Kloberg had a full Rolodex of evil.

For a quarter-century, he was the William Morris Agency of global pariahs, and with clients like these you never had to say, "Break a leg", or at least not within hearing. He was the go-to guy for guys you wouldn't want to go near, the public relations man for men who had little contact with the "public" until the palace guard opened fire on them and little interest in "relations" except when it came to figuring which scheming brothers and cousins it would be prudent to bump off next. Next to von Kloberg, few Beltway insiders had the ear of so many dictators. Not literally, of course: the men who had the ears of Samuel Doe were the fellows who sliced them off and then made him eat them. They kept his genitals for their own light supper, in the belief that the "powers" and "manhood" of the person are transferred to the person whose parts you're chowing down on.

By the standards of President-for-Life Doe and many of his other clients, von Kloberg had a dignified end. Depressed after a failed reconciliation with his Lithuanian lover, he hurled himself from the Castel Sant' Angelo in Rome, the scene of Tosca's operatic suicide, though, unlike Tosca, he took a magazine cover of himself with the first President Bush on the way down. Over the top in death as in life: "Tyrant's Lobbyist, Flamboyant To The End," said *The Washington Post*, "flamboyant" being the agreed euphemism. Perhaps it was the "flamboyance" that explained why he never clinched the deal with Robert Mugabe, the famously homophobic Zimbabwean strongman who prides himself on being able to spot "flamboyance" at 200 yards. But elsewhere among an African elite markedly antipathetic toward flamboyant western gays, von Kloberg found many takers. He was the killers' queen. Mobutu awarded him Zaire's Order of the Leopard, and with decorations like that on your chest you know, flitting from one social event to another up and down the East Coast, that no-one's likely to show in the same get-up. Few others worked so assiduously at turning totalitarian honors into gay kitsch.

"I call it hardwear," he said at the Red Cross Ball in Palm Beach a few years back. "You can only wear four stars at a time, you can't repeat the same country, and you wear a star low on your jacket." He pointed to the next table, where the young male companion of an elderly lady had a star over his heart. "That gigolo over there is wearing it as a pin."

Larry Gelbart has an oft-quoted line about how, if Hitler's still alive, he hopes he's on the road with a musical in trouble. Von Kloberg seemed like an addendum to the gag: if Hitler's musical was in trouble, this guy would be the press agent. He was a man with a foot in both camps, the military junta's camp and the screamingly camp. Even the name was oddly reminiscent of the faux Continentalism of Roger de Bris, director of *Springtime For Hitler* in the Mel Brooks hit *The Producers*. I don't know whether Roger's "de" was an affectation, but Edward's "von" voz. Edward J von Kloberg III may have been the third Kloberg but he was the first "von" Kloberg, after a brief interregnum as the first "van" Kloberg.

The *Almanach de Gotha* touches were grafted on to make him sound more distinguished: he came to regret the hasty adoption of the "van" – as in Dick van Dyke and other eminences – and decided "von" was what he'd been looking for all along, and that he was, in fact, an authentic baron: "Baron Edward von Kloberg III", a "titled European in Washington", as *The Washington Post* once called him. Like Baron von Frankenstein, Baron von Kloberg favored black capes lined with red velvet when out on the tiles: von singular sensation, every little move he made. Like Van Johnson in *In The Good Old Summertime* (1949), van Kloberg favored in the summer months bow ties and straw boaters. Did he mind being a flack for dictators? "Shame is for sissies", he said, in what would have made a good motto for most of his clients. They would have appreciated the whiff of self-invention, too.

Even if one had a mind to, how does a chap go about becoming a specialist in dictatorial representation? Kloberg, as he then was, was born in New York, educated at Princeton, and earned a master's degree from American University, where he stayed on for the next couple of decades rising to Dean of Admissions. Then in 1982, he set up shop as a PR man and never looked back. Within months, he numbered among his clients the governments of Syria, Panama and Lesotho. Or at least that's what he told the bank when applying for the $60,000 loan. When it turned out the references on embassy letterheads were forgeries, the FBI were called in and van Kloberg, as he then was, found himself facing the possibility of a $5,000 fine and two years in jail. But he gave a moving performance in court, explaining that his gambit was born of his "desperation" to save his struggling firm and its 18 employees – even in those days, he favored dictator-sized retinues. Van Kloberg got five years on probation, and did himself no harm with the kind of governments he was hoping to attract: forging ambassadors' letters to sucker the bank has the kind of panache many totalitarian regimes like, in the same way the Soviets are said to have warmed up to Mengistu when he had his best general decapitated and the headless corpse ceremonially paraded through the streets of Ethiopia's second city. It's the willingness to go the extra mile that impresses discriminating dictators, and within a few months of his loan scam van Kloberg was proudly telling *The Wall Street Journal* that his firm "specializes in developing countries and Eastern European countries". That would be Saddam's Iraq and Ceauşescu's Romania.

THE PARIAH GUY

His first big success was Surinam. After reading about its "bloody dictator" in one newspaper after another, van Kloberg wrote to their ambassador in Washington and successfully pitched his services. Within a year of signing with him, they had a new, democratically elected government. How closely these two events are connected depends on whose version you prefer. But van Kloberg worked hard at rehabilitating the country's image – setting up some harmless little photo-ops, cornering key Congressional figures, and telling the bloody dictator in question, Colonel Bouterse, what to say in his big speech to the UN. It was mostly a lot of boilerplate about the country "marching toward democracy" as "the free and democratic Republic of Surinam", but it was a rare example of a dictator taking dictation and it encouraged van Kloberg in his view that he could be a force for good, wooing his unlovely clientele away from the dark side.

That's one view. The other is that these otherwise savvy dictators wound up with little to show for putting van/von on retainer. Like so many other flacks for problematic acts, he'd promise network primetime and feature spreads in *Vanity Fair* and in the end the clippings file would have little in it other than a few letters to the editor in non-major markets, invariably under Kloberg's own name or whichever variant of it he was using at the time. According to the US government's Foreign Agents Registration records, he billed Saddam Hussein for several prominent op-eds that appeared in *The New York Times*. When the journalist Murray Waas called up the authors, none had heard of von Kloberg. Fraud-wise, it's small beer next to Saddam and his Oil-for-Food racket. But even so: bilking the Baathists takes some nerve. He was an expert at schmoozing friendless regimes into picking up the tab for his social life, a one-man Oily-for-Food program he kept running for two decades.

To modify Sir Thomas More, it profits a man nothing to give his soul for the whole world… but for Burma? Guatemala? To look at his client list is to wonder what was going through the minds of his later signings: Did they reject the wimp down the street representing Belgium and New Zealand because it would be damaging to their

145

image as a reviled bload-soaked thug not to be represented by the town's Number One pariah guy? Even more perplexing, signing with von Kloberg was usually a good indicator that the President-for-Life was coming to the end of his term. Mobutu fell and von Kloberg wrote a hagiographic eulogy for the papers, "The Mobutu I Billed" – sorry, my mistake, "The Mobutu I Knew", and then he promptly signed up the fellow who deposed Mobutu, Laurent Kabila. Either it was a clerical error – Kabila had changed Zaire's name back to the Congo – or von Kloberg prided himself on being one of the few members of the Order of the Leopard who could change his spots.

But with the Cold War winding down, beleaguered despots figured they could use a spin-doctor. They were trying to get with the beat and he assured them he could teach 'em to dance the new steps. A charming host who seemed very lonely, he had contacts rather than friends, and in his isolation he gravitated to those more spectacularly isolated. He was never as influential as he claimed, nor even as wicked: *pace* von Kloberg, there are plenty of sissies with no shame, which is why many of his clients didn't want for pals in the State Department and the other bastions of striped-pants foreign policy "realism" whose unreality 9/11 blew apart – and those friends discreetly did far more for them than their flack's letters to the editor ever could. "*E lucevan le stelle*," sings Cavaradossi in *Tosca*, "How the stars seemed to shimmer …and a footstep skimmed over the sand." Edward von Kloberg skimmed lightly over as the sands ran out. He kept the show on the road longer than most of his clients.

The Atlantic Monthly

Doing the decent thing

JOHN PROFUMO
JANUARY 30TH 1915 ~ MARCH 10TH 2006

I T BEGAN LIKE a movie: July 8th 1961. An unusually warm evening at a grand country estate. A girl in the swimming pool. She pulls herself up out of the water. She's beautiful, and naked. A larky lad in the water has tossed her bathing costume into the bushes. And among the blasé weekend guests dressed for dinner and taking a stroll on the terrace one man reacts with more than nonchalant amusement as the girl hastily wraps a towel around her. She leaves with someone else the next day. But not before the man on the terrace has enquired after her name.

It was Christine Keeler. The house was Cliveden, country home of Lord Astor. The name of the fellow who threw away her swimsuit was Stephen Ward, to whom Bill Astor had rented a cottage on the estate for one pound a year. Ward was, formally, a society osteopath and basked in the dingy glow of reflected celebrity: his client list included Winston Churchill, Anthony Eden, and, when in town, Averell Harriman, Elizabeth Taylor and Frank Sinatra. The man in the dinner jacket so taken by the girl in the dripping towel was the Right Honorable John Profumo, Her Majesty's Secretary of State for War. The man the girl left with was another guest of Stephen Ward's, Yevgeny Ivanov.

Miss Keeler was a showgirl at Murray's cabaret club in Soho. Commander Ivanov was the Soviet naval attaché in London. "Showgirl" was a euphemism for call girl, "naval attaché" a euphemism for KGB intelligence officer.

It's hard to devise a precise contemporary parallel for "the Profumo affair" - imagine Donald Rumsfeld is having an affair with one of Mullah Omar's wives? - but in London it became the standard by which were measured all subsequent political sex scandals. They occur with depressing regularity but remarkable variety (straight, gay, three-in-a-bed, auto-erotic asphyxiation, toe-sucking while accoutred in the garb of Chelsea Football Club) and have prompted some cringe-making performances in the House of Commons – one thinks of the resignation statement in 1999 of Ron Davies, Secretary of State for Wales, after getting mugged in the shrubbery of Clapham Common during a comically inept nocturnal foray in search of some Rastafarian "rough trade". "We are what we are," said Mr Davies, echoing the First Act finale of *La Cage Aux Folles* before going on to enter more mitigating circumstances – unhappy childhood, abusive father - than his fellow Labour members were in the mood for. Jack Profumo was less maudlin. With the Prime Minister Harold Macmillan at his side, he rose from the government benches in Parliament and declared flatly: "There was no impropriety whatsoever in my relationship with Miss Keeler."

Given that Miss Keeler was distinguished by a noticeable lack of non-improper relationships, even fellow Tories found this hard to credit. "What are whores about?" scoffed his fellow MP Nigel Birch. The denial was soon proven false, and that's why Profumo resigned – not because he was untrue to his wife but because he was untrue to the House of Commons. The Westminster system – all the "my honorable friend"/"the noble Earl"/"the right honorable member opposite" stuff – is predicated on the assumption of integrity. As a much retailed limerick of the day put it:

> *"Oh what have you done?" said Christine.*
> *"You have ruined the party machine.*
> *To lie in the nude*
> *May be terribly rude*
> *But to lie in the House is obscene."*

In other words, Jack Profumo was done in by the "I did not have sexual relations with that woman" moment. Whether or not President Clinton should have suffered the same fate for his finger-wagging, it would doubtless have been merely a temporary retreat before reemergence for a full-scale redemption-by-talk-show tour, doing the flawed-but-all-too-human shtick to Larry and Oprah, explaining how he'd conquered his demons and how you can conquer yours, too, with the help of his new self-help video, etc. The advance from Random House probably wouldn't have been any bigger, but the book would have been at least partially readable.

John Profumo didn't do any of that. There was no comeback, and no attempt at one. He accepted that his career was ruined and never sought public sympathy. As extraordinary as his downfall was, the aftermath was unique. On June 5th 1963 he resigned from the government, from Parliament and from the Queen's Privy Council. Not long afterwards, he contacted Toynbee Hall, a charitable mission in the East End of London, and asked whether they needed any help. He started washing dishes and helping with the children's playgroup, and he stayed for 40 years. He disappeared amid the grimy tenements of east London and did good works till he died. And, with the exception of one newspaper article to mark Toynbee Hall's centenary, he never said another word in public again.

He was, technically, the fifth Baron Profumo of the late Kingdom of Sardinia, but his family had settled in England in 1880, made their money in insurance and by the time Jack was born were comfortably ensconced as Warwickshire landowners. As a rising politician, he had a sheen and a charm about him that Ian McKellen, in the 1989 film *Scandal*, never quite captured. I don't suppose he thought they'd be making movies about him a quarter-century later, but he accepted it. Profumo is Italian for "scent", which gives the fallen political star a whiff of Ben Jonson: he caught the heady intoxication of cheap perfume one summer's night, and, though he swapped his evening dress for a hairshirt, he understood the smell could never be washed out.

Shortly after Profumo's disgrace, Harold Macmillan resigned for health reasons and was succeeded as Prime Minister by the 14th Earl of Home. But the minister's downfall, Stephen Ward's suicide on the final day of his trial, and tidbits such as "the man in the mask" - an otherwise naked personage who would serve guests at Ward's parties, wore a sign advising dissatisfied patrons to whip him, ate from a dog's bowl, and who was said to be a High Court judge or perhaps another high-ranking cabinet minister – these glimpses of life among "the Cliveden set" took their toll on the Conservatives' reputation and conjured a Britain run by a decadent elite having all the fun the masses never got. In court, it was pointed out to Christine's chum Mandy Rice-Davies that Lord Astor had denied sleeping with her, and Mandy replied, prompting much laughter and a subsequent entry in many dictionaries of quotations, "Well, he would, wouldn't he?" That neatly summed up the British people's view of their rulers and a year later the Tory government fell to a resurgent Labour Party.

A couple of decades on, in my radio days, I wandered into work, and was told by the boss that a colleague was supposed to be interviewing Christine Keeler but that he hadn't shown up and I had to do it. I was old enough to recognize all the names – Profumo, Ward, Mandy Rice-Davies still resonated as cultural markers – but too young to be entirely clear as to who'd done what to whom. It wasn't a great interview. Miss Keeler spoke in a soft breathy whisper, like someone suggesting you might want to come in for a nightcap, which only made her impenetrable footnoting of the case even harder to follow. At one point, she said, "Stephen killed himself because he couldn't live with people thinking he was a ponce", and I remember recognizing "ponce" as a British term of disparagement but not being entirely clear what precisely it was disparaging: a ponce can be a man who lives off a woman's immoral earnings or a male homosexual, and I wasn't sure which Miss Keeler meant, or indeed if she meant both. But even then it seemed a quaintly archaic term, and one that placed its speaker in what was already a time capsule.

In the film *Scandal*, Joanne Whalley had a bland smooth prettiness. By the time I met Christine, the vicissitudes of life had etched a lot more character into the face – ie, wrinkles – but she looked if anything more beautiful than in the iconic photograph of her naked and straddling an Arne Jacobson chair (or copy thereof), an image much parodied by everyone from David Frost to Homer Simpson. She had a kind of fragile sensuality, except when she opened her mouth and revealed a full set of Austin Powers choppers. She was living in poverty in a "council flat" (British for housing project) and had nothing to retail but those few months in the early Sixties, which she did incessantly to diminishing returns, updating her story according to whatever new "evidence" emerged, the most recent being a treasure trove of conspiracy-rich CIA reports positing Ward as a Soviet agent. For all she's got from the attempts to cling to her celebrity, Miss Keeler might as well have joined Profumo at Toynbee Hall and done charity work for four decades.

Still, you could see why a red-blooded male would want to chase her naked round the pool at Cliveden. In 1953, Jack Profumo had gone along to see *The King And I* at the Theatre Royal, and been introduced to Valerie Hobson, who was playing Mrs Anna. Miss Hobson was one of the biggest British stars of the day, and she's very good in *Kind Hearts And Coronets* and certainly a fine-looking woman, but like a lot of other English roses of the period it's a sort of de-sexed good-lookingness, at least on screen. Miss Keeler, by contrast, was very abandoned, though unfortunately not just in bed. If you were running auditions for the role of *grande horizontale* to the ruling class, she's the last person you'd want, almost pathologically unable to keep her mouth shut. With the scandal unraveling, Jack took Valerie to Venice and spilled the truth over lunch. "Oh, darling," she said, in near parodic British, "we must go home and face up to it." And so, like some stoic stiff-upper-lipped sequel to *Brief Encounter*, she did the decent thing and stood by him.

In 1963, "Profumo" was shorthand for establishment hypocrisy. Across 40 years, he reclaimed the narrative, as a story of shame and redemption, of acting honorably, making the best of a sticky wicket and all the other allegedly obsolescent virtues of his class the sex and hookers had supposedly rendered risible. Had Stephen Ward not thrown a teenage girl's bathing suit into the topiary, John

Profumo would have been noted as the last surviving member of the House of Commons to vote in the confidence motion of May 8th 1940, after the fall of Norway. He was one of only 30 Conservative MPs to join the opposition in declining to support the continued leadership of Neville Chamberlain and thus to usher Churchill into Downing Street. That vote changed the course of the war. But instead his place in history is as the man who saw a call-girl naked in a swimming pool.

The Atlantic Monthly

HEIRS *&* *Relicts*

Half dragon queen, half Georgia peach

MADAME CHIANG KAI-SHEK
MARCH 5TH 1898 ~ OCTOBER 23RD 2003

C LAIRE CHENNAULT, the American founder of China's air aces, the Flying Tigers, met his new boss on June 3rd 1937. "A vivacious young girl clad in a modish Paris frock tripped into the room, bubbling with energy and enthusiasm," he recalled. It was "an encounter from which I never recovered," and whatever happened, that "young girl" would "always be a princess to me."

Thus Madame Chiang Kai-shek, half dragon lady, half Georgia peach, and an encounter from which many who should have known better never recovered. Her life is a monument to the power of personality in the great sweep of history. Most people who survive to 105 end up as living anachronisms: their world dies long before they do. But even as a frail centenarian taking her walks in Central Park, unnoticed by joggers and tourists, Soong Mei-ling had the satisfaction of knowing that, geopolitically speaking, we live in a world shaped in part by her extraordinary character.

Bad news comes in threes, and so for the most part did Madame Chiang. She lived in three centuries. She was one of only three women to wield real power in modern China: Ci Xi, the former concubine turned Empress Dowager in the final years of the Qing dynasty; Madame Mao, who was jailed shortly after the death of her husband and killed herself in 1991; and in between, and on a different scale, Madame Chiang. She was one of three sisters, of whom it was said, "One loved power, one loved money, one loved China." Mei-ling was the first; she did love power, though in the objective sense she

155

never had a lot of it. But America so loved her that it treated her as if she did.

And so, in the most remarkable of Madame Chiang's threesomes, China was invited to participate with Britain and America in the 1943 Cairo Conference. Roosevelt was insistent that the Chiangs be invited; Churchill thought it preposterous to pretend that General Chiang's China was - along with Britain, the United States, and the Soviet Union - one of the Big Four world powers; its presence at the conference was "an absolute farce". The reason for this difference of opinion was simple: Churchill had never met Madame Chiang; Roosevelt had. Indeed, after visiting with Mei-ling in New York earlier that year, Eleanor Roosevelt announced that she wanted to "take care of her as if she had been my own daughter" and promptly moved her into the White House, which didn't give Churchill a lot of room for maneuver.

Nonetheless, the British Prime Minister's judgment was the correct one, and the languid old Asia hands at the Foreign Office were calling America's man "General Cash My-cheque" long before Washington noticed how many of the billions it had lavished on his country had gotten hoovered up by the generalissimo's near and dear. In fairness to Chiang, a lot of the money ended up in the hands of his wife's family, who were already fabulously wealthy. Mei-ling's father, Charlie Soong, got rich as a Bible salesman in China and then helped bankroll General Sun Yat-sen's 1911 revolution. He had his children educated in the United States, and the girls went to Wesleyan College, in Macon, Georgia. By the time Mei-ling advanced to Wellesley, her English had acquired a southern lilt. The sisters were said to be the first Chinese girls to go to college in America.

Three decades later she became the first Chinese and only the second woman to address Congress. On a prolonged visit in 1943 she enchanted everyone - the Roosevelts, the Republicans, the Hollywood Committee to Receive Madame Chiang Kai-shek (Rita Hayworth, Ginger Rogers, Shirley Temple, and others), an audience of 20,000 at Madison Square Garden, and one of 30,000 at the Hollywood Bowl.

Had America been an imperial power, Madame Chiang would have been one of a type. The annals of British colonialism are strewn with exotic figures - Indian maharajahs and African princess - who would have recognized Madame Chiang's ornately convoluted English as she denounced the "convulsions and perfervid paroxysms" of the Cultural Revolution or the "dastardly Communist poltroons" who perpetrated the Tiananmen Square massacre. But the United States is not an imperial power, so Madame Chiang had the field of Americanized exotics all to herself. Her husband spoke little English, and she sold herself to both parties as a bridge between two cultures. Other than the American tenor who sang that quintessentially American wedding song "Oh, Promise Me" at their nuptials, to Madame Chiang East was East and West was West, and hardly e'er the twain did meet; for all her love of America, she never troubled herself with whether American notions of liberty or justice would be useful to China. Madame tailored her act to her audience; even the Georgia drawl was variable.

Many consequences flowed from her smash tour of 1943, among them that Cairo Conference, which so inflated the status of General Chiang's China, and (even more of "an absolute farce") the decision to reward the general's insignificant contribution to the Allied victory by giving China one of the five permanent places on the new UN Security Council. Though the British and the Americans had agreed on much in the preceding years, both had their idiosyncratic fetishes: Washington thought that de Gaulle was a poseur and that Chiang would save his country; London thought vice versa. In the objective sense, neither postwar France nor China merited a Security Council seat. But the former was at least a coherent nation-state. Even in the Thirties the Chiangs never ruled China, only a shifting sliver of it. A Japanese puppet emperor reigned in Manchuria; there was a Communist regime in Shanxi; the Soviet Union held Mongolia and Xinjiang; Shanghai and other "treaty ports" were garrisoned and run by Britain, America, France, and Italy; and local warlords carved up much of what was left. Buffeted by these various factions, General Chiang moved his court from town to town according to which of his enemies was chastising him least. Chiang's China was unstable; he was never a likely candidate to hold it together; and it was obvious who the likely successors would be. But the Allies gave him a Security Council seat anyway.

In 1949 the Chiangs left mainland China for the last time and took their government into exile on Formosa, recently returned to the Middle Kingdom by Japan. Mei-ling was no longer the force she once had been in America, but her residual aura helped persuade Washington to endorse an illusion: that she and her husband were the real government of China. Thus for the next two decades one of the five vetoes in the UN Security Council was wielded by a quasi-colonial dictatorship of outsiders on a small insignificant island. The Soviets were so affronted by America's refusal to cede China's seat to the fellows who actually ran China that they walked out of the council and in their absence the UN voted for the Korean War.

Maybe some of this would still have happened without Madame Chiang. But it's doubtful that a conventional, locally raised Chinese wife would have so intoxicated an American audience. And the austere general couldn't have done it on his own. In January of 1938 he was one half of *Time*'s "Man and Wife of the Year", a formulation that tells you what angle Henry Luce was interested in: the American college girl running an ancient civilization.

In 1936 Chiang was kidnapped by Marshal Chang, who wanted him to quit battling the Communists and take on the Japanese. Eleven days after his capture Mei-ling flew to Xian to be by her husband's side and turned her charm on Marshal Chang; within 48 hours the generalissimo was freed. If she'd stayed home, and if Chiang had been killed by his kidnappers, the last half of the 20th century might have been very different. China, the UN, the Korean War, McCarthyism - the fragile skein of history snaked back to a delicate, small-boned lady of fierce determination. At the end of her life a woman who'd come into direct contact with all the great forces that blew through her country - from the emperors to Japanese militarism to communism - found that the most potent was the one that made her dad rich a century ago: China is once again Christianity's most fertile recruiting ground.

"Who lost China?" America's anti-Communists agonized. Nobody. China was never lost. Chiang Kai-shek had never won it in the first place. And if not for its sentimentalization of "a vivacious young girl clad in a modish Paris frock", America might have seen that six decades ago.

The Atlantic Monthly

Polite and cheerful

THE 11th DUKE OF DEVONSHIRE
JANUARY 2ND 1920 ~ MAY 3RD 2004

IN BRITAIN, Digby Anderson has just published a pamphlet called *All Oiks Now* – "oik" being British for a loud, coarse, vulgar, unpleasant common little man, and Anderson's thesis being that this unfortunate breed now has the run of England's formerly green and pleasant land. Writing to *The Daily Telegraph* from Borthwick Castle in Scotland, Lady Borthwick was inclined to agree:

Sir - In the week in which the splendid obituary of the Duke of Devonshire appeared, I am writing to say that I agree with Digby Anderson that this is a country fit only for oiks. Sadly, anyone speaking proper Queen's English is now derided as a toff. This country will rise from its present position near the gutter only when once again we have Members of Parliament who have spent time in the real world, perhaps in the Armed Forces, or indeed are from a landowning family, brought up with a sense of duty to those around them.

A tall, dapper aristocrat, Andrew Cavendish, 11th Duke of Devonshire, fulfilled all Lady Borthwick's criteria for a model public servant: He spoke the Queen's English rather more grandly than Her Majesty. He won the Military Cross for capturing and holding a hill in Italy despite being surrounded on all sides. His family owned thousands of acres of prime land in England, Ireland and Scotland. And he descended from a long line of dutiful patricians: the second Duke was Steward of Queen Anne's Household, the third and fourth were Lords-Lieutenant of Ireland, his grandfather was Governor-General of Canada and his father Under-Secretary of State for Dominion Affairs.

All the same, he would have been reluctant to sign on to Lady Borthwick and Dr Anderson's general line on the depths to which his countrymen have sunk.

For one thing, he disliked rudeness, and, even in the midst of Britain's descent into Hogarthian depravity, believed in looking on the bright side. He was, after all, a founder of the Polite Society, with its Campaign for Courtesy and its polite courteous logo of a gentleman doffing his hat. The Duke decided there was a need for a Polite Society after he thanked a taxi driver for taking him home one night and the grateful cabbie "put his gnarled old hand on my gnarled old hand and said: 'You've no idea the difference a kind word makes.'"

For another, he was a genuine English patriot. In the 1980s, when a London court case brought to light his prodigious philandering, the Duke seemed to think it his duty, even in the midst of momentary public discomfort, to do his bit for the home team. "English girls are the loveliest in the world," he said. "As for a dalliance, well, the French have their strengths and the Italians are very agreeable. But if you want my advice, stick to English women." And so, for the most part, he did.

And the final reason the Duke would have eschewed the Borthwick line is that he had an aristocratic reluctance to make a fuss. He displayed great physical courage in Italy but insisted for the next 60 years that they gave him the Military Cross merely for "being cheerful". As one son of privilege to another, he would have found John Kerry's war-hero campaign commercials utterly cringe-making. He was a modest man – or, at any rate, a man shrewd enough to understand that, in post-war socialist Britain, modesty behooves a duke.

In the 1960s, he served as Britain's Minister of State for Colonial Affairs, a distinction he attributed to the fact that his uncle happened to be Prime Minister (Harold Macmillan). But those were busy days at the Colonial Office: the Duke midwifed 11 newly independent nations, from Malawi to Jamaica, which is no mean accomplishment. Yet he brushed it aside, and, asked how he rubbed along with notoriously uncooperative Afro-Marxist revolutionaries, he was at pains to emphasize how frightfully decent they were. "I got on well with the Africans," he'd say. "They were very jolly." "Andrew is awfully good with natives," observed Uncle Harold.

And so, cloaking a sharp wit and canny instincts in the traditional virtues of diffidence and self-deprecation, Andrew Devonshire somehow survived and prospered as a duke in a very unducal age. They're an endangered species these days – just 24 in the whole of Britain, if you discount the royal ones such as the Duke of York (Prince Andrew) - and by the time of his death Devonshire was the best-known duke in the land.

Insofar as he's known to Americans at all, it's through one of the many graves on the estate – that of Kathleen Kennedy, daughter of Joe, sister of Jack, and sister-in-law of Andrew Devonshire. In 1944, "Kick" married Andrew's older brother, the Marquess of Hartington. Four months later, Hartington was killed in action, leaving Kick a widow and Andrew heir to the dukedom. One of his father's pleasures was to essay some occasional physical exertion on his own behalf rather than leaving it all to the servants, and he was particularly partial to sawing up fallen trees for his fireplaces. While doing this at their seaside home at Eastbourne in 1950, he had a massive thrombosis and died. He was 55, which made it not just tragic but expensive, as he was 14 months shy of his qualification for a reduced level of "death duties". Instead, he left Andrew owing 80 per cent of his inheritance to the government.

Britain in the Fifties was a grim, grey place: wartime rationing was still in effect, under the modified catch-all heading of "post-war austerity". Many peers found it easier to sell the crumbling old stately pile and retire to the Caribbean or the Riviera. Chatsworth has 17 staircases and 56 toilets (or "lavatories", as the Duke would have said). That's great, if you can afford 56 rolls of toilet paper and 56 cakes of soap every time you go to the store, and you've got a plumber on staff. But, besieged by confiscatory class-war taxation, by the 1950s many of England's great country homes were little more than a poky apartment with a couple of space heaters in the middle of a vast abandoned ruin.

The 11th Duke considered his options and determined to save what had been his family's home for four centuries. He sold the Holbein, and a Rembrandt, and the family's prized Anglo-Saxon manuscript, the Benedictional of St Ethelwold. And then he set about playing for time and discovered that the notorious indolence of an effete aristocracy had nothing against the bureaucratic inertia of socialist tax-collectors. He carefully noted how long the Inland Revenue took to reply to his last letter, and made a point of taking as long to reply to theirs, less one day. By this method, which the Revenue never noticed, he dragged out the final settlement of death duties for 17 years.

By the end, Chatsworth was saved. Today, some 400,000 tourists visit the palatial family home at Chatsworth each year and without the Duke and his chatelaine Debo (the most perfectly poised of the Mitford sisters, at least politically) having to go to the desperate lengths of his fellow landowners. The Marquess of Bath turned his place into a wildlife park in order to serve the surprisingly large niche market that likes to see lions and tigers roaming around a stately home. "We stayed upmarket," Devonshire liked to say. Tom Jones will be singing at Chatsworth this summer, but there'll be less panty-hurling than at his Vegas gigs.

The Devonshire strategy was less successful applied to politics. By mid-century, *noblesse oblige* had decayed in Britain's insecure ruling class into a weary fatalism about imperial decline. Just as the Duke accepted he could never retain all his inheritance, so too he assumed that his nation couldn't: as with his father's estate, it was a question of tactical surrenders, retrenchment, holding on to what was feasible. There was a ratchet effect in British politics, and all a Conservative could hope to do was slow it down. In the mid-Seventies, with the country a socialist basket-case, Devonshire's party turned to Margaret Thatcher. She wasn't *noblesse* and she was disinclined to *oblige*: she wanted to reverse Britain's decay, not provide genteel oversight.

The Duke wasn't the only grandee uncomfortable with the new management. Noting the Iron Lady's preference for Jews, Harold

163

Macmillan remarked that hers was the first Tory cabinet with more Estonians than Etonians. In the Eighties, Devonshire left the Conservatives for the new Social Democratic Party, a breakaway of Labour Party "moderates". That was the first occasion I met him, when his sister-in-law introduced us at an art exhibition. He was wry and amusing, but I couldn't help feeling that, though the political analysts' frequent complaint about the SDP was that it was "too middle-class", signing up an 11th duke was approaching the problem from the wrong end. The SDP eventually faded away, and by the end of his life Andrew Devonshire was a supporter of the UK Independence Party, an even smaller breakaway grouping founded to resist Britain's submersion within the European Union. Like Mrs Thatcher, the Duke finally found a ratchet effect he wanted to arrest. The old virtues – chin up, keep muddling through – will only get you so far.

They have dukes in Europe, of course – even in the republics, like France and Germany. But, as his sister-in-law Nancy Mitford once wrote, "An aristocracy in a republic is like a chicken whose head has been cut off: it may run about in a lively way, but in fact it is dead." Whether or not the same holds true for Britain's new oikocracy, Andrew Cavendish, Duke of Devonshire managed to run about livelier and longer than most of the other chickens.

The Atlantic Monthly

Bright young thing with a blind spot

DIANA MOSLEY
JUNE 17TH 1910 ~ AUGUST 11TH 2003

D IANA MOSLEY was the last person alive to know both Churchill and Hitler. The former was married to her second cousin, the latter came to her wedding reception. She was born into that section of English society that takes it for granted one will be related to a fair proportion of eminent men. But, as if to underline the not always acknowledged fluidity of the British aristocracy, she expanded her social circle well beyond traditional confines. Her wedding planner was Goebbels.

She was one of the six famous Mitford sisters. There have been books, plays, TV dramas and a musical about the Mitford girls – or gels – and two-thirds of the sisters have been good enough writers to burnish the legend through any quiet patches. With the exception of Diana, with her pale cheeks and huge china-blue eyes, they weren't really beauties. Nor were they rich: their father, Lord Redesdale, was a broken-down rural peer well off the beaten track of high society. But they were "Hons". That's not an abbreviation for "honeys" but for "Honourables", as in the courtesy title given to the daughters of barons and viscounts. Plotting their escape from dreary provincialism in their childhood hideaway – the "Hons' Cupboard" - the Hon Diana and her sisters determined to marry well.

It didn't exactly work out as planned: Nancy had a terrible, debilitating lifelong love for Colonel Gaston Palewski, aide to General de Gaulle and the randiest man in France, which is saying something; Jessica eloped with Winston Churchill's Communist nephew, and later settled down in America with her fellow leftie Bob Treuhaft; Unity had a pash on Hitler and shot herself at the outbreak of war. Only Debo and Pam made conventional upper-class marriages, one to a duke, the other to a bisexual. Diana ended up with Sir Oswald Mosley, leader of Britain's Fascist party, and wound up spending most of the Second World War in jail. In the Twenties, there were lots of silly giggly girls dashing about Mayfair – "bright young things", as Evelyn Waugh called them in the novel he dedicated to Diana – but only the Mitfords transformed themselves into a collective of distaff Forrest Gumps, always somewhere in the picture at the decisive moments of 20th century history. Even on the West Coast, Jessica and Bob Treuhaft's employees included at one point a young Hillary Clinton.

Diana was my favourite, and hilarious company. Even when she was talking about something ineffably sad, she couldn't steer clear of the jokes for long. Discussing her only brother Tom, killed in the war, fighting for King and country against the Japanese allies of her old friend and wedding guest, she soon turned to happier memories: One weekend as children they'd been motoring with Lord and Lady Redesdale through the Oxfordshire countryside. At school, Tom had a crush on a boy called Milton. As they passed the sign for the village of Milton-under-Wychwood, he sighed, "Lucky Wychwood."

It was when the jokes stopped that one got uneasy. If you're going to have one blind spot, being soft on the Fuhrer and married to his bargain-basement British branch office is not the one to have. I got to know her in her seventies and, as the spidery sign-offs at the end of her letters advanced chummily from "Diana Mosley" to "Diana M." to "Diana", I began to feel a little queasy. "Are you a Jew?" she asked me. "You're *so* clever." Usually, she meant the Jews were clever in always keeping "the thing" – the Holocaust, as she could never quite bring herself to say – in the public eye, unlike the millions killed in the name of the ideology her sister Jessica supported. This is a fair point, and true to this day, when the elites of the western world still brim with shills for genocidal leftists. But it's not a point the public is willing to take from a pal of the Fuhrer's.

The first time I was invited to her home in France I could only afford to take the night boat from Dover, which was even rougher than usual - not the sea, the passengers. I arrived at the Gare du Nord reeking of my own sweat and some adjoining yobs' vomit, and with a pounding headache. And by the time I got to the small suburban station at Lozère, where a rather creepily devoted English retainer was waiting, I'd managed to spill a polystyrene cup of coffee down my front. Lady Mosley kindly produced a dry shirt for me. It was frayed and worn and missing buttons, so I assumed it was the under-gardener's. But it occurred to me, inspecting it on the night boat back, that it could well have been Sir Oswald's: with the English, it's hard to tell.

She used all kinds of expressions I'd never heard before, or at least not in that context. About that brother-in-law, she said, "He rode under both rules", and then laughed. I was trying to think of some appropriate equestrian chit-chat to make in response, when I realized she meant he was a bi-guy. If you could get over the whole Hitler thing, Diana was the best kind of girl: she was always funny, and she was off-hand about her beauty. I sat next to her once when she was wearing a cashmere polo-neck all fluffed up and at one point, in the middle of some anecdote or other, she just carelessly brushed her right breast and de-fluffed it. And I thought it was the most elegant gesture I'd ever seen.

Whoops, I'm doing exactly what she did. When you brought up the Fuhrer, she'd go on about his exquisite table manners, manicured fingers, beautifully fine brown hair, etc. She's surely on to something: the nerdy little misfit he usually gets played as in movies can't be the whole story. I tried to ask her about the concentration camps. "So awful," she murmured, the big blue eyes gazing off into the distance. "One knows it happened, but it's hard to believe really..." Or "rairlehhhhh". Her drawled vowel sounds went on forever, and, not being entirely attuned to them, I'd learned to wait before replying just in case there was a surprise consonant on the end. But in this case the "rairleh" just dribbled away into nothing.

Her husband was a Labour MP who went on to found the British Union of Fascists. Socialism does not always lead to National Socialism, but in the early Thirties statism of one degree or another was all the rage in Europe: Communism, Fascism, Nazism. Even in Britain, liberal democracy was thought by all the great thinkers to be inadequate as an organizing basis for society. Of course, if you weren't a great thinker, the notion that Sir Oswald and his excitable Continental comrades were the chaps to put in charge was utterly risible. In *The Code Of The Woosters*, P G Wodehouse turned Mosley into Roderick Spode, founder of the Saviours of Britain, a movement modeled on Hitler's blackshirts and Mussolini's brownshirts and hampered only slightly by the fact that all the good shirt colours have been taken and they're obliged to go around as the Black Shorts.

"Footer bags, you mean?" gasps a horrified Bertie Wooster.

But Bertie has the measure of the would-be dictator. "The trouble with you, Spode, is that just because you have succeeded in inducing a handful of half-wits to disfigure the London scene by going about in black shorts, you think you're someone. You hear them shouting, 'Heil, Spode!' and you imagine it is the Voice of the People. That is where you make your bloomer. What the Voice of the People is saying is: 'Look at that frightful ass Spode swanking about in footer bags! Did you ever in your puff see such a perfect perisher?'"

There in a nutshell is the history of British Fascism. In the late Seventies, Mosley still expected the people to realize their error and belatedly turn to him. "I am ready to serve," he'd say, gravely, as interviewers tried to keep a straight face. He and Diana spent decades in exile in Paris in a grand house in miniature absurdly called le Temple de la Gloire – the Temple of Glory or, as her more malicious friends dubbed it, the Concentration of Camp. It's a heartless joke, characteristic of the English upper class. But it's the jokes that explain the difference between Britain and the Continent: unlike their European counterparts, the English elite could never take Fascism seriously enough to fall for it.

I had the misfortune to meet some of the Mosleys' shrunken band of followers. Bitter little Cockneys, to whom all Jews were "Yids" and all blacks were "wogs". But, in a sense, their awfulness confirmed Diana's certainties about her husband. The people were too crude and stupid: they needed great men to tell them what to do. That was also why, for the last half of her long life, she was a passionate supporter of the European Union – the latest of the elite's grand plans for the people after the failures of all the others. Her views were indistinguishable from Wim Kok's or Chris Patten's. "Everything is so much more efficient in France than England," Diana told me a few years ago. "The government understands that to govern is to decide. And, if you do that, the people will follow."

I don't know how I'd recover if I'd got wrong the great issue of my times. But, if I needed another reason to loathe the EU, it was that she was gung ho for it. Still, I can't see why the historian Andrew Roberts, a year or two back, was so convinced she was destined to spend eternity in Hell. The opprobrium heaped on Diana for what she did seemed to intensify in proportion to the routine acceptance of similar or worse behavior by anybody else. She didn't kill anyone. She didn't urge the killing of anyone. She didn't betray her compatriots, like that cute little 87-year-old London granny and Communist spy the British Government declined to take action against a few months ago. She didn't take up arms against her own country, like those plucky West Midland Muslims captured in Afghanistan that Ken Livingstone thinks were just celebrating their distinctive cultural identity and Jack Straw wants to spring from Guantanamo.

Granted, Diana got turned on by totalitarianism, but she's a piker compared with world-class thug fetishists like Ted Heath, who still admires Mao, or Pierre Trudeau, who yelled "Viva Castro!" in Havana and regretted the liberation of Eastern Europe, or Jimmy Carter, who's never met a psychotic dictator he couldn't make a case for: Mengistu, Assad, Kim Jong-Il... Ceauşescu? "Our goals are the same," declared Carter. "We believe in enhancing human rights."

When Diana gushed over a monster, she was a silly kid, not head of government. What's Jimmy and Ted and Pierre's excuse?

Diana loved Paris – so well-ordered, so un-American. But the city, its windows undisfigured by those ghastly American air conditioners, was a little too stifling this summer and a day after complaining about the heat she had a stroke. Thousands upon thousands of others died, because the hospitals were understaffed and the government was at the beach. Next time it happens, new Kyoto-compliant regulations will ensure cheap air conditioners remain beyond the reach of the masses.

Diana Mosley was a hoot and I'm surprised at how glum I feel to think I'll never be laughing through one of her indiscreet anecdotes again. The last time I saw her a mutual friend had just died. "So sad," she said. "People die non-stop." I thought she'd go on awhile, and I certainly never expected that she'd be among the many elderly victims of France's lethargic bureaucracy. But it's a cruel joke that she would have been the first to see. The elite, unlike the masses, can usually escape the consequences of big ideas. This summer European Big Government finally caught up with her.

The Daily Telegraph/ The Atlantic Monthly

Swingin' Fascist

ROMANO MUSSOLINI

SEPTEMBER 26TH 1927 ~ FEBRUARY 3RD 2006

B ACK IN THE Sixties, the Bonzo Dog Doo-Dah Band, Britain's leading psychedelic novelty group, recorded a number called "The Intro And The Outro". You know that moment when you see some act live on stage and midway through the set they do an extended if not interminable beginning to the song so the leader can introduce every member of the band individually? Well, that's what the Bonzos did:

> Hi there, nice to be with you, happy you could stick around. Like to introduce 'Legs' Larry Smith, drums...

Only in this case the intro never stopped. After the real band members and a few genuine special guests – "Eric Clapton on ukulele" - Viv Stanshall moved on to some even less likely soloists:

> Princess Anne on sousaphone...
> Looking very relaxed, Adolf Hitler on vibes...
> Yeah! Digging General de Gaulle on accordion...
> Really wild, General! Thank you, sir!

I would have liked to have seen Adolf Hitler on vibes. But the closest I came was one night in the Nineties, in London at a jazz *boîte* called Pizza On The Park: up on stage, looking very relaxed, Romano Mussolini on piano... Not Il Duce himself, but the son of. Mussolini *père* wound up hanging with his mistress from that gas station, Mussolini *fils* preferred to hang with Chet Baker and Lionel Hampton at hot nightclubs. Junior seemed in better shape than pop did at that age, and not just because at that age pop was swingin' in the Piazzale

Loreto rather than at Pizza On The Park. Romano was similarly bald but taller and thinner than Benito. Your initial reaction was that he'd make a much more photogenic dictator than dad, but then you noticed that he was way too mellow. You can get away with being short and looking like you're bustin' your blackshirt if you've got the requisite 24/7 passionate intensity. It was just about possible to imagine Romano as an amused 007 villain – "I'm afraid you're beginning to bore me, Mr Bond" – but not conquering Ethiopia.

The closest family resemblance was the pudgy fingers with which he plunked the ivories through Hoagy Carmichael et al. Romano played, to my ears, like a slightly melancholic Oscar Peterson. Occasionally inspired, he was always efficient: he made the refrains run on time. To be honest, I'd only gone to see him because I liked the whimsy in his combo's moniker – "the Romano Mussolini All-Stars". They weren't all-stars, just solid Italian *molto hip* cats; the only star quality, as he recognized early on in his career, was the enduring potency, or at any rate curiosity value, of his pa's name. But the designation hinted at least at the possibility of some A-list agglomeration of second-generation dictatorial talent. There was a comic in London in those days called Bing Hitler, but I don't believe he was a blood relative – and, come to think about it, he's since dropped the Hitler handle and gone on to great success as CBS late-night host Craig Ferguson. The Fuhrer and Eva Braun died without issue and, according to most experts, without much heavy petting. But if only the Mussolini All-Stars had lived up to their billing: Artie Hitler on clarinet, Miles Tse Tung on trumpet, Woody Stalin, Buddy Franco...

I was introduced to him after the show and, of course, everyone was way too cool to ask about dad or the old days. So instead he made the kind of standard jazz small talk that non-jazz buffs find so tedious – all Dizzy this and Monk that – but with a beguiling accent that made me swear at one point he'd referenced a song called "Fascisnatin' Rhythm". The conversation had a surreal frisson, like running into Uday and Qusay at a pro-celeb golf tournament and chitchatting about

Tiger as you play a couple of holes. If you want to escape the sins of the father, going into jazz is a smart move: unlike men bent on world domination, which by definition obliges one to keep an eye on the far horizon, not least when posing for official portraits, the jazz scene tends to the self-absorbed. Half these fellows are barely cognizant of what continent they're on, never mind who's oppressing it. During his sojourn in Italy 45 years ago, Chet Baker played a stint with Romano at the Bussola in Viareggio. There's a famous story that, after their first set together, it was pointed out to Chet whose son Romano was. The trumpeter went over to the piano and commiserated:

Gee, it's a drag about your old man.

Romano always professed to have no memory of the exchange – "Chet and I never discussed politics" – but Caterina Valente, the Continental chanteuse with whom they toured, claims to have been present and insists it happened.

The prototype Fascist's youngest son was named for the glorious new imperium already under way by the time he was born. Romano had a happy childhood in a close-knit family: four siblings, one duce, one mom, two tortoises, two ponies, two parrots, two gazelles, two lions, a monkey and a jaguar. The youngster had fond memories of his pa's signature pose – fists on hips, jutting jaw, looking either like a visionary leader or a bitch waiter at Coconut Grove when you send back the curly endive. Apparently, dad liked to adopt the stance not just to whip up the masses below the balcony but around the house as well, though more "playfully".

They were a musical family. When he wasn't dictating, Benito liked to play violin for hours on end. But, even at a young age, musically Romano disdained Il Duce in favor of Il Duke: his older brother Vittorio gave him a record of Ellington doing "Black Beauty" – the first jazz Romano had ever heard, and he was hooked. Being decadent and Negro, it wasn't the easiest music to come by in Fascist Italy, but Romano sought it out wherever he could. "I remember the first time I heard a Louis Armstrong record," he said. "The sound was so beautiful I cried." American 78s were available in Rome under Italianized names – Louis Armstrong was sold as "Luigi Fortebraccio". His brother Vittorio would return from trips abroad with the latest Benny Goodman or Count Basie. Romano got more pleasure listening to King Oliver than his dad ever got from listening to King Victor Emmanuel.

In later life, Mussolini Jr would protest that his father's antipathy to jazz was much exaggerated and that he greatly enjoyed Fats Waller. Hard to imagine the great dictator singing along to "Keepin' Out Of Mischief Now" or "Your Feet's Too Big". By 1943, it was Mussolini whose feats were too big: he'd projected Italian power far beyond its credible limits and, after military humiliations and the Anglo-American landings on Sicily, he was fired by the King only to be snatched by the Nazis and installed in Gargnano as head of the "Italian Social Republic". A chippy teenager, young Romano was wont to offend their German benefactors by playing boogie-woogie in their presence. Despite being born to neo-imperial destiny, he was already running away from the circus maximus. After the lynching of his father and the end of the war, he ended up with his mother and sister in exile on the isle of Ischia, where the only jazz was at the local barber shop and he liked to sit in on guitar.

When he returned to the mainland in the 1950s, he performed as "Romano Fall", until he discovered that his father's name, far from repelling customers, was actually a commercial plus. While members of the House of Savoy were forbidden to set foot in the new Italian republic, members of the House of Mussolini were relatively untroubled. It was Romano's musical associations that caused him problems, not his political ones. "At that time it was very dangerous to have contact with him because the police investigated everyone," he recalled, but he was talking about the famously drugged up Chet Baker rather than any old-time Fascist.

If you were making a movie of his life, it'd be a cinch: the young man who finds in wild improvisatory American jazz all the freedom he's been denied by his oppressive Fascist background. In fact, if you asked him, Romano Mussolini would cheerfully concede he agreed with "90 per cent" of his father's policies, and, apropos the murkier ten per cent, there weren't many other Fascist scions who could plead in mitigation that some of their best session players were Jewish. In the last couple of years, he began turning out coffee-table books about daddy that proved big sellers. Alessandra Mussolini, his daughter by his first wife (Sophia Loren's sister), went into politics in the Nineties and, though dismissed as a pleasingly underdressed slice of neo-Fascist cheesecake, has become a player in Italian coalition-building. A couple of weeks ago, Colonel Gaddafi threatened attacks against Rome unless the government paid reparations to Libya for colonialism. Alessandra was having none of it. "If it hadn't been for my grandfather they would still be riding camels with turbans on their heads," she said, "They are the ones who should be paying us compensation, because it was a positive colonization. Fascism exported democracy, as well as roads, houses and schools." It may yet be that Romano was only a musical interlude before the resumption of the family business.

He was proud of his daughter. When she founded her current party, Social Alternative, he chipped in by composing the official anthem, "The Pride Of Being Italian". The lyric's somewhat generic, but Alessandra's recording of it is spirited:

> *Together for the future*
> *The Pride Of Being Italian*
> *The ideals that unite us are our truth...*

Romano Mussolini's funeral is surely one of the few to feature both "When The Saints Go Marching In" (inside the church) and Fascist salutes (outside the church, from Italians pining for a new Duce). It was the first time the twin threads of his life had come together since the last time he saw his father, on the morning of April 17th 1945 at Lake Garda. "I was playing Franz Lehár's *The Merry Widow* on the piano," he wrote. "The composer had given my father the original score, and he reacted with enthusiasm whenever it was played. I thought he would stand and listen to me for a few moments." Instead, the dictator embraced his boy, said, "*Ciao*, Romano," and before going out to the waiting car gave a final salute. Eleven days later, he was caught by Communist partisans, executed, and hung from the Esso station.

His last words to his son: "Keep playing."

Romano did.

The Atlantic Monthly

The Kay agenda

KATHARINE GRAHAM
JUNE 16TH 1917 ~ JULY 17TH 2001

IN ALL MY TIME in the Conrad Black salt mines, the only occasion I've ever been subject to censorship was a couple of years back when I wrote a piece on something or other for *The Sunday Telegraph* in London and included a passing jest about Katharine Graham's Georgetown dinner parties. Nothing rude or vicious, just mildly non-reverential. Nonetheless, the editor requested that, as he was dining with Kay later that week, would I mind if he removed the reference. I agreed. At that time I had not yet given up hope that one day I too might receive the summons to Georgetown to trade high-end Washington gossip with top Beltway power brokers like Vernon Jordan and leading figures in the arts like, er, Diane Sawyer.

But Mrs Graham died last week and I never made the cut. Still, judging from the tone of the drooling eulogies, most commentators are apparently assuming that *The Washington Post*'s proprietress will be continuing her salons in the unseen world and that, come their own demise, they want to make sure they're at the top table with Kay, the Kennedys, Pam Harriman, and not down the déclassé end near the powder room with God, Christ, St Peter and the other losers. The media's sense of proportion is never more out of whack than when bidding farewell to one of its own, but even so the passing of Katharine Graham set impressive new standards of laughability: "The Most Powerful Woman In America", "The Most Powerful Woman In The World", "America's Queen", "Kay's Amazing Grace", "Oh, Kay", "Special Kay"…

No "Kay, Why?", funnily enough, though the question is certainly worth asking. Many obituarists contrasted Mrs Graham's iron sense of integrity re Nixon and Watergate with the more supine approach of her late husband, Philip, who prior to his suicide in 1963 thought nothing of squashing stories in *The Washington Post* unfavourable to his chum, President Kennedy. But that, of course, begs the question: Had the Kennedy and Nixon presidencies been chronologically switched and some minor operatives tied to JFK had broken into the Republican offices, would Mrs Graham's *Post* have thought the story worth pursuing? The paper didn't find Clinton's various illegalities objectionable. At its stablemate, *Newsweek*, Michael Isikoff's original Monica story was sat on for so long that the magazine wound up losing its scoop to the Drudge Report. And the presence at Kay's funeral of Bill and Hill, Ted (Dangerous When Wet) Kennedy, and Marion Barry, DC's cokehead mayor whose mountain of incompetence and corruption the *Post* cheerfully endorsed, strongly suggests that the paper's fearless crusading begins and ends with GOP housebreaking.

No such unpleasantness was allowed to intrude on the coverage, not least by *The National Post*'s own fawning courtier Charles Laurence. Obituary-wise, Kay was the hostess with the mostes', but nevertheless an inevitable hierarchy quickly set in, with points for how recently you'd last seen her ("At lunch last month...") and a bonus for whether she'd come to you (Barbara Walters scored big here, entertaining Kay at her pad in the Hamptons). Many anecdotes were told and re-told and re-re-told: thirty years ago, dining at the home of columnist Joe Alsop, Mrs Graham discreetly rebelled by refusing to join the ladies while the men discussed world affairs over brandy and cigars. As she modestly explained to Larry King on CNN, this brave stand singlehandedly brought about an end to the custom throughout the town. Perhaps Washington was singularly backward in this respect. By this stage, in London, New York, Winnipeg, all the great cities of the world, the ladies were no longer obliged to retire after dinner, a social revolution accomplished amazingly enough without the intervention of Mrs Graham.

One writer stood head and shoulders above the crowd, which admittedly isn't terribly difficult when everybody else is prostrate. The anonymous editorialist at *The Pittsburgh Tribune-Review* evidently returned from lunch drunk and momentarily forgot himself. Possibly while working as a busboy in Washington in the early Sixties he'd been the victim of some casual slight by Mrs Graham. At any rate, summing up her life he started conventionally enough but then wandered deplorably off-message:

> *Born in New York City, the daughter of multimillionaire Eugene Meyer, she grew up privileged. In keeping with her father's fortune, she graduated from Vassar College, where she was involved with the leftist trends of the day ...*
>
> *She married Felix Frankfurter's brilliant law clerk, Philip Graham, who took over running* The Post, *which her father purchased at a bankruptcy sale. Graham built the paper but became estranged from Kay. She had him committed to a mental hospital, and he was clearly intending divorce when she signed him out and took him for a weekend outing during which he was found shot. His death was ruled a suicide. Within 48 hours, she declared herself the publisher.*

That's the stuff! As the *Tribune-Review*'s chap has it, Mrs G got her philandering spouse banged up in the nuthouse and then arranged a weekend pass with a one-way ticket. "His death was ruled a suicide." Lovely touch that. Is it really possible Katharine Graham offed her hubby? Who cares? To those who think the worst problem with the American press is its awful stultifying homogeneity, the *Tribune-Review*'s deranged perverseness is to be cherished. Give that man a Pulitzer!

But, of course, they never do. Instead, with feeble predictability, they gave the Pulitzer to Mrs Graham's own carefully veiled memoir, *Personal History*. Her formula for her publications was succinctly expressed: "Mass With Class" – "perhaps the best three-word definition for what a good news magazine should be," wrote Mark Whitaker in *Newsweek*. But what "Mass With Class" boils down to in practice is the genteel middlebrow conformity that makes so much of the mainstream US media such a world-class yawnfest. "Mass With Class" means you don't ask Hillary Clinton about her husband's perjury and trashing of his female, ahem, acquaintances but only whether she finds it difficult coping with the accusations and if she thinks this is because conservatives have a difficult time dealing with her as a strong intelligent woman in her own right. "Mass With Class" means Dan Rather piously declaring that the Chandra Levy story is too unseemly for the CBS Evening News, no matter that it involves a Congressman obstructing a police investigation.

"Mass With Class" equals "All the news that's fit to print" and it's never more protective than when giving the mass a glimpse of the class. Thus, Mrs Graham's death clippings tell us more in their oleaginous uniformity about the relationship between journalism and politics than the heroics of Woodward and Bernstein ever did. The mourners at her funeral "read like a *Who's Who*", albeit a somewhat obvious one: Alan Greenspan, Bill Gates, Oscar de la Renta, John McCain, Tina Brown. I shall refrain from disparaging the guest list any further as our own power couple, Conrad Black and Barbara Amiel, were also among those present. But the cosiness of this world is American journalism's principal problem: There is "us" and there is "them", the "class" and the "mass", and the media have long since decided which side of the fence they belong on.

Mrs Graham wasn't a crusading journalist taking on the establishment. She *was* the establishment, and poor old Nixon wasn't. She was great at parties, he was hopeless. Awkward, sweaty, no social skills, no small talk. After his resignation, he sat down for several weeks of in-depth TV interviews with David Frost. One Monday morning, as they were waiting for the camera crew to finish setting up, Nixon decided to try a little locker-room buddy-buddy stuff with Frost and asked, "Did you do any fornicating this weekend?" Frostie was doing quite a bit of fornicating in those days, but as he gleefully recounted to pals that's the very last word real guys use, swinger to swinger. By contrast, Mrs Graham always knew *le mot juste*. As her own papers noted approvingly, she dismissed one Reagan administration official as a "starfucker". Maybe he was. But nobody starfucks like the US media, and it would no doubt be deeply satisfying to Katharine Graham that her death gave them an opportunity for the starfuck to end them all.

The National Post

Cruising on autopilot

JOHN F KENNEDY JR
NOVEMBER 25TH 1960 ~ JULY 16TH 1999

N IGHT WAS ALREADY falling as the lean rugged young man in the T-shirt and reversed baseball cap pulled up in his white convertible and strode purposefully across the asphalt.

He knew the risks. He knew he was inexperienced. And older, wiser hands than he had already shaken their heads and walked away that night. But he'd always had a reckless side, a daredevil streak, a need to push the boundaries, to live life to the full and on the edge.

He climbed the steps, sat down and stared at the glowing control panel he barely understood. Then he typed the first line:

America's Golden Child.
To those of us old enough to remember someone old enough to remember where they were when President Kennedy was shot, JFK Jr will always be the son all of us never had...

He was off, his flight of fancy borne upward into the endless haze to cruise smoothly through clouds of hot air:

...family curse... America's royalty... Joe, Rose... Bobby, Teddy... Sergeant Shriver...

The keyboard wobbled beneath him. He knew he was getting into dangerous territory here. He flipped on the automatic spell-check: "Sargent Shriver." Whew. Close call. He peered at the screen: 1,200 words and climbing. It was so smooth, so effortless, but he knew its ease was deceptive: So many other columnists had reached this level, only to spin out of control in the final paragraph and nosedive into the vast inky blackness.

"We all grew up with him," he tapped. *"Well, actually, now I come to think of it, only those of us who were born in Washington in 1960, moved to New York three years later and subsequently spent our formative years on a Greek yacht can really be said to have grown up with him. I personally grew up with Gordy MacKay, who lived next door at 47 Strathcona Gardens and is now operations manager for a mining company in Timmins..."*

God, what was happening? He frantically hit the dump button and tried to get back on track: *"We all grew up with him. All of us. He was the poster child for an entire generation..."* That's better.

The adrenaline coursed through his ventricles. He shouldn't have come this far, but it was too late to turn back. He was still recovering from a foot injury, when he'd dropped the thesaurus on his toe looking up synonyms for "tragedy". They said he was mad to try one more Kennedy column when there were so many others out there, careening around wildly searching for one more obscure distant relative to interview. But he'd had the best training money can buy. He'd passed every test with flying colours. He'd started with a simple "Family Curse" background piece:

The accident happened on the 30th anniversary of Senator Edward M Kennedy's car crash at Chappaquiddick, as well as the seventh anniversary of the ill-fated attempt by cousin Patrick Joseph Joseph Patrick Kennedy Smith Shriver Lawford to open his garage door while playing the traditional Kennedy game of blowtorch catch...

He'd breezed through the "What If?" column:

What if he'd paused a moment longer at that convenience store? What if he'd said, 'You know, maybe I better grab a Diet Dew, too'? And then said to the clerk, 'Hey, buddy, I gave you a twenty, not a five'? And what if, during the ensuing dispute, a tractor-trailer had jack-knifed in the street outside seizing up traffic for 15 blocks? And what if I'd taken that July vacation package to Antigua and I was sitting on the beach right now while that ambitious little creep from the features department was cranking out all this award-winning colour stuff?

He'd done the personal memoir of "The John-John I Knew":

I well remember the last time we met, a chance encounter in the elevator during a fundraiser at the Waldorf-Astoria. I didn't want to bother him - every woman from 16 to 70 wanted a piece of him. But his eyes met mine and, with the gracious lightly worn charm for which he was famous, he said to me: '17th floor, and step on it.' I said, 'I'm not the elevator boy.' He said, 'So what?'

He'd moved on to the "Improvised Aviation Correspondent Routine":

Many experts agree that when you're flying at night across water it's easy to lose sight of whether the big coloured thingamajig on the instrument panel is correctly aligned with the funny-shaped wossname tracking the whatever...

He'd graduated to the "Genetic Theory" column:

According to a report in today's British Medical Journal, nutrition deficiencies caused by the potato famine could explain the recurring predisposition toward recklessness of Massachusetts Irish-Americans of the late 20th century...

But he knew enough to know that he'd only just made it through the Princess Di spirits-of-the-age column:

Like Diana, he looked great in Versace and liked hanging around with George Michael. Er, I mean, like Diana, he had kohl-ringed eyes and was an inspiration to bulimia sufferers everywhere. Er, I mean...

He should have pulled back while he still could: There were so many other ways he could go - Kosovo, the Middle East, a little light foreign policy... But that wasn't his style. He picked up *The National Post*:

Is Media Coverage Of The Kennedy Crash Excessive? See pages A3, A6, A8, A9, A10, A11, B2-B27 and our special pull-out family tree tracing every Kennedy all the way back to Kennadosaurus Rex, the Jurassic era dinosaur whose political ambitions were dashed when he was taking home a young, unmarried stegosaurus-stenographer and decided to eat her.

Suddenly, he saw his piece, laid out in front of him, beckoning like the sirens of old. He felt the thrill of uncharted territory, as he boldly typed on:

"Is my coverage of the Kennedy crash excessive? That was a question I put to myself in a lively debate on the popular late-evening media discussion Me Slumped In Front Of The Keyboard Thinking Oh, God, I've Got Another Kennedy Column To Churn Out. *On the one hand, my Sunday column - 'Goodnight, Sweet Prince' - was perfectly adequate, while my Monday column - 'Did Crazed Whacko John-John Have Death Wish?' - demonstrated my versatility, and my Tuesday column - 'Aren't we all sick of hearing about this pampered socialite mediocrity?' - had a certain chutzpah. But, on the other hand, what about all the stories we're* not *covering? Doesn't anyone want to take a flier on whether Jennifer Aniston and Brad Pitt's relationship is in trouble?*

Phew. He'd made it. He flipped a switch, shut down his computer, wiped the sweat from his brow and felt the wheels humming smoothly underneath his office chair as he taxied over to the percolator for a cup of hazelnut decaf. This was the way he needed to live, pushing the envelope. He folded his invoice to *The National Post*, pushed the envelope and stuck a stamp on it.

He looked out the window again: the endless emptiness of night. He thought there'd be more people: everyone was interested in this story, weren't they? Hanging on every word, desperate for any new tidbit? But there was only an eerie silence, briefly punctuated by the sound of millions switching from CNN back to the Wrestling Channel.

The National Post

George's girl

KAY SWIFT
APRIL 19TH 1897 ~ FEBRUARY 2ND 1993

MOST FOLKS in the show business use their walls to celebrate their own success. Not Kay Swift. As you entered her Manhattan apartment, you saw a drawing of Gershwin, then a poster of Gershwin and, over the piano, a photograph (mounted on Gershwin Music manuscript paper) of Gershwin and Miss Swift riding in Connecticut.

"George brought me that painting over there by Kubim, and also this one," she pointed out to me. "He came with one in each hand - framed - and he said, 'You don't have enough of the right paintings, and I just think these would look fine on your wall.'"

Kay Swift has two claims to a place in American musical history: first, in the Twenties, she was a rare exception to the rule that songwriters had to be grizzled cigar-chewing Lower East Side men; second, as his girlfriend and a fellow composer, she was George Gershwin's closest musical confidant apart from his brother Ira. On the whole, she was less touchy about being described as George's girl than as a "woman composer". "It's like saying, 'Let's have ten people with brown eyes.' Who cares?"

George was the cocky Tin Pan Alley song-plugger with ambitions to cross the tracks; Kay was a socialite, a banker's wife and a conservatory-trained musician who at one point in her life was writing a fugue a week. Without her, he'd undoubtedly have found his translation to the concert hall more laborious and painful. In turn, it was Gershwin songs which awakened her own interest in popular music, songs first heard when a mutual friend brought George to one of her parties. As always, Gershwin played for most of the evening;

then, he stood up from the piano and said to Kay, "Well, I've got to go to Europe now."

On his return, they began a unique personal and professional relationship that lasted till George's sudden death from a brain tumour in 1937 - and beyond. Kay, no matter how you pushed her, refused to voice any criticism of George, beyond an expression of regret that he never married her. They saw each other constantly, but, despite her divorce, those who knew the mercurial Gershwin doubted he would ever wed. One evening, entering the Stork Club, they were spotted by Oscar Levant, who unloaded what became a famous *bon mot* on their romance:

Ah, here comes George Gershwin with the future Miss Kay Swift.

Marriage aside, there was no question of Kay's importance to the composer. At the first night of *Porgy And Bess* in 1935, she sat between George and Ira; he dedicated his *Songbook* to Kay; they played duets and spent so much time at the piano together that, until her last illness, she was the first port of call for any Gershwin scholar who wanted to hear how George would have played any particular piece; the original manuscripts for the Preludes and several other works are written partly in his hand, partly in hers; they shared musical notebooks, jotting down themes and melodies, he starting at one end of the pad, she from the other.

After George's sudden death, she and Ira carefully preserved and numbered all the unused jottings, with Kay filling in the gaps from memory. Gradually and selectively, they began turning the best into new songs - first for the theme for the 1939 World's Fair, next for a Betty Grable film, *The Shocking Miss Pilgrim* (1946). The latter produced a couple of lasting semi-standard additions to the Gershwin oeuvre – "For You, For Me, For Evermore" and "Aren't You Kind Of Glad We Did?" - but, over the years, more than a few of us wondered how much of the music was Gershwin and how much Swift.

"I would say to Ira, 'Look, this theme here would be really good for a main section, and then on this page there's a theme that we

188

could work into a middle-eight,'" she recalled. But, in any kind of music, how the themes are put together is at least as important as what they are: surely, I suggested, she ought to have taken a co-composer's credit. "Oh, no," she insisted. "Every note is George's." Like Ira, she was largely content to neglect her own career to serve what she saw as George's genius.

Her own catalogue includes the music and lyrics for *Paris '90*, a revue for Cornelia Otis Skinner; the song cycle *Reaching For The Brass Ring*; and the score for one of George Balanchine's earliest American ballets, *Alma Mater* (1935), a spoof on the Harvard-Yale football game. But most of us know her for a clutch of songs from the end of the Twenties.

She cracked Broadway in 1929, contributing to the score of *The Little Show* one of its biggest hits. "Can't We Be Friends?" is one of those effervescent swingers typical of the Twenties but with enough surprises - sliding down to a low D - to put it a cut above most of the rest. For words, Kay Swift turned to "Paul James" - a pseudonym for her husband, James Paul Warburg, scion of three great banking families and, as financiers go, not a bad lyricist:

> *I thought I'd found a man I could trust*
> *What a bust!*
> *This is how the story ends*
> *He's going to turn me down*
> *And say Can't We Be Friends?*

It's a neat lyric, though whether it suits the breezily carefree tune is another matter. Sinatra sang it slow and mournful, taking his cue from the words, attempting to infuse it with a solemnity the melody can't really support; most versions, such as Linda Ronstadt's recent record, go with the tune, freewheeling and up-tempo.

Mr and Mrs Warburg landed another hit in 1930 with the title song for *Fine And Dandy*, a number with an irresistible rhythmic device. She never found the notion of bankers on Broadway as striking as it seemed to others. "Bankers invest in the shows, they go to the

189

shows, they throw the first-night parties for the shows," she told me, "so why shouldn't they write them?" Warburg's lyrics earned the praise of Ira Gershwin, but banking called and he and Kay went their separate ways.

She had a theory, based on her friendships with Gershwin, Ravel and others, that composers look like their music. You can see it in George: brash, restless, confident, etc. But Kay Swift always looked to me like what she was - a high-toned banker's wife. She sprang to life, though, when conversation turned to music. "I loved it when Ira sang, because he used to close his eyes tight and, if it was upbeat, he'd do a sort of little dance. He'd screw up his face and go round and round - I don't even think he knew he was doing it," she'd say. "When Ira was pleased with a lyric, he used to run around the room like a squirrel." And then she'd show you. At the piano, she could conjure from memory an old Irving Berlin ragtime novelty that she'd last sung with her brother when they were ten years old.

Unlike George, who was driven, Kay could turn her hand to everything and so never did enough. After his death, she went west and married a rodeo cowboy, an unlikely union which she chronicled in an idiosyncratic memoir, *Who Could Ask For Anything More?* (from a Gershwin lyric, of course). The book outlasted the marriage and was filmed in 1950 as *Never A Dull Moment* with Irene Dunne and Fred MacMurray as Kay and her cowboy. She wed a third time - to a radio announcer - and was divorced a third time.

Almost from their first meeting, it was George who was the most important man in her life. She was a tireless promoter of *Porgy And Bess* after its shaky premiere - but she knew enough, and was trusted enough by George, to suggest a few judicious cuts. And, despite his suffocating ego, she was never far from his thoughts. At the opening of *Strike Up The Band* (1930), in the middle of conducting the overture, he turned round to Kay, sitting directly behind him in the front row, and whispered, "April and Andy" - a reference to her daughters, who liked to do a little dance to one of the score's songs, "I've Got A Crush On You". She never ceased to marvel that any composer, on the first night of a show and on his first stint in the orchestra pit, could find time to recall a small moment of domestic pleasure.

In August 1936, the Gershwins left for Hollywood. Kay saw them off at the airport, having already agreed with George that it would be best if they didn't see or speak to each other for a year; then, when he returned, they would decide their future. The following June, after badgering friends for news of her, he phoned from California and said, "I'm coming back for both of us." A few weeks later, he was dead.

In a room at the back of her apartment there was a photograph. The inscription read, "With love", followed by three bars of music. "Do you know what that is?" asked Kay Swift. I peered closely, and hummed the notes. George Gershwin had written the title phrase of "Bess, You Is My Woman Now."

The Independent

The fifth Nixon

ROSE MARY WOODS
DECEMBER 26TH 1917 ~ JANUARY 22ND 2005

NO MAN IS A hero to his valet. But some of us hope at least to be a hero to our secretary. And even if we're not heroic, even if we can't be Perry Mason, she'll still be Della Street – there to buck up the Chief, to assure him that he's been in tight spots before and he always comes through.

Thus, the White House, May 14th 1973, half an hour before midnight. Today, George W Bush would have been tucked up in bed for a couple of hours, but three decades ago Richard Nixon had things keeping him late at the office. The news wasn't good, and unlikely to get better. That wasn't just the view of political strategists, but even of the leading celebrity psychic, with whom the President's secretary had recently met:

> WOODS: *Jeane Dixon tells us that May and June are going to be pretty bad. June may be worse than May. But everything will turn out to be fine and to be of stout heart and all that....*

> NIXON: *That's why we have been brought into this world.*

> WOODS: *Well, you particularly, and you'd be surprised how many people say, you know, God does bring the hardest problems to the strongest men.*

> NIXON: *That's right.*

When the going gets tough, the tough know how to delegate. When he decided to resign as President, it was Rose Mary Woods whom Nixon told first, dispatching her to the residence to inform his wife and daughters. As he wrote in his autobiography, "I asked her to suggest that we not talk about it anymore when I went over for dinner." So Rose went in to see the First Lady, and told Julie and Tricia, "Your father has decided to resign", and then explained that there would be no further discussion. The President arrived for dinner and they chit-chatted about ...other things. Small talk, which was never exactly Richard Nixon's big strength.

Rose had been known since the Fifties as "the fifth Nixon". But, at the climactic moment of his life, she seemed to be somewhat higher up the rankings: the intimacy, the intensity, the honesty is all between "the Boss" (as she called him) and his secretary, not man and wife. Rose Mary Woods knew more about Richard Nixon than anybody who ever worked with him, and she was just about the only one who never wrote a book about it. Nixon went to his grave in large part unknowable, and he has her to thank for that.

Uniquely, she was famous for 18½ minutes: "the gap" – in the White House tapes. She never claimed to be responsible for accidentally – or "accidentally", according to taste - erasing all 18 minutes and 28 seconds of it, but in the distillation of a defining moment the details get lost. Rose Mary Woods=gap. *The Washington Post's* Tony Kornheiser in a memoir of his father:

> *"What happened to your teeth, dad?" I asked softly. There were gaps. Rose Mary Woods gaps.*

When she died, the wags at Kornheiser's paper ran an appreciation by Hank Stuever complete with its own gap – a chunk of blank white paper in the middle of the article. To mark the 20th anniversary of the President's resignation, Theatre Babylon in Seattle presented an evening of selected dramatic readings from the White House tapes and a playlet called "Rose Mary, That's For Remembrance", followed by intermission – or "a gap in the proceedings".

Rose Mary's gap swallowed the decades either side of it. Scandals are complicated things. To catch fire with a public disinclined to wade through pages of densely investigative journalism, they need an image – and Rose provided it. She said she'd taken a phone call, in the course of which she'd accidentally kept her foot on the tape machine's pedal and accidentally hit the record button, and, even though the phone was a long way from the foot pedal, the explanation could have passed muster. Alexander Haig offered corroboration, of a sort, in trying to reconcile Rose's recollection of a five-minute conversation with 18 minutes of missing material. "Just like a woman," he volunteered genially, "not to realize how long she'd been talking on the phone."

And that might have been good enough, if Rose hadn't gamely essayed a visual re-enactment – her limbs extended to the limit across the length of the office, her left hand reaching backward to the phone, her right forward to the "record" button, one foot straining for the pedal, presumably leaving the other free to snake round the desk, over to the corner and start the Ray Conniff on the eight-track. The big stretch was too much of a stretch for the court, or for the "silent majority", which broke its silence and started guffawing loudly. John Dean called her a "stand-up woman", and she was – if only she'd stayed in that position.

"President Sadat had a belly dancer entertain President Nixon at the state dinner," said Johnny Carson. "Nixon was really impressed. He hadn't seen contortions like that since Rose Mary Woods." And even as the years passed, for an inordinate number of novels set in the Seventies, the secretary became a shorthand for the era. She turns up in Rick Moody's *Ice Storm*, and Delia Ephron's *Hanging Up*, Wally Lamb's *She's Come Undone*, and Robert Ludlum's *Apocalypse Watch* ("I figured we had one of those Rose Mary Woods things"). In Samuel Shem's *The House Of God*, four generations of one family gather for dinner and Rose's turn provides fun for young and old:

> *Spurred on by the news photos of Rose Mary Woods spread-eagled between the foot pedal of her tape recorder and the phone behind her as if awaiting a quick roll in the hay with Nixon, we laughed and chortled together that now, finally, Nixon was going to get*

his... My brother's four-year old daughter, who was learning to play with her toy phone by picking it up and spread-eagling herself and screaming RO-MARY REACH RO-MARY REACH...

When a celebrity becomes a pop culture joke, we still know other things about them, enough to put the gag in a broader context. When a real person becomes a punchline, that's all there is – "The Rose Mary Woods Award for Convenient Technological Incompetence" (an Arianna Huffington crack). The real Rose Mary Woods returned to Sebring, Ohio – a small-town girl who ended her days a spinster of the parish she'd grown up in. The "devoted secretary" was an easy joke even before Women's Lib put the very noun in jeopardy ("Secretaries Week" is now "Administrative Professionals Week", which takes a bit of the zip out of the Hallmark verses). "Cities like Washington," wrote Gail Sheehy, *Vanity Fair*'s self-appointed shrink to the corridors of power, "are magnets for women who devote their lives to caring for public men and politicians, and who, like Rose Mary Woods, do so to the exclusion of any other deep personal tie." But it's one thing to be the stereotypical secretary in love with the boss, quite another to love a boss whose principal characteristic to the media and the other elites is that he's unlovely and unlovable.

She remains the only secretary to get her own *Time* magazine cover, though she looks rather severe on it. She wasn't always. Dr John C Lungren, who first met her on the train – the Dick Nixon Special – in the '52 campaign when he signed on as Dick's doc, remembered Rose as "red-haired, pretty and Irish-Catholic". She was warm and vivacious: my favorite photograph from the Presidential years is not The Stretch but one of her dancing with Duke Ellington, an improbable couple hitting the floor at a White House party to celebrate Duke's 70th birthday, with Dizzy Gillespie, Gerry Mulligan, Dave Brubeck and other hep cats supplying the music. (Nixon's avowedly "square" White House was, in fact, less cheesy than Clinton's

Lite FM programming and more confident than the Kennedys' culturally craven collect-the-set approach.)

There was a man once, a fiancé. But he died when Rose was 17 and thereafter she was all business. She moved to Washington, got a secretarial job with the House committee dealing with post-war reconstruction in Europe, and met a young congressman called Richard Nixon. The granddaughter of an Irish stowaway, Rose was political and ambitious, and, in the absence of non-secretarial outlets for such a woman in the Washington of mid-century, Congressman Nixon became her vehicle. She was tough and plain-spoken. On Tony Lake: "I've watched him. He's a weak character." To Kissinger when he threatened to quit over Al Haig's move to the White House: "For once, Henry, behave like a man," which he never had to take from the Soviets or the ChiComs. She could be tough on the Boss, too. She was the first to tell him he'd lost the 1960 Presidential debate, after her parents called from Ohio to enquire if the Vice-President was unwell.

Not everyone around him wanted a "fifth Nixon": they had more than enough with the first four. After victory in the '68 election, Haldeman, with Nixon's consent, decided to put her in a basement room far from the Oval Office. "Go fuck yourself!" she told the President-elect, for once declining to delete the expletive, and thereafter refusing to speak to him until she'd been moved up closer to the action.

She stayed close, long after everyone else was gone, and, when the man she considered "the greatest President this country has ever had" set about rehabilitating himself as the greatest ex-President this country has ever had, as a geopolitical strategic colossus, the unlikely sage had Rose Mary and time, and not much else.

The secretary who kept the secrets died with them, and left us a Richard Nixon that she helped create. Miss Woods wasn't a speechwriter. Instead, she took words out of the President's mouth, and the substitution – the "expletive deleteds" that fell as furiously as the radio bleeps on a gangsta hit - came to define Nixon as much as anything Ted Sorensen wrote for Kennedy. For all the low cunning and petty thuggery of the participants, the transcripts exemplify the almost touching naivete of the Administration. Whatever their crimes, their mistake spin-wise was stenographic. Asked to transcribe the tapes, Rose approached it like any other dictation assignment: she cleaned up the stumbles and stutters and folks talking over each other, put everything into proper complete sentences, rendered "gonna" as "going to" and excised the "yeahs" and "ers" and "ums". That's what you want in a secretary if you're dictating a letter to the chairman of the Rotary Club. But it was a disaster for the Oval Office tapes: the cool clinical precision of the language makes Nixon and co sound far more conspiratorial, ruthless and viciously forensic than the incoherent burble of the originals.

But nothing was as damaging to the President as the "expletive deleteds". According to his British biographer Jonathan Aitken, "the tapes were censored with Hannah Nixon in mind". "If my mother ever heard me use words like that she would roll over in her grave," he said. Words like what? "Dammit" and "Jesus" mostly. So Rose loyally took out everything that would have crossed the late Mrs Nixon's profanity threshold, and as a result readers assume every expletive deleted isn't "Goddamn" or "that bastard" but "cocksucker" or "motherfucker". Hannah Nixon's boy went down in history as one of the foulest-mouthed sonsofbitches ever to open his yap, even though Rose swore she'd never heard him swear. In the end, the perfect secretary was too perfect.

The Atlantic Monthly

BODY & Spirit

Man of taste

WILLIAM A. MITCHELL
OCTOBER 21ST 1911 ~ JULY 26TH 2004

WILLIAM A Mitchell never became a household name, but most households you can name have something of his in it – Cool Whip, quick-set Jell-O, egg whites for cake mix... He gave American astronauts the first space-age beverage (Tang) and impressionable adolescents one of the great urban legends (Pop Rocks). Bill Mitchell's inventions are not to everyone's taste. Once, for a BBC show about Thanksgiving, I served Martha Stewart a pumpkin pie with Cool Whip, and she wasn't happy about it. As it happens, Martha and Bill Mitchell both have Nutley, New Jersey in common. In the year of Martha's birth, 1941, Bill Mitchell started work as a chemist at General Foods and briefly lived in Nutley. As he was developing Cool Whip, Martha's parents were developing the anti-Cool Whip.

Business-wise, the former beats the latter. Originally developed as time-saving substitutes for various elementary kitchen needs, the Kraft/General Foods repertory has multiplied and mutated, and the products which Mitchell and his colleagues developed live happily within a self-contained universe. To make Kraft's Classic Angel Flake Coconut Cake you need a 7 oz bag of Baker's Angel Flake Coconut, a package of yellow cake mix, a package of Jell-O White Chocolate Instant Pudding, and a tub of Cool Whip. Sometimes you put Cool Whip in the Jell-O, sometimes you put Jell-O in the Cool Whip. But it's an all-or-nothing world. It would be unsettling and intrusive to replace the Cool Whip with Martha's recipe for *crème anglaise*.

And yet, if you're at a county fair or a church bazaar and you buy the local fundraising cookbook, you notice how in a relatively short period (Cool Whip, the world's first non-dairy whipped topping, dates back only to 1966) Bill Mitchell's products have become the great staples of "down-home cooking" and traditional "family recipes". In *The Tunbridge Volunteer Fire Department Cookbook* from Tunbridge, Vermont, for example, Mary Vermette's excellent "Pudding Dessert" requires for the first layer 2 sticks of oleo, 2 cups of flour, 1 cup of chopped nuts (mix and bake); for the second layer, 1 cup of confectioner's sugar, 8 oz of cream cheese, 1 cup of Cool Whip (combine and spread on the first layer); for the third layer, 2 small packages of instant pudding and 2 ½ cups of milk (mix and spread on the second layer); and for the fourth layer more Cool Whip sprinkled with chopped nuts. I made it and ate it in the interests of research, and had such a good time I clean forgot what it was I was meant to be researching.

Still, you don't have to eschew Mitchell's products as ostentatiously as Martha Stewart does to feel that they might not be the best for one's health. They were certainly good for Mitchell's: he was 92 when he died, and long after his retirement from General Foods continued to chip in ideas for his daughter Cheryl's company, California Natural Products. To a chemist, the line between "natural products" and "processed foods" is somewhat fuzzy. Starch technology, which is indispensable to the convenience food industry, goes back to ancient times. Bill Mitchell's contributions to the science stand at an innocent mid-point between the separation of starch from grain first noted by Cato in 170 BC and the brave new world of genetically modified food that so terrifies the Europeans and the anti-globalists. Some of Mitchell's inventions were specifically for children (Increda Bubble carbonated gum), but even the grown-up ones are child-like: they're designed not just to shorten cooking time but to extend the sweet tooth of grade-school birthday-partygoers through adult life. Cool Whip is a little too sweet, a little too sugary ever to be mistaken for "natural". By "sugary", of course, I don't mean sugar: Looking through the ingredients, one finds nothing labeled as such but plenty of palm kernel oils and sorbitan monostearate and "less than two per cent of sodium caseinate". In the European Union, they give all these additives "E numbers" – E912 (ontanic acid esters), E1202 (polyvinylpolypyrrolidone), E1442 (hydroxy propyl distarch phosphate), to name some of my all-time favorite numbers - which make it sound like the random draw of a megabucks lottery. Who, other than Bill Mitchell and a few other specialists, understands the precise combination which makes it just slightly too sweet enough? If you put in 2.4 per cent of sodium caseinate, would it all go to hell?

He was born in 1911 in Raymond, Minnesota, spent his early years on a farm, and then, after the death of his father, moved into the town of Rocky Ford. By eight, he was picking peas and beans for local farmers; by 13, he was subbing for the older melon-packing boys; by 18, he'd rented land from the American Beet Sugar Company and was growing corn and tomatoes. That autumn, he went to junior high during the day, helped with the harvest for American Beet Sugar all night, and slept from 4.30 to 6.30am. After working his way through college, Bill got a research job at an Agricultural Experiment Station in Lincoln, Nebraska, whose lab promptly blew up leaving him with second and third degree burns over most of his body.

His first big success came with a tapioca substitute developed during World War Two when, as the Associated Press put it, "tapioca supplies were running low". War is hell. In fact, tapioca, a starchy substance in hard grains from cassava, came mainly from the Far East, and, with supply lines disrupted, that presented problems for packaged food. You can be sniffy about preservatives in peacetime, but in war an army marches on its stomach and food is a national security issue. Mitchell, in developing an alternative to tapioca, helped facilitate the huge expansion of the processed food business in the Forties and Fifties.

Some innovations were happy accidents. Pop Rocks began in the Fifties, as an attempt to create an instant carbonated drink that went awry. Though they took 20 years to reach the market, they were a huge hit with kids: when you put the fruit-flavored candy in your mouth, it triggered the carbonation, creating a mini-explosion complete with sound-effect. Almost immediately, rumors started about their potentially lethal effects. It was said that, if you ate Pop Rocks while sipping a Coke, the candy would react with the beverage and the carbonation combination would cause a massive gas explosion blasting apart your stomach. That was what had happened to Little Mikey, the cute boy in the Life cereal commercials. He'd popped a couple of Pop Rocks while chugging a Pepsi and he'd exploded in a horrible death. That's how come you didn't see him on TV anymore.

Little Mikey didn't explode. Nor did his career, which is why, like many child stars of TV commercials, you never saw him on anything once the ad stopped running. But a quarter-century after becoming the confectioner's equivalent of the *Abbey Road* LP cover Little Mikey was working as an account manager at a New York radio station. Bill Mitchell and General Foods took out advertisements in 45 newspapers, and the FDA set up a special hotline, but the stories persisted. It's apparently true that a shipment of Pop Rocks managed to blow the doors off an overheated delivery truck. But turning your stomach into Bikini Atoll was strictly an urban myth. If there was anything to it, the jihad would be bulk ordering.

There's something rather appealing about dangerous food. Instantly dangerous, that is, not cumulatively. America has the most regulated food in the developed world yet it also has the fattest people in the world, with the exception of the hearty trenchermen of Nauru and a few other dots in the Pacific. There surely is a cautionary tale in the limitations of big government, at least in respect of its ability to constrain big citizens. Not all of this is due to Bill Mitchell's contributions to the American diet, but in his last years, serving as *éminence grise* to his daughter's company, he seemed more health-conscious than at General Foods.

When Cheryl Mitchell persuaded her then husband to grow some dahlias on their land, it was her dad who suggested roasting their inulin-rich tubers. It produced a brown substance with a coffee-like taste which the Mitchells began marketing as Dacopa, a coffee substitute with health benefits. It never caught on in a big way. Mitchell didn't foresee that, in an age of convenience foods, coffee would head in the other direction and become the ultimate inconvenience food. In the old days, you'd say, "Gimme a cup o' java" and the waitress would slide it over the counter. Now you stand around for 20 minutes as the guy juices up the espresso, lovingly spoons on the froth, gives it a shot of hazelnut flavoring, sprinkles it with cinnamon, adds a slice of pepperoni and a couple of zebra mussels, and instead of a quarter it's $5.95. In its sheer simplicity, Dacopa seems to belong to a lost world. A decaf Pop Rocks latte would have had a better shot.

But in his heyday, Mitchell always understood that a successful "convenience food" is a blend of convenience and delight. He never made the mistake of Princess Ozma's scientific advisor, H. M. Wogglebug T.E., in L Frank Baum's Oz books:

> *He took a bottle from his pocket and shook from it a tablet about the size of one of Ojo's finger-nails.*
>
> *'That,' announced the Shaggy Man, 'is a square meal, in condensed form. Invention of the great Professor Wogglebug of the Royal College of Athletics. It contains soup, fish, roast meat, salad, apple-dumplings, ice cream and chocolate-drops, all boiled down to this small size, so it can be conveniently carried and swallowed when you are hungry and need a square meal.'*
>
> *'I'm square,' said the Woozy. 'Give me one, please...'*
>
> *'You have now had a six course dinner," declared the Shaggy Man.*
>
> *'Pshaw!' said the Woozy, ungratefully. "I want to taste something. There's no fun in that sort of eating."'*

Even devising crystal mixes for space-shot beverages, Bill Mitchell subscribed to the fun of eating. Unlike Professor Wogglebug, in creating food in the rhythm of modern life, he wasn't defeated by it. He's part of the taste of America, the stuff that gets under your skin – from the not entirely "home-made" pies rotating at the diner to the red, white and blue Jell-O salad at the Fourth of July fireworks. That's how he deserves to be celebrated: take 1 pkg of Jell-O, throw in 1 pkg of Cool Whip, add Tang, mix, lob in a couple of Pop Rocks, and stand well back.

The Atlantic Monthly

Big appetite

IDI AMIN

CIRCA 1925 ~ AUGUST 16TH 2003

FOR IDI AMIN, in defiance of Sir Donald Wolfit, comedy was easy but dying all but impossible. A month ago, he was in a coma and not expected to make it to the end of the week, and newspapers were dusting off their 1970s obituaries and hoping they'd got all his titles and honorifics in the right order: His Excellency Field Marshal Idi Amin Dada, VC, DSO, MC, Conqueror of the British Empire and King of Scotland. But the King wasn't dead, the Conqueror refused to conk. The old monster emerged from his coma and resumed what, by the standards of most ex-Presidents-for-Life, was a remarkably long retirement.

Still, let us assume that reports of his death are not yet again exaggerated. It's amazing how far a sense of humour will take a dictator, at least in the eyes of the west. No one remembers Milton Obote, the dour LSE Marxist Amin deposed and who subsequently deposed him. The Obotes were ten a penny in that first generation of British-educated Afro-Marxist economic illiterates. But Idi had style. The defining image of him is a 1975 photograph of his arrival at a reception for ministers from the Organisation for African Unity: as the band plays Colonel Bogey, His Excellency is borne aloft in a sedan chair balanced with some difficulty on the shoulders of four spindly Englishmen from Kampala's business community, while another humbled honky walks behind holding the parasol. It's the precise negative of a thousand colonial daguerreotypes from Victorian illustrated weeklies. When it came to the white man's burden, the British could talk the talk. But that night the 300lb Amin made them walk the walk.

"Well-disposed to Britain," the diplomatic cables back to Whitehall had reported. Well, up to a point. The mother country never quite succeeded in imparting to Idi the value of representative government or the rule of law, but he'd got the hang of the dressing up. Amin's neighbour and nemesis Julius Nyerere kept a copy of Evelyn Waugh's *Black Mischief* on his bedside table. But Idi didn't read it, he lived it. If you can overlook the corpses - which was hard to do when they were bobbing down the Nile by the dozen - Amin remains the best of the post-colonial jokes.

Today, grievance-mongering African Studies professors like to talk of the lingering "psychic damage" of colonialism, not a concept many of us have much time for after four decades of Afro-kleptocracy. But, with hindsight, Idi seems genuinely to have suffered psychic damage from colonialism. He was born, circa 1925, near the Sudanese border: his dad, a Kakwa, skipped town; his mum, a Lugbara, became a groupie of the King's African Rifles. Young Idi joined the regiment as soon as he was old enough and, under the patronage of several Scots who'd taken a shine to him, rose to become one of Uganda's first black officers - though the phrase doesn't seem quite right for a man who'd lived in a British milieu almost his entire life. To the end, he was said to sleep with a favourite portrait of a kilted George VI – "my old commander-in-chief" - over his bed.

The problem for Idi was that by the Seventies his late Majesty's daughter and her woeful mid-reign Prime Ministers - Heath, Wilson, Callaghan - had no inclination to command anybody. Instead the Queen was out on the road night after night in ramshackle outposts giving speeches on how one-party states demonstrated the rich diversity of the Commonwealth. Idi was the perfect post-imperial parody, the mediocre colonial corporal who'd somehow wound up with the keys to the officers' mess, the British subject still seeking approval from the mother country even as he trampled its legacy. The details were exquisite, right down to the head of his secret police, the not-quite-pukka "Major Bob" Astles.

All the wise old Africa hands in the Commonwealth Office thought Idi was the coming man. Much better than that ghastly Obote. So, in a cautionary tale on the limitations of expertise, they quietly approved his 1971 coup, British intelligence fretting only that he might be too obviously pro-British. What they don't seem to have noticed is that he was bonkers. Or, if they did, it didn't bother them.

George W Bush, campaigning on the problems of inner-city schools, liked to talk about the "soft bigotry of low expectations". That's what Uganda got from London: Good heavens, this is Africa, old man. What do you expect? After Obote the doctrinaire ideologue, Amin was an Idi-ologue, in it strictly for himself. Much more our cup of tea. Publicly, he was sold as the "gentle giant". Privately, the High Commission considered him "benevolent but tough". The more condescending diplomats regarded him as an "idiot savant", though he was mostly heavy on the "idiot" and the "savant" moments were rare, if choice: one of his last acts as dictator was to warn the Prince of Wales not to marry Lady Diana. "You will live to regret this," he wrote.

But what he really was was a psychopath. In eight years, more than 300,000 Ugandans were killed. He enjoyed personally decapitating his enemies, and on one occasion he and a few family friends passed a pleasant farewell dinner with the severed heads of two opponents propped up at their places round the table. He had the second of his five wives murdered and dismembered, and then ordered the pieces retrieved from a burlap sack and stitched together so he could show her off to their children. The expatriate community he regarded as mainly a source of potential hostages, such as the adventurer and writer Denis Hills, whom he arrested and sentenced to death. After being advised to do so by God, he expelled all the Asians and destroyed his country's economy. Then he decided to invade Tanzania, and that was the end.

A convert to Islam, he escaped to Saudi Arabia, where, officially, he had been on "pilgrimage" for the last quarter-century, living on a stipend from the royal family. At least in this instance, unlike their more recent subventions, the House of Saud began giving money to a mass murderer *after* he'd stopped killing. He was apparently a devout Muslim, Allah providing the slap of firm discipline the King's African Rifles, the Queen and Ted Heath never quite had the stomach for. In Britain, where *Private Eye* used to issue comedy singles in his name, he might as well have been in a coma for 20 years rather than the last week: he's the one Seventies act who's never been revived, except for odd once-a-decade stories when one of his wives turns out to be serving stewed goat and cow hoof in gravy at a caff in West Ham. (It was "Suicide Sarah", who met Amin when she was a teenage go-go dancer with the band of the Ugandan Army's Revolutionary Suicide Mechanised Regiment.)

It seems strange to think of Idi among the Wahhabis. He wasn't King of Scotland in Jeddah, just "Dr Jaffa", an affectionate title deriving from his consumption of oranges, the cannibal having turned fruitarian. One wonders whether Idi looked at the Saudis' export of their toxic ideology to Pakistan, Indonesia, Chechnya, Amsterdam, San Diego and pondered what he might have accomplished if he'd been a little less entertaining. He never had a plan, he never had a point. So hundreds of thousands of Ugandans died for no particular reason, except that in the Seventies we were reluctant to do anything about anything in case a little local difficulty escalated into a proxy war between the big powers. And Amin was never called to account for his bloody reign because he was shrewd enough to flee to the one rogue state no western nation ever puts any pressure on, even today.

Asked about his cannibal appetites, he liked to complain that human flesh was a little too salty. Hard to believe he'd have said that if he'd eaten bland, insipid Mr Callaghan instead of just metaphorically chewing him up and spitting him out on Sunny Jim's pitiful Kampala kowtow to get Denis Hills off the hook. Even in that pre-Thatcher, pre-Falklands era when anybody could cock a snook at the toothless British lion, the rise of Idi Amin remains a particularly extreme symbol of a great nation's paralysis. His coma ended a lot quicker than post-war Britain's did.

The Sunday Telegraph

The Swedes' swingingest swinger

VILGOT SJÖMAN
DECEMBER 2ND 1924 - APRIL 9TH 2006

FOR A BRIEF moment, he was the most famous Swedish male on the planet. Before Björn Borg, before Benny and Björn from Abba, before …well, hang on, let me have a think – ah, yes, before Sven-Göran Eriksson, outgoing manager of the England soccer team, before all those famous Swedes, there was Vilgot Sjöman. In the late Sixties, he loomed large – not in the same sense as Anita Ekberg and Bibi Andersson but in the same general vicinity. Sjöman made a movie called *Jar är nyfiken - gul,* or *I Am Curious (Yellow),* or in some billings, eschewing parantheses for the colon, *I Am Curious: Yellow.* As it happens, the colon was one of the few bodily parts not on display in the film, but pretty much everything else was. The British censors snipped 11 minutes out of it and US Customs seized the prints when they showed up here and *I Am Curious* was banned, which only made Americans even more curious, and by the time it was unbanned in 1969 Vilgot Sjöman was a *cause célèbre* and his $160,000 film was a monster smash.

You can't buy publicity like a government lawyer demanding to know before the Supreme Court whether the leading lady's lips had actually touched the party of the first part's parts. "I have a feeling," answered Sjöman non-committally, "that it was possible for her just to have her lips a couple of millimeters above the penis." Below the title but above the penis, Lena Nyman, the Swedish Hummingbird (as she was dubbed), was the art-house darling of the year. Liberated by the court from the attentions of the Customs service, *Curious,* though

211

playing only in New York and New Jersey, quickly became the highest-grossing foreign-language film in America - a record it held for almost a quarter-century.

I saw the movie some years later in high school. I was one of a stampede of adolescent boys that signed up for the Film Society when they announced a screening of *I Am Curious (Yellow)*. The Film Society didn't waste its time with westerns or musicals or Buster Keaton retrospectives; it specialized in vaguely arty films with extensive nudity. "What is this *I Am Curious* thing?" some unfortunate classmate would ask, and the others would shoot him a pitying glance and pass him the famous photograph from the picture, of Sjöman's young protagonists embracing on a bed, and he'd stare at it with a faraway look and breathing through his nostrils, like a sweating horse.

I Am Curious (Yellow) was an adult film. I don't mean in the debased contemporary sense of industrially depilated porn starlets with unfeasible implants engaging in joyless mechanical thrashing. I mean in the sense that, aside from the sex scenes, it included an interview with the Swedish minister of trade. If that's not "adult", what is? It was certainly more adult than many of us new members of the Film Society were in the mood for. There were interviews with Yevgeny Yevtushenko and Martin Luther King, and Miss Nyman also questioned passing Swedes in the street about the Vietnam War and demilitarizing the Swedish armed forces. But in between these longeurs the leading lady was certainly a game gal, and in a remarkable range of locations, including in a pond, up a tree and outside the Royal Palace in Stockholm.

If I recall correctly, the connection between the interviews with Olaf Palme et al and the sex-in-a-tree bits was that, while Lena Nyman's character – a sociologist called "Lena" – believes in both political freedom and personal freedom, the film explores the ironies and contradictions between her commitment to pacifism in the political sphere with her commitment to aggression in the sexual sphere.

Or something like that. Norman Mailer hailed it as "one of the most important pictures I have ever seen in my life". Aside from the nudity, Sjöman also flashed key words from his political philosophy up on screen: "NONCOOPERATION", "FRATERNIZATION", "SABOTAGE". It pioneered a new cinematic concept: sex in a political context. Hitherto, there had been no context whatsoever in most movie sex: In the Fifties, it was heartily earnest paeans to naturism. In the Sixties, Russ Meyer and others inaugurated porn with plot. I once had to host a BBC featurette on softcore Europorn, and after the first couple of films I was an expert in the conventions of the genre: The bisexual countess discovers the new stable-girl sleeping naked in the hay loft and there then follows a sort of Scandinavian pre-echo of the current "What Not To Wear" reality shows, as the countess arranges a fitting session for the stable-girl's new wardrobe, to the accompaniment of elevator music and occasional interjections – "That pipphole bra would rilly suit you, ja?"

Vilgot Sjöman, by contrast, kept his eye on the sociopolitical ball. "Do we have a class system in Sweden?" Lena Nyman asks her fellow Swedes. "It depends on the people," she's told. "Undress them and they're all the same. Dress them and you have a class system." Undress them while talking about the class system and you have a boffo smash: Sjöman conclusively demonstrated that the biggest bang for the buck was in sex with context. In the years afterwards, actresses lined up on talk shows to explain that they wouldn't have done this or that explicit nude scene if it hadn't been "totally in context". With the right sub-text and political theme, you could hardly restrain your leading lady from climbing out of her clothes and getting into context.

Not all critics were impressed. Rex Reed dismissed Sjöman as "a very sick Swede with an overwhelming ego and a fondness for photographing pubic hair". But pubic hair was thin on the ground in the late Sixties and, if it takes a sick Swede with an overwhelming ego to make this artistic breakthrough, so be it. I once asked Victor Lowndes, Hugh Hefner's head honcho at the Playboy Club in London, about this important matter – his girlfriend had been the first centerfold to be shown with pubic hair – and he replied, "Well, we've all got it, haven't we?" Judging from today's *Playboy*, apparently not. But back then the combination of pubic hair and discussions of Swedish politics proved to be box-office dynamite. It would have been a stretch to assert that you were only there, as with your *Playboy* subscription, for the interviews. But, as Vincent Canby of *The New York Times* observed at the belated premiere of *I Am Curious (Yellow)*, "the crowds were large, mostly middle-aged and ruly".

With his intense Nordic mien and thick-rimmed spectacles, Sjöman was an unlikely cementer of the gloomy Swedes' sudden reputation as the Sixties' swingingest swingers. The son of a construction worker, he left school at 15 to work for a cereal company and then as a prison orderly before, already in his thirties, coming to America to do film studies at UCLA. In his early days, he was a playwright, writing unproduced plays, some of which he would then adapt into novel and film form. And even when he got hep to the sex racket he was hampered by an undue attachment to the "well-made play". If you overlooked the bestiality and incest and whatnot, much of his pre-*Curious* work was as conventionally structured as standard West End or Broadway drawing-room fare. His last film before the bonanza was *My Sister, My Love* (1965), based on *'Tis Pity She's A Whore*, set in 18th century Syskonbadd and starring Bibi Andersson as the eponymous 18th century sis gone bad with Per Oscarsson as the twin brother with whom she's enjoying a vigorous incestuous relationship. The critics yawned: unconventional sex in a conventional narrative structure; you'll have to do better than that.

Some years ago, I visited the British director Derek Jarman on the set of his *War Requiem*. Racked by Aids and wheezing and coughing somewhat distractedly, he quite out of the blue named *My Sister, My Love* and its startling ending – a new life retrieved from death – as one of the films that had made the most profound impact on him. And, unlike Norman Mailer, I'd wager he meant it, for why otherwise mention it? By then, Vilgot Sjöman was an all but forgotten one-hit provocateur.

He followed *I Am Curious (Yellow)* with *I Am Curious (Blue)*, whose material was in effect leftovers from the first film. "Yellow" and "blue" are the two colors of the Swedish flag, and the idea of the two films was that in combination you got a complete picture of the state. *Blue* – or *Jag är nyfiken - blå* – concerned itself, according to Sjöman, with the church, prison camps, government and so forth, which practically speaking boiled down to *Yellow* with a lot less sex. To fans of the first, *Blå* was a big blah. Some critics argued that *Yellow* was a man's film and *Blue* was a woman's film, but, if you did as Sjöman suggested and laid them end to end, you noticed more people were getting laid end to end in the first film. *I Am Curious (Yellow)* was the blue film, *I Am Curious (Blue)* was the red film – socialist politics leavened fitfully by Sjöman's camera lovingly lingering on the sweetly chubby Lena, his muse.

And that was it. Having been raped by a German Shepherd in Sjöman's *491* and had her oral sex technique analyzed by the US Supreme Court, Lena Nyman figured she'd exhausted the director's range of possibilities and went off to become one of the most respected serious actresses at the Royal Dramatic Theatre in Stockholm. Sjöman, on the other hand, went off to make *Till Sex Do Us Part*, a farce with a hit title it couldn't live up to. He kept busy – lots of books, not so many films, and with diminishing returns. In the wake of *I Am Curious* came more films for the curious – *The Devil In Miss Jones*, and *Last Tango In Paris*, with suburban audiences lining up to see Brando bark "Get the butter!" And then came video and the Internet and the mainstream sex film faded away as quickly as it had appeared. New stars mostly declined to take their clothes off, and, even with his on, Brando looked as if he'd have been better advised to yell, "Get the I Can't Believe It's Not Butter!"

It seems hard now to recall what the fuss was all about, and indeed, from the bemused tone of some obituaries, Vilgot Sjöman might as well have been a director of silent movies or singing-cowboy pictures or some other obsolete genre. Cinematic sex, like so much real sex, was over almost as soon as it had begun. By the Nineties there was no surer way to laughingstock status in Hollywood than some ill-considered "erotica". Joe Eszterhas' reputation never recovered from *Showgirls* and poor Sharon Stone and Paul Verhoeven were reduced to blaming the failure of *Basic Instinct 2* on cowardly moviegoers unwilling to go against the new Puritanism of the Bush tyranny. Apparently, we're no longer curious, but we are yellow.

The Atlantic Monthly

A feel for politics

STROM THURMOND
DECEMBER 5TH 1902 ~ JUNE 26TH 2003

STROM THURMOND, the only centenarian senator in American history, is dead, and in a day or two we'll see whether the undertakers have successfully dealt with a potential problem that might, ah, arise: in the words of a favourite Washington aphorism (coined, I think, by the late John Tower), "When ol' Strom dies, they'll have to beat his pecker down with a baseball bat in order to get that coffin lid closed."

There's the epitaph a lot of us guys would like. Some eulogists will speak about his heroism in war. Others will deplore his 1948 presidential campaign as the segregationist candidate. But to many of us, Strom will be fondly remembered as South Carolina's most indestructible ladies' man. In his early 90s, the wizened Republican with the fiery orange hair-plugs made an ill-advised attempt at bipartisan outreach and groped fellow Senator Patty Murray. In his late 90s, he had a little light petting session with, um, me.

This was my only close encounter with him, and a lot closer than I'd expected. It was the first day of the Clinton impeachment trial and, in a chaotic melee by the elevators, I was suddenly pushed forward and thrown between Thurmond and California Senator Barbara Boxer.

Ol' Strom had just cast an appreciative bipartisan eye over the petite brunette liberal extremist. Ms Boxer gave an involuntary shudder. I'd been squashed between the two for about five seconds when I became aware of a strange tickling sensation on my elbow. Glancing down, I was horrified to see an unusually large lizard slithering up and down my arm. On closer inspection, it proved to be Strom's hand. Presumably he'd mistaken my dainty elbow for Barbara's, but who knows? What a great country! In how many other

217

national legislatures can a guy just wander in off the street and find himself in a tripartisan squeeze being petted by a 97-year-old Senator? I can't speak for Patty Murray, but I found the mild electric frisson not unpleasant.

A senator is only as old as the woman he feels, and, until he started hitting on *Telegraph* columnists, that's one thing Strom always had a feel for. He's also the only American to have been elected to national office by a write-in-campaign. And the only Senator to have spoken for 24 hours and 18 minutes continuously, back in 1957 when he filibustered the civil rights bill and had an aide standing with a bucket in the adjoining cloakroom so he could relieve himself while keeping one foot on the Senate floor and still speaking - an unusually literal illustration of LBJ's political aphorism that with certain types (Robert F. Kennedy, J Edgar Hoover) "it's better to have 'em inside the tent pissing out than outside the tent pissing in."

And, of course, Strom is the only circuit court judge in South Carolina history to have made love to a condemned murderess as she was being transferred from the women's prison to death row. This was Sue Logue, the only woman in the state ever to be sent to the chair, but not before she'd been sent to the back seat of Strom's car for a lively final ride. It was a particularly bloody murder case that had begun when Mr Logue's calf had been kicked to death by some other feller's mule. Things had escalated from there. Strom was said to have had a soft spot for Mrs Logue, whom he'd hired as a teacher back when he was School Superintendent. She didn't meet the minimum qualifications for the post, but she was said to have had unusual "vaginal muscular dexterity". Nothing could be finer than to be in Carolina with a muscularly dextrous vagina.

I mention this not merely to be salacious and gossipy - perish the thought - but only because, after profiling a thousand politicians from Al Gore to John Prescott to Wim Kok, one is naturally grateful for a subject with whom one can introduce the phrase "vaginal muscular dexterity" without it feeling shoehorned in. I may use it again before the column is out.

Strom was the best thing about that weird impeachment racket. Bill Clinton's legal team had been seated just in front of the old boy, and, during each break in the trial, Strom was at pains to demonstrate his, er, evenhandedness. He'd wobble up to the President's two lady lawyers, pat them down, tickle their elbows, stroke their hands, and refuse to let go until the gavel came down and the proceedings resumed. Watching from the gallery, I thought, "That's the way he used to treat me, the ol' three-timin' no-good dawg." Cheryl Mills, Mr Clinton's fetching African-American attorney, smiled nervously, no doubt marvelling at how far the Senator had come since his 1948 segregationist campaign for the White House and, indeed, how far he was willing to go to demonstrate in a very real sense his personal commitment to integrating with the black community. Her colleague, the President's other cunningly planted jailbait nymphette, 41-year old Nicole Seligman, stared thoughtfully at Strom's flame-coloured hair plugs and made a mental note to warn her client that this is what he'll look like in half-a-century if he doesn't cut out the womanizing.

What strange days they were. There were rumours that Larry Flynt, *Hustler*'s head honcho, had been working with Clinton operatives to provide the President with an insurance policy lest the numbers got a little close: he'd promised to hunt down video evidence of any amorous adventuring by hypocritical senators minded to convict.

Naturally, we in the media were eager to see what Flynt might produce. I turned up one morning to find my colleagues immersed in a scandal from an unexpected corner – "Thurmond In World's Oldest Love-Child Shocker!" Apparently, someone had alleged that, in 1923, Strom had fathered a child by a black woman. It seemed unlikely even Larry Flynt could have video evidence, though perhaps he had an authentic silent movie of the incident with full piano accompaniment and ornately bordered dialogue cards saying, "Why, Mistuh Thurmond suh, what are you doin' here at this hour?"

In the end, like most everything else, it only added to Strom's legend. South Carolina's junior senator, Fritz Hollings, now 83 but

219

thanks to Strom the oldest junior senator in history, complained sourly that Thurmond was no longer "mentally keen". On the basis of the few exchanges I had with him at the trial, Strom seemed one of the sharper guys: Jim Jeffords is a third his age, but try getting a coherent sentence out of Jim when his aides aren't around. Fritz Hollings, feeble frontman for Disney and the other big entertainment conglomerates in their assault on the world's copyright conventions, is far more of an extinct dinosaur than Strom. Considering that only 100 folks get to be Senator out of a talent pool of almost 300 million, there's a lot of mediocrities in there. Strom Thurmond, as Democrat or Republican, D-Day war hero or squire of generations of Miss South Carolinas, is the size of fellow a United States Senator ought to be.

He retired in January, after a 100th birthday some folks worried he might never get to see. In those far-off days of spring 2001, when the Senate was split evenly between the parties and South Carolina's sultan of swing was a mere whippersnapper of 98, the ghouls of the press were running a round-the-clock Strom deathwatch: All it would have taken was a particularly nubile intern bending over the photocopier in a low-cut top and the 50-50 Senate would have fallen to the Democrats.

As events transpired, it was Jim Jeffords who flipped the Senate, after the President had allegedly snubbed him by not inviting him to the Teacher Of The Year reception. Jim's flounce may well have saved Strom's life. Before Jeffords flew the coop, Tom Daschle and his troops had decided they'd waited long enough for ol' Strom to kick off, and it was time to hasten the process by keeping him on the floor hour after hour in one frivolous roll call after another. The Monday before the Jeffords defection, some of the old boy's Republican colleagues were worried that Thurmond wouldn't last the night and Jim would soon be getting not invited to the Funeral Of The Year reception.

But not for the first time Strom had the last laugh. That centennial birthday party set off a chain of events culminating in the fall of Senate Majority Leader Trent Lott. Aside from the ill-advised remarks on segregation that cost him his job, Lott also made a joke about the centenarian sex fiend attending the opening of Hooters, a restaurant chain with skimpily attired waitresses, and suggested that Strom replace Bob Dole's dog in a Pepsi commercial in which the said pooch gets over-excited at the sight of an underdressed Britney Spears.

The National Organisation for Women denounced the pervasive sexism of Strom's knees-up. The longest-serving senator in history could hardly have asked for a better curtain call: a 100th birthday bash that prompts feminist outrage. In an age of dull politicians who merely follow their polls, Strom at least had one worth following.

The Daily Telegraph

PARTINGS & Sorrows

The paladin of palimony

MARVIN MITCHELSON

MAY 7TH 1928 ~ SEPTEMBER 18TH 2004

L IKE MANY implausible characters, he was at home in the fiction of Jackie Collins. In *Hollywood Wives*, one of their number discovers that her husband is having an affair with her best friend, a Miss Karen Lancaster:

> She escorted him to the door. 'Tomorrow I am phoning Marvin Mitchelson,' she announced grandly. 'By the time I am finished with you the only milk you'll be able to afford is from Karen Lancaster's tits!'

As withering put-downs go, it doesn't quite work. But the Mitchelson detail has the ring of authenticity. In real life, it was he who did most of the milking – not just of his clients' unfortunate husbands, but of the case itself, for every last drop of publicity. He was a faded name by the end, which must have distressed him. But for two decades he was a genuine celebrity – the celebrity who changed the way other celebrities live. He was the lawyer who seized the opportunity in evolving attitudes to divorce – or, at any rate, celebrity divorce. In the old days, Hollywood handled splitsville discreetly, the studios could usually square things with Hedda and Louella, and the discarded spouse got a one-way ticket on the oblivion express. But, in Mitchelson's hands, divorce was just part of the show and he expected his stars to perform. And happily for him some of his movie-star clients made much better clients than they ever did movie stars. In the oft-retailed surefire alimony gags of the period, he's the unseen presence. Zsa Zsa Gabor on her fifth husband:

> He taught me housekeeping. When I divorce, I keep the house.

In fairness, the man who taught Hollywood women housekeeping was Mitchelson, who represented Zsa Zsa on two-sevenths of her divorces. He performed the same service for two of Alan Jay Lerner's eight wives. Lerner wrote many musicals, but there was one plot he liked so much he kept writing it over and over: young unformed woman taken in hand by older worldly man. That's the gist of *My Fair Lady* (1956), *Gigi* (1958), and, eventually and inevitably, *Lolita My Love* (1971), which proved to be one reprise too many of "Thank Heaven For Little Girls". In life, Lerner found the happy endings harder to come by. A serial monogamist, he discovered that little girls don't always grow up in the most delightful way. Sometimes they grow up, grow out of love, and someone gives them Marvin Mitchelson's phone number.

That's what the lawyer made his specialty - the Alan Jay Lerner woman: the young unknown taken up by an older more powerful Hollywood man. Mitchelson represented Mrs Marlon Brando and Mrs Bob Dylan and by the end of it the husbands had top billing in more senses than one. He made his name 40 years ago with Hollywood's first "million-dollar divorce", representing Pamela Mason against her husband James. A "million-dollar divorce" sounds almost quaint in an age when Britney's minders make sure she always has the photocopied pre-nup with GROOM [YOUR NAME HERE] tucked in her purse when she's out for a cocktail on a Saturday night. But it was big news back then: Mitchelson subpoenaed dozens of witnesses and threatened to reveal in court James Mason's more recherché sexual exploits. The actor was glad to settle.

His mother worked hard to see him through law school, and for a while he was a doughty champion of the poor. He was proudest, he said, of winning the right of indigents to legal representation in a case before the US Supreme Court in 1963. But he had a flair for tabloid publicity, and after the Mason case, he chose to be a doughty champion of the prospectively poor – the ex-trophy wife. For *Camelot*, Alan Lerner wrote a song called "How To Handle A Woman". Easier said than done. The real problem is how to handle a woman who gets Marvin Mitchelson to handle her divorce. Indeed, *How To Handle A Woman* would have made a much better title for Mitchelson's autobiography than the one he plumped for - *Made In Heaven, Settled In Court*. On a TV special back in the Seventies, Bob Hope sang a duet of "How To Handle A Woman" with special guest Richard Burton. "One thing's for sure," cracked Hope over the final chord. "We won't ask Lee Marvin."

The Marvin case was Mitchelson's big expansion of his franchise, the one that introduced a new legal concept: "palimony". Michelle Triola had lived with Lee Marvin at Malibu Beach for seven years without benefit of clergy, but Mitchelson saw no reason why lack of marriage should be an obstacle to a divorce settlement. To back up the innovation, he disdained fusty concepts such as legal principle and opted for one-liners: palimony was "a commitment with no rings attached". Not bad. Even better, the Los Angeles Superior Court bought it: live-in lovers could sue for financial support. The ruling, declared Mitchelson, was "the biggest setback for showbusiness since John Wilkes Booth."

It was great news for Mitchelson, less good for his client. Instead of a multi-million dollar settlement, Miss Triola was awarded a crummy hundred grand for "re-training" (in her pre-Marvin days, she had been a "singer") and lost most of that on appeal. But, as a general rule, regardless of whether his client won the case, the lawyer always emerged with some kind of victory. Lee Marvin was everybody's all-time great grizzled, squinty tough guy, but he ended his days as a butt for lounge-act divorce gags. Following the same trajectory, Adnan Khashoggi was everybody's all-time great international man of mystery, the numero uno of shadowy billionaire arms dealers and confidantes of the big-time Saudi royals. But then his relationship with his wife Soraya, a London waitress' daughter whom he'd married at 19, hit the rocks. In accordance with Islamic law, Adnan told Soraya "I divorce thee" three times, the third making it final. In accordance with non-Islamic law, Soraya called Mitchelson.

He demanded a settlement of $2.5 billion, based on the fact that Khashoggi spent a quarter of a million bucks a day and she was the mother of five of his children. But he also worked the case assiduously through the Fleet Street tabloids: Soraya had already married and divorced another husband, who was the ex-boyfriend of a daughter she'd had out of wedlock before marrying Khashoggi, and was having an affair with Winston Churchill, a prominent MP, grandson of the former Prime Minister, and rumored father of her seventh child. For a while *The Guinness Book Of Records* included the case as the world's most expensive settlement - $950 million. Those in the know said it was up to $948 million south of that, but, whatever the check he had to write, it was nothing compared to the damage to Khashoggi's reputation and the permanent diminishment of his status with the House of Saud.

That was the Mitchelson trick. He Zsa Zsaed everyone. No matter how cool, refined or sinister you were, by the time he was through with you you sounded like a bit-part in a Jackie Collins. Only Groucho Marx gave as good as he got. When his third wife, Eden Hartford, sued for divorce in part because he'd threatened to kill her, Groucho countered that there was no point giving her the house as her sloth made her unsuited for housekeeping, he'd ponied up all the money she'd ever asked for including a hundred bucks a month for her mother, and in fact he'd been giving her an allowance before he even married her. "Since I'm a very bad lay, she was entitled to this," he said in his deposition. Mitchelson got a million dollars for Miss Hartford, but Groucho, like Zsa Zsa, kept the house.

He moved with the times. As film stars faded, he turned to rockers. As marriage faded, he pushed palimony. When Aids arrived, he represented Rock Hudson's under-informed lover. Just as lack of a wedding certificate was no reason to forgo the divorce, so lack of paternity was no reason to forgo the paternity suit. He sued Robert De Niro on behalf of the daughter of an old girlfriend, dismissing as irrelevant DNA tests proving the actor couldn't be the father. "She loves him," said the lawyer. "She feels he's her dad." No matter what kind of relationship or non-relationship you had going, you were on the hook to somebody for something. Because of lawyers like Mitchelson, Hollywood marriage brokers dreamt up the pre-nup, a device he despised.

In court, he could reduce you to tears, or worse. "I once reduced a witness to death," he claimed. "He had a heart attack while I was cross-examining him... I did mouth-to-mouth resuscitation in court and thought about giving up law for the rest of the evening." But most of the time Mitchelson just made you feel queasy in a non-fatal way. He was a terrible ham, weepin' an' a-wailin', breaking down, cracking up, collapsing in a coughing fit, whatever it took. He had a two-tone Rolls and drove a Merc with the license plate PALIMONY. He paid $605,000 for the Duchess of Windsor's amethyst and turquoise necklace and announced he'd bought it in honor of his mother.

In the Nineties, it all caught up with him. A fortune built on the personal failings of others fell victim to his own: he was charged with fraud, his staff said he was addicted to cocaine, two clients accused him of rape, he was convicted of tax evasion, lost his license, and in 1996 went to federal prison, where he ran the law library and helped fellow inmates with their appeals. On his release, he was broke and worked as a paralegal.

He would have done well out of gay marriage, which after just a few months in Ontario has already led to the first gay divorce. Somewhere in Beverly Hills there's a turkey baster lying abandoned in the kitchen drawer of a famous Hollywood single mom he could probably have won a landmark $10 million settlement for. Instead, in the time between the restoration of his license and the onset of his final illness, he won one last great pay-off - $216 million for the estranged wife of a minor Saudi royal.

And, for all the cocaine-fraud-rape-tax accusations, there was one mess he managed to avoid. He leaves a widow, Marcella, his wife of 45 years.

The Atlantic Monthly

The marrying kind

OWEN ALLRED
JANUARY 15TH 1914 ~ FEBRUARY 14TH 2005

"I HATE TO BE hated. I think everybody does. I want to be part, but I want to be myself and live the way I believe, the way the Lord told me to do.

"Now does that make me an evil person?"

Well, it depends who's talking. A nice middle-aged gay in a committed relationship, with a weekend home in Connecticut where he serves as a popular long-time usher at the local "open and affirming" Congregational Church? Alas not. Owen Allred was a proponent of a far less fashionable minority marriage cause: he was the patriarch of the United Apostolic Brethren, Utah's second-largest polygamous group, a church with an estimated 5,000-7,000 believers, many of them living a confetti throw from Mr Allred's home in Bluffdale on the edge of Salt Lake City. Seven thousand doesn't sound like a lot, but there are more polygamists in Owen Allred's municipality than gay Vermonters who've ever been to their Town Clerk for a "civil union" permit.

I say "home", though *The New York Times* preferred "compound". The precise point at which a "ranch", "bungalow" or "18th century saltbox with many original features" becomes a "compound" is best left to realtors – "Extensively remodeled compound with drop-dead views of ATF agents at the tree line calling for back-up." But the *Times* seems to use the term as universally accepted shorthand for "wacky cult", and certainly Owen Allred attracted his share of lurid headlines over the decades. He came from a long line of Mormons – his great-grandfather walked with Brigham Young on the original trek to the Great Salt Lake – but Owen knew how to move with the times, the kind of stern fundamentalist patriarch who, when his church needs financing to buy the recreational hangout of the old Vegas mob, is savvy enough to route the deal through Belize. Two years ago, a judge ruled that he'd laundered thousands of dollars and his church had swindled one and a half million out of Marsha Jones, a one-time South American movie star and Detroit hood's moll who changed her name to "Virginia Hill" in honor of Bugsy Siegel's squeeze. Poor old "Virginia" could handle the mobsters but got taken to the cleaners by the Mormons.

As presiding elder and the only "living prophet" of his church, Mr Allred was said to have learned the sacred Mormon rites directly from God. Others said he got 'em from a fellow called Fred Collier, who had a genealogist pal with access to the archives of the Church of Jesus Christ of Latter Day Saints. Fred's wife Bonnie pulled a Sandy Berger and smuggled microfilm of the holiest texts out in her bra and then passed them on to Allred. A third version by disenchanted polygamist and Nixon-era Secret Service Agent Rod Williams holds that he, Williams, stole the LDS holy ordinances for Allred. The living prophet conceded Williams brought them over to the house, but he told him to take them right back.

Owen came to the role of living prophet late in life, only being designated as such after the Brethren's previous leader, his brother Rulon Allred, was murdered in 1977 when rival polygamists from the Church of the Lamb of the God went on a killing spree, after their leader Ervil LeBaron had been excommunicated by his brother, leader of another polygamous sect, the Church of the First Born. There are men who cope with the stresses and tensions of multiple marriages but apparently go bananas at the thought of multiple polygamous sects. Ervil had his teenage bride Rena pump seven bullets into Rulon at point-blank range mainly because his brother had gone into hiding and he thought this would flush him out and he could kill him at Rulon's funeral. But 2,600 people turned up and LeBaron's posse decided it would be impractical to launch the bloodbath.

Yet the mob moll/Belize bank/homicidal child-bride/sects 'n'violence segments of Eyewitness News do an injustice to Mr Allred. For a presiding elder living in a compound, he was droll, urbane and politically shrewd: Mormon polygamist-wise, this was not your father's patriarch. An open and engaging chap, he was especially open about all the engaging: he held press conferences and testified in legislatures on multiple marrying. He was very adroit at reminding his fellow Utahans that, regardless of how many practicing polygamists there are in the state, those part of a broader polygamous inheritance are far more numerous, and include Senator Orrin Hatch and Mike Leavitt (then Governor, and now President Bush's Health and Human Services Secretary), both men whose family history is little different from the Allreds'. Born in Idaho, the son of the Speaker of the state's House of Representatives, Owen Allred was excommunicated from the LDS in 1942, when he took his second walk down the aisle. By the end, he'd married eight wives, fathered 23 children, raised another 25 step-children, and had over 200 grandchildren.

In an age which deplores unreconstructed homophobes foolish enough to conflate gayness and pedophilia, we're happy to assume that, if some hatchet-faced patriarch with nothing but a compound in one of the less chic zip codes can find eight women prepared to marry him they must be 14-year old cousins he keeps in the cupboard under the stairs most of the week. One of Owen's nieces, Dorothy Allred Solomon, wrote an exposé of her life within the church, under the title of *Daughter Of The Saints: Growing Up In Polygamy* or, if you prefer (as the publisher evidently did), *Predators, Prey And Other Kinfolk: Growing Up In Polygamy*. Mrs Solomon couldn't quite live up to the latter billing. She was the middle child – 24th of 48 – of Rulon Allred, and the vicissitudes of her life seem to derive from the secrecy and isolation that necessarily attends such communities – the psychological damage of the polygamous closet.

But, if you've got 48 kids and only one is disaffected enough to go public, that's a better strike rate than most celebrities manage, or, indeed, many two-child monogamous couples. At Allred's funeral, six of his sons carried his coffin and as many daughters celebrated his memory with a rendition of "Oh, My Papa" and, given that most of them aren't exactly spring chickens, I doubt that's because he was keeping them chained out in the dog pound. There's less verified child abuse among all the Utah churches than among priests who passed through Cardinal Law's diocese in Boston. It was the state that permitted marriage at the age of 14, and Owen Allred who campaigned for the legislature to raise the age to 16. "For 50 years now," he said, "the rule among our people has definitely been that girls should not even start courting until they are at least 17." At 88, he told *The New York Times*, "People have the wrong idea that we're old-time kooks who prey on young girls. I suppose I'm guilty of that. My youngest wife is 64. My oldest girl is 93." They lived in four houses, lined up side by side, and all eight marriages were till death did them part.

He died on Valentine's Day. And before you add "which must have saved him a fortune at the florist" or "he collapsed under the weight of the stack of heart-shaped chocolate boxes he was carrying", Mark Woods, *The Florida Times-Union*'s sports columnist, did most of the polygamous Valentine gags three years ago, finding himself in Salt Lake City for the Olympics and in need of a Utah-themed romantic column. So he called up Owen Allred:

> *He wouldn't come to the phone. The man who answered said that Allred's not doing any interviews these days. And that he was busy.*
>
> *I bet.*
>
> *Eight wives. Do you buy valentine gifts in bulk? ('Yes, the same message, just change the name to Sally.')*

Etc. For feminists, the practice of polygamy is inherently abusive. But to guys it's mostly an easy laugh – the Old Testament elder who's hit the swingers' jackpot. Journalists kept his number handy when they needed a quote for a light item on a Utah brewery's introduction of Polygamy Porter (slogan: "Why have just one?"). Mr Allred was not minded to order a crate for his next wedding toast: "We do not believe in alcoholic drinks of any kind," he said.

Utah is said to operate a "don't ask, don't tell" policy on polygamy, the conventional wisdom being that the likes of Allred are left alone because of official sympathy. That may have been true once, but I doubt it's the reason now. I was told recently that provincial officials in British Columbia have decided to let be their own polygamous community of Bountiful because of a general feeling that, if they hauled everyone before the judge, by the time it wound up at the Supreme Court of Canada all their lawyers would have to do is read out the judges' recent ruling giving the go ahead for same-sex marriage. Whatever the merits of gay nuptials, it's hard to see why, if gender is irrelevant, the central immutable feature of marriage should now be the number of participants.

The gay activists get all huffy about being compared to some stump-toothed backwoods wives-beater. And that might suffice if it were just a matter of Owen Allred and his ilk. But last summer *Le Monde* leaked a government report revealing that polygamy was routinely practiced in Muslim ghettoes in France. An informal survey of the Islamic communities of Ontario found much the same. In Britain, the Inland Revenue is considering recognizing polygamy for the purposes of inheritance law, so that a Muslim husband's estate can be divided tax-free between several wives. And if it's a Muslim who finally makes it to an American state Supreme Court with a polygamy case, bet on the traditional deference to "multiculturalism".

Unlike the overtaxed Islamists of the United Kingdom, Owen Allred did not believe in legalizing polygamy. He fretted that if the law were changed it would be practiced more carelessly – as legal monogamous marriage is - and its holiness would be diminished. His detractors said he'd figured out that, like bootleg hooch, it's more profitable outside the law. As things stood, Allred had sole authority to bless polygamous unions and you had to agree to tithe your income to him before he'd give you the nod. A ten-dollar permit from the municipal courthouse could have dramatic implications for the Brethren's coffers.

"It takes twice as good a man to have two wives as it does to have one," Allred liked to say. On another Valentine's Day, February 14th 2001, he brought over a hundred polygamists to the state legislature for the biggest public hearing on the subject in Utah's history. "The man who wants several women to be his sexual partners," said Allred, "can have children by them, and the state will support those children. He remains free of any legal accusation - until he marries more than one wife. Marry them, and he becomes a criminal."

Owen Allred was born in 1914, barely a generation after the LDS abandoned Joseph Smith's injunction to go forth and multiply multiply. For the best part of a century Allred kept it going, ensuring polygamy's survival into an era of hitherto unknown "rights to privacy" and modish "tolerance" and "multiculturalism". Demographic reality suggests that the new face of plural marriage in North America will not be Owen Allred's or his kind. Still, he might take some comfort in knowing that his sacred covenant and/or lifestyle choice is almost certain to endure and prosper in the years ahead.

The Atlantic Monthly

Wendy's house

WENDY WASSERSTEIN
OCTOBER 18TH 1950 ~ JANUARY 30TH 2006

"WE'RE ALL CONCERNED, intelligent, good women," says the eponymous Heidi of *The Heidi Chronicles*. "It's just that I feel stranded. And I thought the whole point was that we wouldn't feel stranded."

Or as another woman says, in *Isn't It Romantic?*, "No matter how lonely you get or how many birth announcements you receive, the trick is not to get frightened."

Get the picture? A decade and a half ago, when *Heidi* first hit, an American journalist living in London told me she could never understand why these characters were always so unhappy – and then she went to interview the author. And she took one look at her and it explained the whole play in a way that casting Joan Allen and Jamie Lee Curtis as Heidi never quite could. "She's like a bag lady, a derelict," my journalist friend told me. "You feel like saying, 'Get your hair done, lose weight, don't dress like you've been sleeping in the street.' But, if you did, there wouldn't be any play."

She wasn't wrong. Wendy Wasserstein was a disheveled mess, a cuddly giggly bundle of a scarecrow – at least on the few occasions I met her – but she was a hard person to dislike. She once told me she'd met Colin Powell at the opening of the Cameron Mackintosh production of *Carousel* and "I was very impressed by him, even though he's a Republican". She did her trademark giggle as she said it: she meant it, but she was self-aware enough simultaneously to be parodying stereotypical Manhattan liberalism. Though she subscribed broadly to the general pieties - and was supposedly Hillary Clinton's favorite dramatist (did Dick Morris focus-group that one?) - she did not reside in the bilious cocoon of her old college pal Frank Rich. If she was, as pegged early on, a "feminist misogynist", she was jolly about it: in contrast to so many playwrights of her generation, there was no bitterness in her work. The Pulitzered and Tonyed August Wilson, who also died recently, was corroded by self-inflicted resentments, culminating in his demand that all theatres in cities with majority black populations be "converted" (ie, appropriated) into "black theatres" - the white staff retired and replaced by black administrators who would hire black authors to write black plays with black characters played by black actors staged by black directors. The white man's participation would be limited to paying for it through government funding. Defensive about his own light skin, Wilson observed, "When you look at me, it's obvious the white master visited the slave quarters" – which is a curious remark for the son of a German-American, who, as far as one knows, didn't meet his black bride by strolling over to the slave quarters of his Pittsburgh bakery. Wilson's peculiar obsessions overwhelmed his drama.

By comparison, Miss Wasserstein, particularly in the last decade of her life, had many reasons to be sour, but, at least professionally, never was. In that respect, she was somewhat Shavian. In most others, she was closer to a feminist Moss Hart – brisk and professional, full of good lines, with rather more going on underneath than in a Neil Simon romp. Her death is a loss to Broadway, and not just in a sentimental dim-the-lights-on-the-Great-White-Way sense. The American theatre makes a fuss about the deceased because it's a way to grab on to a last shaft of a dimming luster: when a Jule Styne or a Gwen Verdon dies, you remember the great days – the opening nights of the Fifties, the decade that unrolled like one glorious unending season. But Wendy Wasserstein didn't peak in the Fifties; that's when she was born. She was supposed to represent the theatre's future – or at any rate a viable present. In 1992, *The Sisters Rosensweig* opened to an all-time record advance for a straight play on Broadway: three million dollars. "My work is often thought of as lightweight commercial comedy," she told *The Paris Review*, "and I have always thought, no, you don't understand: this is in fact a political act. *The*

Sisters Rosensweig had the largest advance in Broadway history. Nobody is going to turn down a play on Broadway because a woman wrote it or because it's about women."

I don't know that they ever did. The play *Rosensweig* consciously evoked, *Three Sisters*, was "about women". But, in fairness to that grand assertion, Miss Wasserstein was the first female writer to win a Best Play Tony all her own (for *Heidi*). And, regardless of general application, after *Sisters* certainly nobody was going to turn down a Wasserstein play. Like Fosse or Simon, she was now a brand, and bankable. Producers and theatre owners always tell you that it's women who want to go to the theatre; the men don't want to be there – it's something improving they have to suffer through. Some impresarios, like James Nederlander, deduce from this that you have to give hubby something to keep him awake – a flapper in a negligee was the way they did it back when the "tired businessman" was a more critical part of the demographic. From a commercial point of view, Miss Wasserstein's work took a more straightforward approach: well, if it's women who come to the theatre, give 'em women's theatre. She offered the legit equivalent of the "chick flick", and she was the most successful female exponent thereof. Back in 1989, when *The Heidi Chronicles* was on Broadway, there was a London import also on the boards: *Shirley Valentine*, a one-woman play starring Pauline Collins and written by Willy Russell. A Liverpudlian crowd-pleaser, he spent the Eighties churning out one hit after another – *Shirley, Educating Rita, Blood Brothers* – all about the vicissitudes of life for women of a certain age. Where, one wonders in hindsight, was the British Wasserstein? There were female playwrights in London, but, like Caryl Churchill, they were too busy cranking out savage indictments of the Thatcher terror to be bothered with "women's plays". Miss Wasserstein found a niche, and New York theatergoers embraced her as they had no other for many years.

It wasn't a cynical calculation on her part. She wrote what she knew, but she did it well, and there was an awful lot of barely disguised autobiography in there. Her first play, *Isn't It Romantic?*, and her TV

238

adaptation of John Cheever's *The Sorrows Of Gin* were low-key successes. But *Heidi* made her reputation: tracking the social changes prompted by feminism through several decades in the life of an art historian, from Sixties bra-burning through Seventies consciousness-raising to the Eighties and the paradox of the unfulfilled "superwoman", Heidi Holland ends the play cradling her baby – no father or husband in sight, and none needed for aught than filling the beaker with the relevant bodily fluid. The thought recurs in *An American Daughter* (1997), in which the pro-life conservative gay pundit offers to donate his sperm to the childless African-American Jewish breast-cancer doctor. Both scenes prefigured the birth, in 1999, of Miss Wasserstein's own daughter, the identity of whose father she never disclosed. Life, as it often does, outpaced art with ease: unlike Heidi, Wendy gave birth three months prematurely to a daughter terribly underweight. "Although I remain a religious skeptic, I had a kind of blind faith," she wrote in her book *Shiksa Goddess*. "I believed in the collaboration between the firm will of my one-pound-twelve-ounce daughter and the expertise of modern medicine." But such a birth in a 48-year old woman took its toll. She died of lymphoma at 55, and the little girl will grow up with Wendy's brother.

"There's nothing wrong with being alone," wrote Wasserstein in *Isn't It Romantic?* in 1983. At one level, her entire career seemed to be an explanation for the dissatisfactions in her life arising from having that career. Though *The New York Times* suggested that Heidi Holland was the cultural progenitor of the *Sex And The City* gals, the truth would seem to be almost the opposite: that Miss Wasserstein's work was obsessed with the price you pay for a certain kind of life; what she intuitively felt as dissatisfactions, the *Sex And The City* crowd regard as the perks.

The daughter of a wealthy textile manufacturer, she saw plenty of Broadway plays growing up. "I remember going to them and thinking, I really like this, but where are the girls?" Where indeed? She went to college and fell in with the theatrical crowd, and wrote a camp romp with Christopher Durang called *When Dinah Shore Ruled The*

Earth. And after that she never needed to ask, "But where are the boys?" She had a coterie of male friends – confirmed bachelors, as they say – whom she called her "husbands", and who squired her around town, personally and professionally. With one of them, the British director Nicholas Hytner, she made a movie expressly addressing that frequent plaint of the single New York female: Why are all the best men gay? It must have sounded like a great high-concept movie when she conceived it in the Eighties. By the time it arrived on screen as *The Object of My Affection* in 1998, it seemed small and tired. Straight men's fantasies about lesbians don't extend much beyond the two-girl discount-special while you're in town for the convention, but the notion that a straight woman and a gay man are somehow the ideal couple is apparently a more credible fantasy and a recurring theme in the Wasserstein canon. Almost all her work is a simultaneous meditation on the frustrations, for women, both of having a traditional heterosexual relationship and of not having one, and in the course of said meditation some gay pal queens around the room being witty, sensitive, supportive – the ideal object of one's affection. In *The Sisters Rosensweig*, the youngest sibling is a travel writer living with a bisexual theater director.

Chàque a son goût, chàque a son gay. Even as fantasy, the fag/hag couple seems less an alternative to boring suburban marriage than a more extreme version of it: the gal sits at home while the guy's out having sex with whomsoever he wants. Straight men might well wonder why chicks extend this dispensation only to homosexuals - and anyway, in practice, most women who tiptoe down this primrose path wind up looking like pathetic masochists. On stage, *The Object Of My Affection* could have worked. As standard Multiplex filler, starring Jennifer Aniston from "Friends" as the Brooklyn social worker who takes up with a cherubic young gay soulmate, it played like a romance that could never take flight. From a cinematic point of view, at the core of such relationships is an element of making do, not a quality helpful to romantic comedy. Paul Rudd was very charming as the uncloseted first-grade teacher and dance-class partner, and I can well believe he's the ideal man - at least if you're Wendy Wasserstein and looking for someone to go to Broadway openings with. When Miss Aniston's character discovers she's pregnant by her boorish hetero sometime boyfriend, she asks the gay guy to raise the child with her. He's happy to play daddy, though he draws the line at anything as beastly as vaginal intercourse.

You had to be awful quick to catch *The Object Of My Affection* in theaters. On the night I saw it, the crowd figured 20 minutes in that the premise didn't stand up, after which they were increasingly resentful, on the reasonable grounds that no-one wants to see their favorite girl next door (which Miss Aniston then was) boxed in by the concept. It was a sobering moment: Wendy Wasserstein was supposed to be the American playwright who "got" the modern woman. But up on the big screen she seemed largely estranged from American life and just another insular Manhattanite with creepy pathologies unshared by the wider world.

By this point, her career had peaked commercially. A rare bona fide celebrity in the contemporary theatre, she was a gregarious woman who loved the circuit – the opening nights, the galas, the parties. In *The New Yorker*, Nancy Franklin said Miss Wasserstein was "ruled by a kind of celebrity mathematics; she seems connected to everybody who is anybody by a mere two degrees" – but the net effect of that was that she seemed increasingly disconnected from everybody who wasn't anybody. *An American Daughter* (1997) featured a fictional TV anchorman modeled on the real TV anchorman (and Wasserstein chum) Forrest Sawyer. She called the character "Timber Tucker". Cute, but perhaps the most explicit acknowledgement of the difficulties she was having in reconciling her twin impulses to satirize and to schmooze. Perhaps, like Sheridan Whiteside in *The Man Who Came To Dinner*, Timber Tucker will enjoy a life independent of his inspiration. But with this play Wasserstein seemed finally to cross the line from spokesperson for a generation of women to spokesperson for a generation of well-connected women who mix with celebrities and politicians.

Still, she had a good ear for the inanities of the age: one character has written the post-feminist bestseller *The Prisoner Of Gender*, while another has penned a standard college text called *Toward A Lesser Elite*. In *An American Daughter*, the President is polling the American people on which domestic pet they would prefer the First Family to acquire: call 1-800-VOTE-DOG or 1-800-VOTE-CAT and make sure your voice is heard. Given that Bill Clinton had a poll taken to decide where he should go on vacation (the respondents wanted something rugged and outdoorsy, so he hiked in the Rockies and his numbers went down, after which he stuck to Martha's Vineyard and the Hamptons), Miss Wasserstein is barely exaggerating. But it was a rare example of Broadway mockery of Clintonian spinmeistering. She could see the comedy in her own side, which is more than most of her comrades can do, yet in her first explicitly political play she was reluctant to do anything with the subject other than splash around in the shallows.

On the other hand, her last play, *Third*, was fascinating. Opening at Lincoln Center only a few weeks before the author's death, it's set at a New England liberal arts college and explores the relationship between, in the blue state corner, a professor of literature called Laurie Jameson (Dianne Wiest) and, in the red, a Midwestern wresting jock called "Third", as in Woodson Bull III (Jason Ritter). The obituarists said it was "about" plagiarism, but it's not: it's about doubt. The plagiarism – Third is believed to have stolen his paper on *King Lear* – is merely the pretext. Laurie is a smart intelligent woman who prides herself on her sensitivity and compassion, but she gets everything wrong. Fenced in by a lifetime of feminist groupthink, she can't see Third as a human being, only as a repository of her prejudices: he's a preppy Waspy Republican, so he must be privileged and selfish and heartless ...and a plagiarist. And so she hauls him up before the Commissars on the "Committee of Academic Standards" as a necessary sacrifice in order to build a world free of sexism, racism, classism and every other ism calcified in her politically correct bones. He is "a walking red state" in her "hegemonic-free zone".

She's not quite such a walking blue state – or at any rate walking compendium of college-town clichés – as that sounds. That's the point: she really is shrewd and insightful and kind and informed, but in the stultifying homogeneity of the American academy somewhere along the way it all curdled into bigotry. Not the bigotry of "racists" and "sexists" and "homophobes", but bigotry nonetheless. And her realization of that is the first fresh thought she's had in 30 years.

It was interesting to see left-wing drama critics struggle to wrap their heads round the piece: the Republican guy is attractive and engaged, so, er, the play's real theme must be sexual and personal not political and cultural... On the right, you long for the satirist in Wasserstein to rise to gleeful, savage heights – like Neil Simon, after he fell out with his analyst Mildred Newman, author of *How To Be Your Own Best Friend*, and parodied her as a platitudinous celebrity shrink and author of *Love Yourself, Fuck Them*.

But Miss Wasserstein hasn't undergone a deathbed conversion. She's not a Republican, not a conservative, not a member of the religious right. She's just someone who late in life has come to question her own assumptions about who's "intolerant" and "reactionary". The play can be faulted on structural grounds: it's set against the background of the Iraq war, there are Lear parallels, Laurie herself is undergoing menopause and perpetually struggling to ward off hot flushes. It's as if the playwright knew this was her last chance to say everything she hadn't yet said. But the fact that the blue state of mind is middle-aged and intellectually exhausted and the red state of mind is young and sharp is surely telling. It's a unique work in the Wasserstein catalogue: no gay walkers, no alternative family models, just a conventional marriage Laurie couldn't make work. One wonders what assumptions Wendy Wasserstein would have been questioning in the years ahead.

Instead, she fell gravely ill during rehearsals at Lincoln Center. I would have liked to have seen her next play.

The New Criterion

The least worst man

SID LUFT
NOVEMBER 2ND 1915 ~ SEPTEMBER 15TH 2005

S ID LUFT WAS the nearest Judy Garland came to the man that
didn't get away. By the end, the nights were bitter, the star had
lost her glitter, but he was hanging in there. The longest lasting
of her five husbands, he played Mister Judy Garland from 1952 to
1965 - or half her adult life, if one can call it that. Unlike his
predecessor, he was not "musical", in either the artistic or euphemistic
sense; unlike his successor, he was not voraciously gay. A scrappy
gravelly little guy known as One-Punch Luft, he was an all but unique
figure: a rare friend of Judy who wasn't a friend of Dorothy. And, as a
result, folks can't figure out what he saw in her. For a long time, the
received wisdom was that he was a sleazy opportunist who'd hitched
himself to her coat-tails and then milked her as long as he could. Yet,
insofar as there was a Second Act to Garland's career, he was its
impresario: *A Star Is Born*, the great Capitol albums, Carnegie Hall and
the London Palladium, the TV specials and weekly variety show that
get closer than anything to the real Judy, all these are from the Luft
years.

In fact, he was making headlines long before he met his alleged
meal ticket: "Boy, 12, Walking Arsenal" reported his hometown paper
back in Westchester County. In those days, it wasn't the easiest
neighborhood for a Jew, which is why young Sid was packing heat at a
tender age. At the local rink, an older kid whacked him with a hockey
stick and barked, "Hey, Jew, get off the ice!" So he took boxing lessons
and did weight lifting to the point where at age 19 he could walk up
the stairs on the palms of his hands.

That proved less useful in Hollywood, where even the tough
guys condescended to him. Once, at a party at Ira Gershwin's, he

244

began an observation with the words "Culturally speaking…" Humphrey Bogart cut in: "What right do you have to say 'culturally speaking'? You weren't really exposed to much culture as a young man, were you?" said Bogie, warming to his theme. "I lived on Park Avenue, my father was a doctor, my mother was an artist, so if I say 'culturally speaking', people will take it to be the truth. But you, Sid?"

"That does it," said Sid. "Let's take this outside!"

Bogart put on his glasses. "You wouldn't hit an old man, would you?"

If he never quite fit in in Hollywood, he'd spent a lifetime not quite fitting in anywhere else, either. Boxer, brawler, boozer, businessman, and good at all but the last of those, Luft had been in California since the Thirties, save for service in the Royal Canadian Air Force, for which he volunteered after the outbreak of war – ie, well before Pearl Harbor. His timing was rarely that good: a perpetually failing entrepreneur, he got his good ideas mostly too soon or too late, and the rest of the time mooched along on the fringes of glamour. By the end of the Forties, he'd started and folded a custom car company, been a test pilot, a nondescript talent agent, producer of a couple of B movies with elderly child stars Jackie Cooper and Jackie Coogan, and husband of a Hollywood starlet. After seven years, the starlet (Lynn Bari) was divorcing him on grounds of cruelty, because he had a habit of leaving the house to buy the evening paper at six and coming back with it in the wee small hours.

Judy Garland, by that point, had gone to Oz and back, been Andy Hardy's sweetheart and Fred Astaire's dance partner, married a top bandleader (David Rose) and a top movie director (Vincente Minnelli). Luft wasn't a top anything. As one gossip columnist put it, "So Sid Luft is what a girl finds over the rainbow?" They were the perfect couple: her career had self-detonated and his never ignited.

As their daughter Lorna Luft tells it, they met at Billy Reed's Little Club in New York, where Judy was dining with a male friend, Freddie Finklehoffe. Sid never forgot the moment. She was wearing a gold coat, black dress, pillbox hat, and she had him at "Hello". "When you met her, she'd say 'hello', and you'd fall down. The voice would kill you. In a sense, you would drop dead every time she talked to you." Which is what her date would have preferred. "Get lost," Finklehoffe told Luft. But Luft didn't, not for 15 years.

"I love Judy," he said when they married. "I want to protect her from the trauma she once knew. I don't want her to be bewildered or hurt again. I want her to have happiness." And, for a while, she did. There are two Judy Garlands: The first was the moon-faced little girl who got swept up by that Kansas twister and did the show right here in the barn for as many years as MGM could strap her breasts down and do whatever else was needed to keep the child star a child. That Garland was gone long before 1950, when Metro finally fired her. The second Judy went straight from Andy Hardy's barn to premature middle age, and emerged as the most dynamic stage presence since Jolson, a ballad singer whose taste in songs was second only to Sinatra's, a great comedienne, and a rueful raconteuse. That was Luft's gift to the rest of us.

He got her back into movies, too, producing her comeback picture, *A Star Is Born*, the story of a young rising star and a fading self-destructive one, with an actress who'd been both all but simultaneously. At the end, with her husband Norman Maine (James Mason) having taken his one-way walk into the sea, a teary Vicki Lester (Garland) takes the microphone and announces: "Hello, everybody... This is... Mrs Norman Maine." She got an Oscar nomination for the role and, if she'd won, she'd have been more than happy to start her acceptance speech with "This is Mrs Sidney Luft." But she was pregnant with her son Joey and on Oscar night she was in the maternity ward with a camera crew parked outside. They weren't needed and, as Grace Kelly went up to accept her award for *The Country Girl*, Luft looked at the TV technicians dismantling their equipment and told his wife: "Fuck the Academy Awards. You've got yours in the incubator."

The sweet talk didn't last. Every star is fleeced by hangers-on to one degree or another. If you're a celebrity prone to erratic behavior and no-shows and "health problems", it's worse, because at any one time you've got half-a-dozen contractual disputes and suits and counter-suits. The Lufts had money problems from day one and always needed the next deal to pay off the mess hanging over from the last deal. For the first half of their marriage, Sid was Judy's business manager, and thus got the blame. For the second half, he handed it off to others and then found himself on the outside as everyone else bled her dry. The best at it was David Begelman, a peerless Hollywood embezzler who eventually blew his brains out.

Meanwhile, in between bust-ups and reconciliations, Judy was finding consolation elsewhere. She'd go round to Sinatra's pad and hector Frank into having sex with her. He'd planned a quiet night sitting in his orange mohair sweater reading Bennett Cerf only to look down and find Judy trying to pull his pants off. One night her TV producer Bill Colleran was round at her place watching the show when he noticed her hand on his crotch. "I can't," he protested quaintly. "I'm married." Judy flounced across the room and sighed, "Nobody wants to fuck the legend."

Sid Luft did. But, as the "reconciliations" grew shorter and the gaps between longer, he became a Hollywood synonym for "loser". Bob Hope worked him into the Oscar act, merely the latest variation on his standard emcee's gag ("Welcome to the Academy Awards – or, as it's known at my house, Passover"). On Oscar night 1962, Hope closed the show with: "There'll be a victory celebration at the International Ballroom at the Hilton Hotel. I'll be there at a special table with Sid Luft and Eddie Fisher."

Back in 1943, when he was a test pilot for Douglas, Luft took one of the first A-20s on a ferry flight to Daggett, California. On his final approach, a fuel line fitting broke. He got the plane down but, with the left engine on fire, had to crawl out through the flames. He got most of the way before realizing he was caught by the leg straps of his harness. Hanging out the cockpit upside down, he had to crawl back inside the burning plane to free his feet from the straps. In the final years of his marriage to Garland, he must have occasionally felt he

247

was reliving that moment on an endless loop: He'd try to exit but snag on something on the way out and crawl back in to get burned up all over again.

In the end, the security guards threw him out of the house. Judy took the kids to London and married a guy called Mark Herron. He recommended a young pianist called Peter Allen to Judy, and Judy in turn pressed him on her daughter Liza. Herron carried on a sexual relationship with Allen during their respective marriages to Judy and Liza. One is all for being broad-minded and sophisticated about these things and Peter Allen was certainly a fetching young Aussie hunk back in those days, but, measured only by the careless damage to others, Sid Luft can stake a plausible claim to being the least worst man in Judy Garland's life.

He remained in Hollywood and, though no ship ever quite came in, he stayed afloat. A couple of years ago, my colleague at the *Telegraph* in London, Michael Shelden, asked him how he did it. "Well," said Sid, "I made money on horses and - oh, yeah - I once helped a guy try to sell Indonesia an air force."

Easier than managing Judy, I'd bet.

He proved the canniest steward of her legacy. The TV specials and weekly shows are out on DVD, and *A Star Is Born* is lavishly restored with the half-hour Jack Warner cut out, and watching them you can almost forget the camp grotesquerie the Garland story's dwindled down to in the hands of Liza and David Gest. Like daughter like mother, Judy assaulted Sid, but he didn't sue over it. And so history repeats itself: if Judy's decline was the tragedy, Liza's is a farce. Which, when you think about it, is even sadder.

Like many men about town in Swingin' London, Lionel Bart, composer of *Oliver!*, was reported on his death to have been "romantically linked to Judy Garland", a lovely formulation which tells you exactly where his real interests lay. But Sid Luft really was romantically linked to Judy and never quite severed his affections. "She was only five foot tall - just a shrimp of a girl, really - but she had a very sensuous body and, up close, her skin was like porcelain, pure white. I was crazy about her. She had incredibly kissable lips… You don't fall out of love with somebody like her."

The Atlantic Monthly

The local angle

PAULA YATES
APRIL 24TH 1960 ~ SEPTEMBER 17TH 2000

I FEEL THE *National Post* didn't really do justice to Paula Yates, the ageing peroxide-and-pink-tulle "rock chick" whose sudden death in London we reported last week. Paula was the ex-wife of Irish rock star Sir Bob Geldof, late of the Boomtown Rats, and the ex-consort of Australian rock star Michael Hutchence, late in a more permanent sense, and was widely admired by many distinguished Americans, including Andy Warhol, who hailed her first book - a collection of photographs entitled *Rock Stars In Their Underpants* - as "the greatest work of art in the last decade". (The decade in question was the Seventies, so he may well be right.)

But never mind the Yanks, Aussies, and Paddies. The trick in journalism is to find the local angle: What care we for 2,000 dead in a Bangladeshi flood unless the deceased include a couple from Sudbury on a retirement cruise? So today this column is pleased to bring you our exclusive Canadian content - *Paula Yates: The Diefenbaker Connection*. That's to say, Paula was the great-granddaughter of Dief's first campaign manager, back in Prince Albert in the Twenties. Small world, eh?

I think it's safe to say Paula had never heard of her great-grandfather's famous friend. Not because she was, as widely assumed in the obits, an airhead. One may deplore her lack of form in citing Sir Bob's smelliness as a reason for her divorce (apparently he had little interest in personal hygiene, even by British standards). One may disagree with her taste in babies' names (her four daughters are called Fifi Trixibelle, Peaches Honeyblossom, Little Pixie and Heavenly Hiraani Tiger Lily -- eat your heart out, Moon Unit Zappa). One may question the wisdom of her angry rejection of the coroner's suicide verdict after Mr Hutchence was found hanging in a Sydney hotel room. She instead insisted that he had been engaged in an act of auto-erotic asphyxiation that had gone awry: This was all the rage at the time, the British Conservative MP Stephen Milligan having recently been found dead completely nude except for a pair of stockings and a garbage bag on his head; friends explained that Paula had plumped for this theory only to spare her daughter's feelings over the suicide.

But, whatever one feels about a world where auto-erotic asphyxiation is considered a polite evasion, Paula Yates was far from stupid. A few years back, she used to co-host a British TV program called "01" on which I would review West End shows. Off-camera, Paula was very well-informed and rather perceptive on Ibsen and Shaw. But once the cameras started rolling you'd never have known it. She had decided long ago - back around the time she posed for *Penthouse* - that an expertise in Ibsen or Shaw or, indeed, anything could be immensely damaging to one's career prospects. And she was right. Look at me. On the other hand, I'm not dead from an overdose of vodka, heroin and bathroom cleaner.

Paula wasn't a dumb blonde but she played one on TV. In that sense, she showed a shrewder appreciation of the medium's limitations than a genuine airhead such as, say, CBS lamebrain Dan Rather. However, there are two good reasons to believe that, despite her many areas of knowledge, she had nevertheless never heard of John Diefenbaker: One, nobody in Britain's ever heard of any Canadian prime minister other than Trudeau; two, Paula was unaware she was half-Canadian until three years ago when, at the funeral of TV host Hughie Green, the principal eulogist dwelt not on Hughie's achievements in broadcasting or his wartime record but chose instead to reveal that among his lesser-known accomplishments the celebrated legover artist had fathered Paula Yates. Hughie was the unctuous frontman of "Opportunity Knocks!", a hugely successful British talent show on which he introduced the world to any number of stellar talents from a margarine sculptress to Mary ("Those Were The Days")

Hopkin. In any event, when opportunity knocked for Hughie with Paula's mum, he decided not to look a gift horse in the mouth.

Hughie's family were staunch Prairie Tories who named him after his godfather, Sir Sam Hughes, Canada's Minister of Militia during the Great War. He'd spent his early years here, but left school at 12 and went on the London stage. Then Hitler intervened, Hughie joined the RCAF and spent the war ferrying aircraft across the Atlantic. Afterwards, he tried to make it in Hollywood, but his acting career never recovered from *The Magic Of Lassie* (1950). So he went to Britain and became a huge telly star, discovering along the way that being on TV in a country with only two channels offered boundless, ah, social opportunities. It was while enjoying one such opportunity in a Welsh hotel owned by her parents that he sired Paula.

Finding out who your real father is from the newspaper accounts of his funeral is bound to be disorienting. "Tormented Star Tells Of Her New Anguish!" screamed the tabloids, though, actually, Paula sounded rather stoic. "I would have preferred Tom Jones," she said, mainly because she'd always thought "Opportunity Knocks!" was crap. For 37 years, she'd believed her father was Jess ("The Bishop") Yates, the organ-playing host of a top-rated religious show called "Stars On Sunday". The Bishop's career had come to a sudden end when he was discovered also to be playing his organ with a 16-year-old girl. Nonetheless, he was the only dad Paula had ever known, so she had DNA tests done. Yes, indeed: Hughie Green was her father. Her mother, a former beauty queen who now lives in France writing erotic novels and books about cats and goes under the various names of Helene Thornton, Heller Thornton and Heller Torren (she was born Elaine Smith), continues to deny that Hughie is Paula's dad, claiming that someone switched the DNA in the lab, though she does vaguely remember waking up in bed one night a few weeks after the wedding with husband Jess on her left and Hughie on her right.

Jess had the last laugh, becoming producer of Hughie's game show, sacking Hughie's favourite singer, forcing him to wear a purple tie (this was the pre-Regis era) and eventually getting him cancelled.

Hughie denounced the new school of TV shows as "filthy and salacious", though in 1978 he accepted the part of talk-show host Bob Scratchit in a soft-porn movie called *What's Up, Superdoc?* The last time I saw him he was trying to sell a new game-show format called "Find The Lady", in which the audience had to identify which of the 16 women was a transvestite.

One of the (on balance) beneficial effects of celebrity in Britain is the pull of respectability. A few years ago, I happened to be attending the annual summer party thrown by another TV host, Sir David Frost, and was deep in conversation with Paula's soon-to-be-ex, Sir Bob Geldof, and the lyricist Sir Tim Rice, who'd just won an Oscar for "A Whole New World" from *Aladdin*. "Jaysus, that's a shite song," said Sir Bob. "How much you going to make from it?"

"Oh, about six million quid," said Sir Tim airily. I may be doing the song an injustice: possibly it was six hundred million. Sir Andrew Lloyd Webber approached: "Sir Timothy!" he cried, with mock formality.

"Sir Andrew!" responded Sir Tim, with an elaborate Gilbert-and-Sullivan bow.

"Do you realize," Sir Bob said to me, "you're the only one of us without a fokking knighthood, you useless fokker?"

Sad but true. It's been years since Sir Bob made a decent CD. Indeed, his last decent CD was so long ago it was a decent LP. He probably doesn't even enjoy oral sex from groupies in limos these days, which was how he happened to meet Paula. He collects art, has a TV production company, does his bit for charity. Yawn. Even Madonna, since moving to London, has begun giving prissy interviews deploring the excess of sexual exploitation in our culture. Some material girls handle their blonde ambition better than others.

The last I heard, Paula Yates' half-brother, Hughie Green's son, was living in Montreal. Probably a wise move. I have no lessons to offer from the respective fates of Hughie and Paula, other than the observation that it's probably better to name your child for Sir Sam Hughes than to call her Heavenly Hiraani Tiger Lily. Both Paula, her men, her mum, her assumed dad and her real dad led weird joke lives of such lurid intensity that they seem only to exist for the purpose of filling up the tabloids. But before the rock stars in their underpants, the auto-erotic asphyxiation, the margarine sculptress, the soft-porn movie, the Bishop locking his little girl in the closet while he played his Wurlitzer, before all that, there was a perfectly ordinary Canadian family out stumping for John Diefenbaker in Prince Albert in 1925. Which is a useful reminder that even Fleet Street's cartoon celebs started out, long ago, as real human beings.

The National Post

WHIPS *&* Scorns

Old-school copper

JACK SLIPPER
APRIL 20TH 1924 ~ AUGUST 24TH 2005

"H E WAS ALWAYS affable and very much a gentle giant," said Bruce Reynolds. "He was one of the old school," agreed one of Mr Reynolds' colleagues.

Gentlemen publishers? Art dealers? Yes, Mr Reynolds has a small antiques business in south London these days, but he was being quoted in his capacity as mastermind of Britain's Great Train Robbery. His colleague is a rather less revered member of the United Kingdom's criminal class. And the man they were eulogizing was Slipper of the Yard - Detective Chief Superintendent Jack Slipper, the last British police detective to become a household name. If *Slipper Of The Yard* sounds vaguely like a 1950s British movie – black-&-white crime thriller, decent old stick of a copper, girlfriend one of those burly English birds radiating health rather than sex, you catch it late at night in some motel and stick around waiting for the gunfire to start, but it never does, except for a single shot in the final reel when the sweaty rodent-like villain panics – well, Jack Slipper certainly looked the part of the Scotland Yard man. Ex-RAF, he was a tall man with copper-sized boots (size 12 in British, 14 in American) and a bristly pencil moustache. The 'tache was standard-issue for police detectives when he started, though his was a rare survivor by the time he retired in 1980.

If Slipper was indeed an old-school copper, Reynolds and co were old-school robbers, remnants of not exactly an age of innocence, but a time many Britons now look back on fondly: the cops didn't carry guns and neither did the robbers; the former were known as the "Old Bill", the latter were "diamond geezers", and, when the Bill collared one of the ne'er-do-wells, he'd say, "You're nicked, chummy" and the geezer would respond, "It's a fair cop, guv." The moral contradictions of this era of British crime are summed up in misty Cockney reminiscences of the psychopathic Kray twins: Lovely boys, proper gentlemen, always treated everyone with perfect manners – well, except for the people they killed. Years ago, I used to date a nurse at the Royal London Hospital and, after her shift, we'd go for a drink round the corner at the Blind Beggar, an East End landmark famed for one night in the Sixties when Ronnie Kray strolled in the pub and shot his gangland rival George Cornell between the eyes. The jukebox was playing the Walker Brothers' Number One hit "The Sun Ain't Gonna Shine Anymore". "The sun ain't gonna shine for him anymore," said Ronnie.

Nor, in the end, for British gangland's reputation as a playground for lovable rogues. Today, London has worse property crime than New York, the diamond geezers have been succeeded by Jamaican drug gangs – "Yardies", with Uzis – and, if you take the East London Line to Whitechapel for a pint at the Blind Beggar, remember that since the July 7th bombings the Metropolitan Police have a shoot-to-kill policy on the Tube. But somewhere in its folk memory much of Britain still holds a soft spot for the lads responsible for the events of August 8th 1963. That's when Bruce Reynolds and his comrades pulled off the Great Train Robbery, seizing the Royal Mail express from Scotland to London as it passed through Buckinghamshire and getting away with £2.6 million in used notes, which was quite a sum in 1963 and today translates to about $75 million.

They'd cleaned out the train without firing a single gunshot, but the driver, Jack Mills, was uncooperative and one of the gang brutally whacked him with a cosh. Nevertheless, at a time of imperial decline abroad and government scandal at home the public seemed to take a perverse patriotic pleasure in the crime. *Pace* Dean Acheson, Britain may have lost an empire but it had found its rolling stock - stripped clean with immense boldness and panache. "Britons may not admit they are proud," wrote *The Daily Telegraph* of Sydney, "but in private many are thinking 'For they are jolly good felons'."

If only they'd planned the post-robbery phase as efficiently. Investigation of the Great Train Robbery fell to the Sweeney – the Metropolitan Police's mobile armed-robbery division, the Flying Squad ("Sweeney" is Cockney rhyming slang: Sweeney Todd = Flying Squad). Among the six detectives assigned to the case was a junior sergeant called Jack Slipper, who got his first break when a woman called Charmaine Biggs went on a shopping spree in a fancy West End store and paid in cash. Her husband was a petty criminal called Ronnie Biggs, and when he returned home on September 4th Detective Sergeant Slipper was waiting for him. The Great Train Robbery had been cracked within a month. The following April Biggs and the others were sentenced to 30 years in jail.

He didn't stay long. After 15 months, Biggs escaped from Wandsworth Prison, getting over the wall with a rope ladder and then dropping into a waiting furniture van with a hole in its roof. He skipped to France, then Spain, Australia and finally Brazil, where in 1974 he renewed his acquaintance with Slipper of the Yard. Tipped off by a *Daily Express* reporter that Biggs was holed up in Rio, the detective flew out on a secret mission to recapture his man. The fugitive opened his hotel room door to be confronted by a most unBrazilian-looking cove with a familiar pencil moustache. "Long time no see, Ronnie," said Slipper, a line he'd apparently rehearsed.

"Fuck me," said Ronnie, a more spontaneous reaction.

That's a vernacular expression indicating amazement, not an invitation – and, in any case, the position was already taken, by a samba dancer called Raimunda, as Slipper was shortly to discover. The copper and his junior colleague, Sergeant Jones, cuffed their man and took him to the Copacabana police station. Big mistake. Slipper had neglected to look into whether Britain and Brazil had an extradition treaty – they didn't – and by the time the authorities came to make their decision Raimunda had revealed she was carrying Ronnie's child. As the soon-to-be-father of an impending Brazilian citizen, Biggs could not be deported. With the spectacular front-page undercover swoop reduced to an interminable extradition case, the coppers took a plane back to Heathrow. In the middle of the flight, when Sergeant Jones got up to head for the washroom, a *Daily Mail* photographer pounced. The picture appeared in the following day's paper: Slipper dozing next to "The Empty Seat", as the headline put it. Slipper of the Yard was now Slip-Up of the Yard, a bungler who let Britain's most wanted man slip through his fingers. Biggs' Javert was transformed overnight into Inspector Clouseau.

They made a BBC drama about the incident a few years later, and Slipper successfully sued over his portrayal as a bumbling flatfoot. He complained about material such as the scene in a Rio bar where he orders "uno beero and another uno beero", and then turns to his sergeant and mutters, "You see what we're up against, Peter. They only talk Brazilian down here." The screenwriter Keith Waterhouse recalls Slipper as a minefield of malapropisms who told him, "No one minds a bit of dramatic licentiousness, Keith, but you have made me out to be a right prat."

By then Slipper of the Yard was the Tom Hanks figure in *Catch Me If You Can* – an earnest plodder in a raincoat. And Biggs, though no Leonardo diCaprio, was the larky chancer who'd got away with it, and escaped dreary old England for a life of dramatic licentiousness in Latin America – non-stop booze'n'birds and an endless parade of fawning tourists and minor celebrities. He had a cameo in the Sex Pistols movie *The Great Rock'n'Roll Swindle*, and made a record with the German rock band Die Toten Hosen. One of the last gatherings of the old London underworld was Biggs' 70th birthday, when Pretty Boy Roy, who killed a man with his bare hands, and Dodgy Dave Courtney, who attacked five Chinese waiters with a meat cleaver, jetted in to pay court. The gifts included a pair of slippers in honour of Ronnie's flatfooted nemesis.

In fact, Jack Slipper was a brilliant policeman, and had been ever since he was a young officer on traffic duty outside the Royal Albert Hall and leapt on his bike to take down a thug who'd slashed a guardsman's throat. He completed his probation at CID (the Criminal Investigation Department) not in the standard three-to-four years but in what's still an all-time record of just over two. He may have dressed "old school", but he was a very modern policeman. He destroyed the London underworld's "honour among thieves" by assembling a network of "supergrasses" – highly-placed gangland informers. And he cracked one important case after another, from a triple-slaying of unarmed Shepherd's Bush policemen in 1966 to a £12 million Bank of America robbery.

Nevertheless, he accepted that fate had yoked him to the man that got away, and that he'd forever be the straight man in the Biggs'n'Slipper double-act. Happy to fly out to Japan in 1985 for a Nippon Television special, he chit-chatted amiably with his nemesis via satellite link-up to Brazil. "How are you getting on?" asked Slipper, sounding to *The Guardian*'s Tokyo correspondent like a genial headmaster running into an old pupil.

"I'm getting on very well indeed," said Biggs. A few years later, a retired Slipper went to Rio to see for himself. "His villa was bog-standard and in the wrong end of town. His swimming pool was so black with algae even a stickleback couldn't live in it. He was flogging T-shirts to tourists to make a living."

Ronnie's Brazilian son had been a child pop star, Little Biggs, for a couple of years, but that was over. And in the end sun-drenched days and bossa-nova beach babes in minimal thongs are small consolation if you're pining for a warm pint and a Marmite sandwich. Over a beer, Slipper asked, "So Ronnie, does crime pay?" Biggs shook his head. "I've left my family and my home. I've got nothing left." In 2001, broke and sick, he returned to Britain after 13,068 days on the run to serve his remaining 28 years in jail - because the prison hospital was the only way he could get access to medical treatment. The Great Train Robber had finally hit the buffers.

Golfing away in retirement, the dogged copper said he wouldn't join the police now, it was "too political". Today's famous British bobbies are self-flagellating administrators, like the former subordinate of Slipper's turned Metropolitan Police Commissioner, Sir Ian Blair, and his deputy, Brian Paddick, "London's senior gay policeman". For Blair and Paddick, policing seems to involve mainly berating themselves for their force's "systemic racism" and "homophobia". Out in the shires, chief constables respond to the July 7th bombings by issuing mandatory green ribbons to their officers so they can show solidarity with British Muslims worried about "Islamophobia". Jack Slipper was "old school" enough to think that the best form of community outreach was to lower the crime rate. And there's not been much of that in the British police recently: long time no see, as he would have said. Slipper of the Yard will be the last detective so styled. To today's Scotland Yard, it sounds vaguely parodic. Which, of course, is a big part of the problem.

The Atlantic Monthly

Death of a salesman

ARTHUR MILLER
OCTOBER 17TH 1915 ~ FEBRUARY 10TH 2005

TTENTION must be paid. That's the line. And, if you missed
it this last week, well, you weren't paying attention. It was the
headline in *The Christian Science Monitor*, and *The New York
Times*: "Attention Must Be Paid." California's *Contra Costa Times* went
with: "'Attention Must Be Paid' To Playwright". And *The Chicago
Tribune* saved it for the slow-motion elephantine punchline of its
opening paragraph: "The Man who wrote *Death Of A Salesman* died
Thursday. And attention must be paid."

In Britain, they paid even more attention. For a couple of
decades, the National Theatre's given the impression it would be happy
to stage *Arthur Miller's Notes To The Milkman*, preferably as a trilogy.
There is, of course, an Arthur Miller Centre for the Advancement of
American Studies at the University of East Anglia, which is located – as
his most recent biographer Martin Gottfried puts it – "in Norwich,
outside of London". Close enough - and, proximity-wise, certainly
closer than the British director David Thacker's assessment of Miller as
just below Shakespeare. "He is as great as any writer in the history of
playwriting," declared Thacker.

The attention-getter comes from Linda Loman, in her famous
speech rebuking her sons for disdaining their father, the eponymous
salesman facing his eponymous death:

> *He's not the finest character that ever lived. But he's a human
> being and something terrible is happening to him. So attention
> must be paid. He's not to be allowed to fall into his grave like an
> old dog. Attention, attention must be finally paid to such a
> person.*

If there were other memorable lines in the Miller oeuvre, his obituarists seemed disinclined to wander over to the dictionary of quotations and look them up. And in fairness – like "Bob Hope: Thanks For The Memories!" and "Sinatra: He Did It His Way" – the ubiquitous send-off did capture, in its relentless hectoring, something of the essence of the man and his writing. The other word was "moralist": He was the "Moral Voice Of The American Stage" (the *New York Times* headline) with "A Morality That Stared Down Sanctimony" (another *New York Times* headline: you can never run enough Arthur Miller appreciations). "Moralist" in this instance is code for "leftie". For some reason editors and critics were a little touchy about the suggestion that there might be any partisan political characterization to his decade-in decade-out unchanging "indictment of the sad, hollow center of the American Dream" (*The Atlanta Journal-Constitution*).

That, by the way, would be a better name for his Centre for the Advancement of American Studies: the Arthur Miller Sad Hollow Centre of the American Dream, Norwich, near London. But that's why attention's paid: The author of *The Crucible* gave the American left its enduring metaphor for the McCarthy era – the witch hunts – and, indeed, for the post-9/11 Bush-Ashcroft reign of terror, and for terrors yet to come. It's the all-purpose portable metaphor for anti-Americanism.

I tired of his plays long before the politics. In London in the Eighties and Nineties, there seemed to be a new Arthur Miller every month, until they all blurred into one unending premiere – *The Ride Down Mt Morgan*, *The Last Yankee*, *The American Clock*, *Broken Glass*, *The Last American*, *The Ride Down Broken Glass*, *The Last Yankee Down Mt Morgan*, *The American Yankee*, *Broken Clock*, all playing like scenes that Elia Kazan or Jed Harris cut from the out-of-town try-outs of his early hits, all circling back not just to the same broad themes but the same plot – loss of respect of one's children – and the same resolution - suicide – and, when the cupboard got really bare, the same character – his ever marketable ex-, Marilyn Monroe. Broadway, wisely, decided that if every new Miller piece played like a revival, you might as well stick to reviving the old stuff.

On his trips to Britain, he liked to say that London still had "plays" whereas Broadway only had "shows". Given that at the time London had *Cats* and *Starlight Express*, and Broadway had nothing to compete, this didn't seem a very helpful distinction. But it's a useful insight into what's wrong with his playwriting. All his plays could do with being a bit more of a show – that's to say, fine, wallop us over the head with the big preachy indictment of the hollow American Dream for an hour or two, but then lighten up for ten minutes; give us something witty, playful, flirtatious. Vary the tone, vary the tempo. But, as Noel Coward might have observed after visiting the Arthur Miller Centre for Sad Hollow Indictments, "Very flat, Norwich."

Happily for him, Miller's utter humourlessness was taken merely as further evidence of his great "moral" seriousness; his tin ear for the rhythm of American speech was mistaken for poetry; and nobody seemed to mind that, excepting Willy Loman, his characters were thin, and his female ones even more emaciated, especially the ones based on Marilyn. "It is astonishing," wrote *The New Republic*'s Robert Brustein in his review of *After The Fall* (1968), "that he could live with this unfortunate woman for over four years and yet be capable of no greater insights into her character." It requires some perverse skill to be able to demolish even Marilyn Monroe as a stage presence, but in his multiple attempts Miller never failed to snuff her candle in his windiness. In the reflected glow of their celebrity marriage, Marilyn humanized him to the American public a lot more than he ever managed to humanize her on stage.

But there were always the revivals. The playwright's most lucrative year was 1984, when Dustin Hoffman starred in *Salesman* on Broadway. Miller may have disliked shows, but he understood show business. He and Hoffman cut themselves in as co-producers with Robert Whitehead, who did most of the actual producing. After the opening, the other two strongarmed Whitehead into agreeing to a dramatic reduction of his share of the take – Hoffman and Miller would each get 45 per cent of the production's profits, leaving ten for Whitehead. "Arthur likes money," said Whitehead. And there are few surer get-rich-quick schemes than a savage indictment of the cheap hucksterism at the heart of the American Dream.

"Willy was a salesman," says Charley at the climax of the play. "He don't put a bolt to a nut, he don't tell you the law or give you medicine. He's a man way out there in the blue, riding on a smile and a shoeshine."

Frances Fitzgerald lifted the line for her account of President Reagan in his Star Wars phase – *Way Out There In The Blue*, the simpleton salesman riding space-age fantasy missiles on a smile and a shoeshine. But missile defence is here and the empty suit, the "amiable dunce", brought down the Soviet Union.

Even in his disparagement, Miller was right to grasp that the salesman is a critical American archetype. In the dictatorships he admired, from the USSR to Cuba, you don't need them: there's no competition, no choice, nothing on the shelves, and every checkout line in the supermarket is perforce for five items or less. And, in a one-party state, politicians don't need to be salesmen, either – or at least not to their own people: Gorbachev and Castro were very canny in the way they flattered Miller, understanding that a man of such unbounded self-regard judged the health of nations and political systems in the same way he did the health of the American theatre – by how fulsomely they acknowledge his genius. And Fidel and Gorby were applauding long after Broadway had fallen silent.

He wasn't amiable enough to be an amiable dunce but he was the most useful of the useful idiots. It was an inspired move to recast the Communist "hysteria" of the 1950s as the Salem witch trials of the 1690s. Many people have pointed out the obvious flaw – that there were no witches, whereas there were certainly Communists. For one thing, they were annexing a lot of turf: they seized Poland in 1945, Bulgaria in '46, Hungary and Romania in '47, Czechoslavakia in '48, China in '49; they very nearly grabbed Greece and Italy; they were the main influence on the nationalist movements of Africa and Asia.

Imagine the Massachusetts witch trials if the witches were running Virginia, New York and New Hampshire, and you might have a working allegory. As it is, Miller's play is an early example of the distinguishing characteristic of the modern western left: its hermetically sealed parochialism. His genius was to give his fellow lefties what's become their most cherished article of faith – that any kind of urgent national defence is, by definition, paranoid and hysterical. It was untrue in the Fifties and it's untrue today. Indeed, the hysteria about hysteria – the "criminalization" of "dissent" - is far more hysterical than the hysteria about Reds.

The Crucible will survive because it's the clip-on bow-tie of left-wing agitprop: whatever suit you're pressing you can attach it to and it functions no better or worse than to anything else, mainly because it's perfectly pitched to the narcissism of the left. As for *Salesman*, I agree with *The Wall Street Journal*'s Terry Teachout that it works because, underneath its pretensions to forensic realism, it's grossly sentimental. What else is that "attention must be paid" moment about? But I'd happily have a bet with David Thacker that in 20 years even the subsidized Brits will have given up on their favourite heavy-handed doctrinaire American leftist. And round about 2020 the Arthur Miller Centre will be running a week of lectures headlined, "Why Is Attention Not Being Paid?"

The Spectator

The last Edwardian

MICHAEL WHARTON
APRIL 19TH 1913 ~ JANUARY 23RD 2006

IN HIS FAMOUS Publisher's Statement in the first issue of *National Review*, William F Buckley Jr declared that his magazine "stands athwart history, yelling Stop". I'm not sure he meant it even then, and certainly he's availed himself of many innovations of the modern age in the years since, including television and computers.

By contrast, Michael Wharton did mean it. He had no use for television, and never watched it unless he happened to be in a room in which the "receiving apparatus" was present. His conservatism was founded on the proposition that "all change is for the worse", and thus history should have stopped round about the year he was born – 1913. For a British writer truly determined to stand athwart the march of time yelling stop, there are two ways to go: you can create an idealized Edwardian England, as P G Wodehouse did, though he preferred to live on Long Island. Or you can revel in your latterday dystopia, inventing a range of fantastical characters emblematic of England's decline. That's the path Michael Wharton chose, under the pseudonym "Peter Simple" in the country's bestselling broadsheet *The Daily Telegraph*.

For 49 years – from New Year's Day 1957 to the column filed four days before his death in January - Wharton chronicled British life as a satirical fantasia through the eyes of Dr Spacely-Trellis, "the go-ahead Bishop of Bevindon" and author of *God The Humanist*; the environmental consultant Keith Effluvium; Dr Heinz Kiosk, psychiatric advisor to the Ministry of Agriculture and many other prestigious bodies, with his great cry of "We are all guilty!"; Mrs Dutt-Pauker, "the Hampstead thinker", and prototype of what Americans would call "limousine liberals", who champions the world's most deserving causes from her North London mansion Marxmount; the hard-hitting Fleet Street columnist Jack Moron, "The Man Who Knows It All", with his mostly unheeded clarion call, "Wake Up, Britain!"; Sir Herbert Trance, of the British Boring Board of Control, whose deliberations, reported by Wharton's correspondent "Narcolept", determined which modish transgressive cause was now sufficiently tedious to be admitted to the torpor of their hallowed if drowsy precincts. For the country's burgeoning "race relations industry", Wharton invented the Prejudometer, which simply by being pointed at any individual could calculate degrees of racism to the nearest prejudon, "the internationally recognized scientific unit of racial prejudice".

If the professional grievance industry, tabloid blowhards, trendy clerics, eco-zealots, pampered progressives and psychobabbling social-pseudo-scientists seem rather obvious targets in 2006, well, most of Wharton's cast of characters were in place by the early Sixties, and he had the melancholy satisfaction of spending the next 40 years watching the real world remorselessly close the gap with satiric invention. The "go-ahead Bishop of Bevindon" eventually acquired a "partner", Dr Mantissa Shout, but the gay Bishop of New Hampshire's explanation to the Episcopal Synod that sex with his own long-term partner was "sacramental" must have had Simple fearing for the future of satire. Decades ago, Wharton invented a pliable media-friendly "moderate" Conservative of no fixed beliefs – Jeremy Cardhouse, leader of the Tories for Progress Group – only to see him at the very end of his long life triumphantly anointed as head of the apparently real British Conservative Party under the name "David Cameron".

For most of his time there, the *Telegraph* was not known as a home of "good writing". Indeed, it was a point of pride: The paper had no op-ed page and scarce any columnists save for the pseudonymous Wharton. Battered by imperial decline, the "permissive society" and later "political correctness", his middle-class readership were appreciative of Peter Simple, if not always clear on the point of intersection between reality and the author's imagination. A reference

269

to the book *The Naked Afternoon Tea* by Henry Miller prompted many complaints from frustrated readers that the volume appeared to be unavailable in any store.

Much of Peter Simple's world revolved around "the Stretchford conurbation" in the industrial heart of England, a grim conglomeration of boroughs, from Nerdley to Soup Hales, centered on "lovely sex maniac-haunted Sadcake Park", "the iron lung of Stretchford", and the dozens if not hundreds of universities with which the conurbation was endowed. There was no conceivable ethnic minority unrepresented among its terrace houses. In 1991, Harold Pinter, who is a real person and not a fictional character, decided to oppose the grotesque half-millennial celebrations of Columbus' discovery – whoops, "discovery" – of the Americas by launching a group called "Five Hundred Years Of Resistance". Immediately, Stretchford's Aztec community, descendants of settlers who'd crossed the Atlantic in stone boats in the Dark Ages and settled in the West Midlands of England, announced their support for Pinter's campaign. Their leader, a 43-year old 25th-year sociology student at Nerdley University, offered the playwright the high honor of being the principal sacrifice on their anti-Columbus step-pyramid, assuming their grant from Nerdley Arts came through.

Stretchford's mercantile establishment coped with a changing Britain as best they could. At the start of the Iraq war in 2003, Sir Edwin Goth-Jones, chairman of the Stretchford Tourist Board, announced plans for VI Day – Victory over Iraq:

> *My aim is to stage a celebration which will be worthy of the victory of good over evil but at the same time will avoid triumphalism... In the event of victory by Saddam Hussein, the above arrangements will be cancelled. No monies can be refunded.*

Wharton himself was opposed to the invasion of Iraq. He despised the "war on terror" as an obvious bit of weasely obfuscation. There was no neo- in his conservatism and his antipathy to Bush was muted only by his more generalized dislike of the American imperium, reflected in his reprinting of "thoughtful" editorials from *The Feudal Times And Reactionary Herald*. On the 2003 trip to London by the President - or, as the *Feudal Times'* editors put it, "the leader of the North American rebel colonists":

> *Many of our readers will recall the visit of a previous rebel leader, Woodrow Wilson, in 1918... It followed the disastrous entry of American forces into the Great War as it neared its end, which let loose a whole series of calamities when the colonists' leader, in his self-righteous folly and ignorance of world affairs, preached 'self-determination for all nations' and approved the tragic collapse of the Austro-Hungarian Empire and other noble and historical institutions, with consequences that are with us to this day.*

Which was more or less how he felt. Like Wodehouse, his idealized England was the last Edwardian summer, the sun-dappled lawns of 1914. The first volume of his autobiography, *The Missing Will*, begins with a superb evocation of his ancestral home – the great house and gardens, the long gallery with its portraits of ancient forebears – and young Michael's earliest childhood memory, the telegram from the Western Front bearing the news that his brother, the Viscount, was dead.

And then the scene dissolves, and Michael Bernard Nathan is born in rather more modest circumstances in Shipley to a German-Jewish father and a mother with a broad working-class Yorkshire accent. It was after Oxford in the early Thirties that he adopted his mum's maiden name of Wharton. No friend of Israel, indifferent to charges of racism and anti-Semitism, Wharton-Nathan would be an easy case for a Dr Heinz Kiosk: the exile who doesn't quite fit in who converts himself into a parodic English xenophobe only to discover that he too no longer fits in. His second volume of autobiography includes a passage where he threatens to cut his son off without a penny for changing his surname back to Nathan. Is he really that twitchy about his Jewishness? Or is it just another joke? Or is not making it quite clear which it is the best joke of all?

In the course of his 92 years, Wharton wrote millions of words and said hardly any. W F Deedes, the model for William Boot in Evelyn Waugh's great novel of British journalism *Scoop* (1938) and still a columnist at the *Telegraph* today, went to interview the elderly cherub for his 90th birthday and had to crowbar out every three-word response – most of them "I suppose so" and similar. "You were a Colonel in the last war?"

"Yes, but only in Intelligence," he replied, as if, wrote Deedes, "it had been reserved for men of low mental ability". Even then, he found himself oddly drawn to his nation's enemies. In an idle moment, he invented a fanatical one-eyed general in Hirohito's Imperial High Command consumed by a visceral hatred of England after a brief stay in Harrogate. He genuinely admired the Serbs, as the chaps who held the line against the marauding Turk so gallantly, but other than that he had a preference for unsympathetic lost causes – Ulster Unionists, white Rhodesians, etc. He had a sneaking respect for the bloodier aspects of Islam, but the British left embraced the jihad so wholeheartedly it was hard for him to get a word in.

The gulf between Wharton and Peter Simple was largely unknown to his devoted suburban readers. For several decades of his adult life, he operated an "open marriage". His memoirs detail his second wife's 20-year affair with another well-known journalist, "a man I liked and admired, an honorable man", who eventually comes to Wharton and says: "I will ask you a question. If you answer 'yes', the affair will go no further. Do you love Kate?"

Wharton mulls it over and answers: "No." The scene has odd echoes of that cruel moment in Evelyn Waugh's cruelest novel, *A Handful Of Dust*, and it makes you wonder whether Wharton might also have had a great novel in him. He pondered that question, too – after all, his equally fictional columnar colleague at the *Telegraph*, Bridget Jones, jumped to hard covers and the silver screen. But he consoled himself in later years with the thought that, even if he had been a hugely famous novelist, he'd undoubtedly have outlived his success and been washed up by now. Instead, he kept going up to the Friday before his death on the Monday. In the last days of his life, two of the four leadership candidates for the Liberal Democrat Party were outed for consorting with rent boys and calling gay chat lines, and a gay Conservative leapt to their defense by arguing that sexual recklessness went hand in hand with political courage, citing as evidence his own experience of oral sex in the office of a Minister of the Crown.

It was a good week for a satirist to check out.

As he wrote of Alderman Foodbotham, "the 25-stone, crag-visaged, iron-watch-chained, grim-booted perpetual chairman of the Bradford City tramways and fine arts committee":

According to legend, he did not die, but lies asleep in a convenient cave, awaiting the blast of a horn, mill-hooter or other appropriate instrument which will summon him to wake and save his city and his country in their hour of greatest need.

But the hour is late and few believe in the legend any longer.

The Atlantic Monthly

SHATTER'D & *Sunder'd*

A death in Iraq

KENNETH BIGLEY
1942 ~ OCTOBER 7TH 2004

FOR THE FIRST time in all my years with the Telegraph Group, I had a column pulled today. The editor expressed concerns about certain passages and we were unable to reach agreement, so on this Tuesday something else will be in my space.

I'd written about Kenneth Bigley, seized with two American colleagues but unlike them not beheaded immediately. Instead, sensing that they could exploit potential differences within "the coalition of the willing", the Islamists played a cat-and-mouse game with Mr Bigley's life, in which Fleet Street, the British public, governments in London and Dublin and Islamic lobby groups in the United Kingdom were far too willing to participate. As I always say, the point is not whether you're sad about someone's death, but what you're prepared to do about it. What "Britain" – from Ken Bigley's brother to the Foreign Secretary – did was make it more likely that other infidels will meet his fate*.

I suppose the *Telegraph* felt it was a little heartless. Well, tough. This is a war, and misplaced mawkishness will lead to more deaths. In August 2001, I wrote as follows about the first anniversary of 9/11, when coverage was threatening to go the way of Princess Di and mounds of teddy bears:

> *Three thousand people died on September 11th, leaving a gaping*
> *hole in the lives of their children, parents, siblings and friends.*
> *Those of us who don't fall into those categories are not bereaved*

---

* A couple of weeks later, the kidnapping and murder of Margaret Hassan, proved the point. Mrs Hassan was an aid worker, an Iraqi citizen, married to a native Iraqi, and she was opposed to the Bush-Blair intervention. But she chanced to have been born in the United Kingdom, and for her captors – after the Bigley media fest – that was enough.

and, by pretending to be, we diminish the real pain of those who really feel it. That's not to say that, like many, I wasn't struck by this or that name that drifted up out of the great roll-call of the dead. Newsweek's Anna Quindlen 'fastened on', as she put it, one family on the flight manifest:

> *Peter Hanson, Massachusetts*
> *Susan Hanson, Massachusetts*
> *Christine Hanson, 2, Massachusetts*

As Miss Quindlen described them, 'the father, the mother, the two-year old girl off on an adventure, sitting safe between them, taking flight.' Christine Hanson will never be three, and I feel sad about that. But I did not know her, love her, cherish her; I do not feel her loss, her absence in my life. I have no reason to hold hands in a 'healing circle' for her. All I can do for Christine Hanson is insist that the terrorist movement which killed her is hunted down and prevented from targeting any more two-year olds. We honour Christine Hanson's memory by righting the great wrong done to her, not by ersatz grief-mongering.

That's the way I feel about Ken Bigley. Here's the column the *Telegraph* declined to publish:

WHETHER OR not it is, in the technical sense, a "joke", I find myself, with the benefit of hindsight, in agreement with Billy Connolly's now famous observation on Kenneth Bigley – "Aren't you the same as me, don't you wish they would just get on with it?"

Had his killers "just got on with it", they would have decapitated Mr Bigley as swiftly as they did his two American confrères. But, sensing that there was political advantage to be gained in distinguishing the British subject from his fellow hostages, they didn't get on with it, and the intervening weeks reflected poorly on both Britain and Mr Bigley.

None of us can know for certain how we would behave in his circumstances, and very few of us will ever face them. But, if I had to choose the very last last words I'd want to find myself uttering in this life, "Tony Blair has not done enough for me" would be high up on the list. First, because it's the all but official slogan of modern Britain, the dull rote whine of the churlish citizen invited to opine on waiting lists or public transport, and thus unworthy of the uniquely grisly situation in which Mr Bigley found himself. And, secondly, because those words are so at odds with the spirit of a life spent, for the most part, far from these islands, first as a "ten pound pom" in Oz and New Zealand, and later in more exotic outposts of empire. Ken Bigley seems to have found contemporary Britain a dreary, insufficient place and I doubt he cared about who was Prime Minister from one decade to the next. Had things gone differently and had his fate befallen some other expatriate, and had he chanced upon a month-old London newspaper in his favourite karaoke bar up near the Thai-Cambodian border and read of the entire city of Liverpool going into a week of Dianysian emotional masturbation over some deceased prodigal son with no inclination to return whom none of the massed ranks of weeping Scousers from the Lord Mayor down had ever known, Mr Bigley would surely have thanked his lucky stars that he and his Thai bride were about as far from his native sod as it's possible to get.

While Ken Bigley passed much of his life as a happy expat, his brother Paul appears to have gone a stage further and all but seceded. Night and day, he was on TV explaining to the world how the Bigley family's Middle East policy is wholly different from Her Majesty's Government – a Unilateral Declaration of Independence accepted de facto by Mr Blair's ministry when it dispatched Jack Straw to Merseyside to present formally his condolences to the Bigleys, surely the most extraordinary flying visit ever undertaken by a British Foreign Secretary. For their pains, the government was informed by Paul Bigley that the Prime Minister had "blood on his hands". This seems an especially stupid and contemptible formulation when anyone with an Internet connection can see Ken Bigley's blood and the hand it's literally on holding up his head.

It reminded me of Robert Novak of *The Chicago Sun-Times* back in May, quoting "one senior official of a coalition partner" calling for the firing of Donald Rumsfeld on the grounds that "there must be a neck cut, and there is only one neck of choice."

At pretty much that exact moment in Iraq, Nick Berg's captors were cutting his head off - or, rather, feverishly hacking it off while raving "*Allahu akbar!*" - God is great. The difference between the participants in this war is that on one side robust formulations about "blood on his hands" and "calls for the Defence Secretary's head" are clichéd metaphors, and on the other they mean it.

Paul Bigley can be forgiven his clumsiness: he's a freelancer winging it. But the feelers put out by the Foreign Office to Ken Bigley's captors are more disturbing: by definition, they confer respectability on the head-hackers and increase the likelihood that Britons and other foreigners will be seized and decapitated in the future. The United Kingdom, like the government of the Philippines when it allegedly paid a ransom for the release of its Iraqi hostages, is thus assisting in the mainstreaming of jihad.

By contrast with the Fleet Street-Scouser-Whitehall fiasco of the last three weeks, consider Fabrizio Quattrocchi, murdered in Iraq on April 14th. In the moment before his death, he yanked off his hood and cried defiantly, "I will show you how an Italian dies!" He ruined the movie for his killers. As a snuff video and recruitment tool, it was all but useless, so much so that the Arabic TV stations declined to show it.

If the FCO wants to issue advice in this area, that's the way to go: If you're kidnapped, accept you're unlikely to survive, say "I'll show you how an Englishman dies", and wreck the video. If they want you to confess you're a spy, make a little mischief: there are jihadi from Britain, Italy, France, Canada and other western nations all over Iraq – so say yes, you're an MI6 agent, and so are those Muslims from Tipton and Luton who recently joined the al-Qaeda cells in Samarra and Ramadi. As Churchill recommended in a less timorous Britain: You can always take one with you. If Tony Blair and other government officials were to make that plain, that would be, to use Mr Bigley's word, "enough".

And, if you don't want to wind up in that situation, you need to pack heat and be prepared to resist at the point of abduction. I didn't give much thought to decapitation when I was motoring round the Sunni Triangle last year, but my one rule was that I was determined not to get into a car with any of the locals and I was willing to shoot anyone who tried to force me. If you're not, you shouldn't be there.

Perhaps it's easy to say that. Ken Bigley, after all, was blasé about personal security. Tootling around Iraq in his very conspicuous SUV, he told chums, "I'm not afraid. You only die once." In the end, he revised his insouciance, grasping for a shot at a second chance. I know the Ken Bigley on display these last few weeks is not the measure of the man. But that's all the more reason why in dangerous times and dangerous places one should give some thought to what they used to call a "good death". None of the above would have guaranteed Mr Bigley's life, but it would have given him, as it did Signor Quattrocchi, a less pitiful end, and it would have spared the world a glimpse of the feeble and unserious Britain of the last few weeks. The jihadists have become rather adept at devising tests customized for each group of infidels: Madrid got bombed, and the Spaniards failed their test three days later; the Australian Embassy in Jakarta got bombed, but the Aussies held firm and re-elected John Howard's government anyway. With Britain, the Islamists will have drawn many useful lessons from the decadence and defeatism on display.

SteynOnline

A death in Jordan

MOUSTAPHA AKKAD
JULY 1ST 1930 ~ NOVEMBER 11TH 2005

WHEN JOHN Carpenter sold the idea for *Halloween* to Moustapha Akkad, he pitched it to him in one line: "Babysitter to be killed by the bogeyman." "The babysitter part grabbed me," said Akkad, "because every kid in America knows what a babysitter is." The movie became the highest-grossing independent film to date and spawned the most successful of the several franchises in which undeserving victims are butchered at random in archetypal small towns.

By the time the bogeyman came for Moustapha Akkad, he had bigger fish to fry – mass slaughter not of stock types in hick burgs, but of powerful and well-connected elites in Amman's western hotels. On November 9th, a team of suicide bombers dispatched by Abu Musab al-Zarqawi across the Jordanian border self-detonated at the Radisson, the Grand Hyatt and the Days Inn. Akkad was in the country for a high-society wedding and greeting his daughter Rima in the Radisson when Ali Hussein Ali al-Shamari and his wife reached within the folds of their clothing for the explosives belts. The California-raised Rima died first, her father two days later. And so the jihad claimed among its five dozen latest victims Hollywood's most prominent Arab-American.

Like a lot of youngsters, Akkad decided early on that he wanted to be in pictures. The odds aren't helped if you happen to be growing up in Aleppo, in French Syria. But at 18 his father packed him off to Hollywood with $200 in one pocket and the Koran in the other, and the division of his coat contents neatly summed up his work over the next 50 years. Moustapha Akkad made two kinds of movies. As a producer, he delivered slashers to the teen market with an efficiency that made him a very wealthy man: the original *Halloween* cost

$300,000 in 1978 and grossed $47 million. As a director, he wanted to be an Arab David Lean and specialized in films that used Hollywood stars to explain Islam to a wider audience – *The Message* was the life of Mohammed and starred Anthony Quinn; *Lion Of The Desert* celebrated plucky anti-colonial Bedouin fighters, played by Quinn, Oliver Reed and John Gielgud, with members of Arab Equity relegated mostly to the roles of excitable extras; and at the time of his death he was developing a film about Saladin with Sean Connery. It was Akkad's misfortune to have the benign intentions of this half of his canon perpetually tripped up on the way to the multiplex: *The Message* was targeted by angry Muslims who thought the infidel fornicator Quinn was playing Mohammed rather than his uncle, and *Lion Of The Desert* suffered in America from the twin PR setbacks of opening a few months after the Iranian hostage siege and being co-financed by Colonel Gaddafi.

Nonetheless, Akkad persevered. "Islam right now is portrayed as a 'terrorist' religion in the west and by doing this kind of movie, I am portraying the true image," he said of his Saladin project. Long before September 11th, he was always good for a quote bemoaning how Hollywood represented Muslims only as terrorists. "We cannot say there are no Arab and no Muslim terrorists," he told *The New York Times* in 1998. "Of course there are. But at the same time, balance it with the image of the normal human being, the Arab-American, the family man."

He half got his way: movies about the Arab "family man" are still thin on the ground, but the Muslim terrorist has all but disappeared – the film of Tom Clancy's *Sum Of All Fears* de-Islamicized the bad guys and turned them into German neo-Nazis, and Sean Penn's *The Interpreter* eighty-sixed the Muslims and made them terrorists from the little-known African republic of Matobo. Post-9/11 Hollywood perversely recoiled from its preferred villains of the Eighties and Nineties and now your poor Arab thespian can't even get gainful employment as a crazed jihadist. Meanwhile, Akkad saw the Islamophile half of his work gain a new lease of life as Oriental works in an Occidentally accessible form: according to Queen Noor, the Pentagon bought "100,000 copies" of *The Message* to show to US troops before they left for Afghanistan.

And, in the end, for all his efforts, the fellows who murdered Akkad were the most stereotypical Muslim terrorists of all: they behaved more like the psychos in his slasher movies than the noble Bedouin in his Islamic-outreach pictures.

The original *Halloween* introduced us to its highly resilient protagonist in a memorable and effective way: the hand-held Panaglide camera (a state-of-the-art novelty in 1978) roams around; it's as if we're the ones silently prowling the house, entering the kitchen, selecting the knife from the drawer, taking up a plastic clown mask and then pulling it on, so that now we see the action only through two eyeholes – up the stairs, into the bedroom; the girl dishabille at her dressing table turns, half-irritated, and the knife goes in, again and again and again.

The film-maker in Akkad might have found something similar in the husband-and-wife suicide-bomber team who killed him: Mrs al-Shamari entering the Radisson, the camera's eye nervously darting around, shuffling through to the ballroom; the guests standing about, Muslims holding their wedding party in a semi-westernized style, the ladies with bright glossed lips, and coiffed hair bursting through their perfunctory head coverings. What does the jihadist think? Is she disgusted? Or just concentrating on her mission? She struggles with the cord on her explosives belt, but it jams, and she tugs more frantically, and her husband sees her fumbling and pushes her out of the room, either in what passes for gallantry in the death cult or because he's concerned she'll jeopardize the operation. And then he pulls his cord, and he and the wedding party explode.

But Moustapha Akkad made Muslim movies and violent movies and ne'er the twain did meet. His mentor was a master of the latter, Sam Peckinpah. In the late Fifties, the director had in mind a film on the Algerian revolution and asked UCLA to find him someone who knew the turf. The only graduate they had from that neck of the woods was Akkad. The French gave up on Algeria and Peckinpah gave up on the picture, but he kept the young Syrian in tow for a movie called *Ride The High Country* (1962). At dinner in Hollywood, Akkad kept getting asked what he thought of American food, American houses, American girls, so he sold a series to CBS in which a group of foreigners talk about their reactions to American life. Then he did a travel show with Cesar Romero, and pretty soon he had the career they'd said back in Aleppo was impossible: he was a Hollywood moviemaker.

Akkad prided himself on his "duality". "In my house, I am a pure Arab," he told *The Star* in Jordan two years ago. "When I step out, I am thinking like an American." The "pure Arabs" who killed him despise that kind of flexibility, and some Americans would raise an eyebrow at quite how pure an Arab he was in the privacy of his own home. In an interview with Luke Ford for his 2002 book *The Producers*, he agreed with the author's estimate that Hollywood's muscle was "70 per cent Jewish", but reckoned he got along fine as long as you steered clear of certain subjects. "The media runs the world," he said. "No tanks or planes. The media and the public companies. This is what *The Protocols Of Zion* is all about. The Zionists, last century, were persecuted in Europe. So they immigrated to America. They had a target. They were united. They did not permit [statements] critical of Zion. They went all the way to control the world and to control the minds of the people through the media. There's a lesson to learn from them."

Anyone who's spent any time in the Middle East will have heard that, from Saudi businessmen and Bahraini doctors and Palestinian intellectuals and other urbane educated Arabs of the kind you find in the bars and lounges of Hyatts and Radissons. But the professed admiration for the cunning of the Zionists is a more unexpected cliché from a man enriched by Hollywood whose children went to Los Angeles high schools filled with the progeny of liberal Jews. With hindsight, Akkad's "duality" seems more like professional schizophrenia. And, though he claimed *Halloween* was nothing more than a savvy commercial decision, for a schlock horrorfest it was, at it happens, very Middle Eastern in its pathologies. Its principal character Michael Myers (no relation to *Austin Powers'* Mike Myers, though they're about the same age) begins his impressive tally of corpses with what can be read as a textbook Muslim "honor killing": Michael stabs his sister to death after she's had sex with her boyfriend. Its conflation of sexual insecurity and male violence is at least as relevant to Arab culture as it is to alienated losers in small-town America. The only difference is that, unlike the various unprosecuted perpetrators of honor killings from Jordan to Pakistan, it's Michael Myers who eventually winds up getting decapitated, in one of *Halloween*'s many sequels. "With *H20* we chopped off his head," exulted Akkad, while leaving himself a loophole. "But was it really his head?"

The "duality" of Mustapha Akkad finally came together in one freakish finale at the Amman Radisson. Yet he'd encountered terrorism once before, nearly 30 years earlier. Many Muslim scholars were outraged by *The Message* – or, as it was then called, *Mohammed, Messenger Of God*. Though Akkad had observed the prohibition against representations of the Prophet, even a rumored glimpse of his shadow (which the director had at one time considered) provoked objections. Hamaas Abdul Khaalis, formerly a Seventh Day Adventist called Ernest McGhee, decided to do something about the abomination. A dozen Muslims seized three buildings in Washington, DC, and took 120 hostages, including (in an early example of the many internal contradictions of the Rainbow Coalition) the future mayor, Marion Barry. He was one of a couple of dozen injured. Jewish hostages were abused. A reporter was killed.

Khaalis had several demands, including a ban on Akkad's movie and the transfer of Muhammed Ali, among others, to his custody. The ambassadors of Egypt, Iran and Pakistan stepped in and drew the kidnappers' attention to Surah 5:2-4 from the Koran:

> *And let not the hatred of some people in shutting you out of the Sacred Mosque lead you to transgression and hostility on your part. Help ye one another in righteousness and piety.*

286

And it worked: Khaalis threw in the towel. Alas, by November 9th 2005, Islamic terrorism had refined its techniques beyond intercession. Explaining the success of the *Halloween* franchise, Mustapha Akkad said, "If you're locked inside a house and there's somebody there who wants to kill you, that could happen to anybody. You can relate." It was the bogeymen closer to home he couldn't relate to.

The Atlantic Monthly

SANCTITY & Space

Moonstruck

BART HOWARD
JUNE 1ST 1915 ~ FEBRUARY 21ST 2004

CCORDING to Johnny Mercer, "Writing music takes more talent, but writing lyrics takes more courage." What he meant was that a tune can be beguiling and melancholy and intoxicating and a lot of other vagaries, but there comes a moment when you have to sit down and get specific, and put the other half of the equation on top of those notes. A songwriter spends his life chasing the umpteenth variation of "I love you", and that takes courage because there's usually a good reason why no one's used your variation before: the thought's too precious, or clunky, or contrived.

Topicality isn't much help. The American telegraph and telephony songs of the 1890s ("I Guess I'll Have To Telegraph My Baby") and the airplane songs of the oughts ("Come, Josephine, In My Flying Machine") seemed like smart moves at the time, but this is one area where the fundamental things apply as time goes by. Moon/June/stars above/so in love, etc.

So in 1953 Bart Howard sat down to write a love song and, for once, as he put it, "it just fell out of me". In 20 minutes, he had a number that was full of all the usual stuff – moon, stars – and yet not so much topical as prescient. It's the only hit he ever wrote, and he didn't need another. He called it "In Other Words".

Never heard of it? That's because Howard didn't know what he was sitting on. What hits you aren't the other words, but the first five:

Fly me to the moon...

You might know it by Peggy Lee, or Tony Bennett, or Dion and the Belmonts, Astrud Gilberto, Marvin Gaye, Diana Krall, or any one of a few hundred others. You might know it from the opening of Oliver

Stone's valentine to the "decade of greed", *Wall Street*: the trains and ferries and buses feed the workers into the city, hundreds and thousands of stick figures, pouring up from the subway tunnels and on to the teeming sidewalks of Lower Manhattan. And above the skyscrapers Count Basie plays and Sinatra sings:

Fly Me To The Moon
Let me play among the stars
Let me see what spring is like
On Jupiter and Mars...

The song makes the scene. Without it, it's nothing: for what's drearier and more earthbound, more literally everyday than commuting? But not when it's accompanied by Basie and Sinatra and a Quincy Jones arrangement that starts low-key with bass and tweeting flutes and surges into blaring brass rocketing into the skies. It's what Nelson Riddle meant when he called his preferred 4/4 swing for Sinatra the "tempo of the heartbeat". It's what Bono had in mind when he said "Frank walks like America. Cocksure." And, of course, it's what Gordon Gekko renders more bluntly in his "greed is good" speech: all the possibilities of the day ahead, all the dreams and ambitions of the anonymous figures on the street articulated in music and, like the buildings, reaching for the stars.

By then, "Fly Me To The Moon" had served as the soundtrack for the fulfilment of the grandest dream of all: In 1969, Buzz Aldrin took a portable tape player up there with him, and "Fly Me To The Moon" became the first moon song to get to the moon itself. "The first music played on the moon," said Quincy Jones. "I freaked."

And none of this is anything Bart Howard had in mind for his song. "I didn't know what I'd written," he told me a few years ago. On his death, NPR's Michelle Norris announced that they'd be paying tribute to "the man who wanted to see what spring is like on Jupiter and Mars". But that's exactly what Howard didn't mean. He couldn't have been less interested in what spring is like on Jupiter and Mars. His little-heard verse sets up the premise:

MOONSTRUCK

Poets often use many words
To say a simple thing
It takes thought and time and rhyme
To make a poem sing
With music and words
I've been playing
For you I have written a song
To be sure that you know what I'm saying
I'll translate as I go along…

Fly Me To The Moon
And let me play among the stars
Let me see what spring is like
On Jupiter and Mars
In Other Words
Hold my hand
In other words
Darling, kiss me…

In other words, Howard wasn't reaching for the stars, but trying to bring the airy, high-flown sentiments of romance back down to earth. He called the song "In Other Words" because that's what it was about – what we're really saying underneath all the "Moonlight Becomes You" starry-eyed hooey. He wrote it for Mabel Mercer, whose accompanist he was in the post-war years, at Tony's on 52nd Street. In its first decade, "In Other Words" was picked up by all Manhattan's cabaret darlings – Kaye Ballard, Felicia Sanders, Portia Nelson. They sang it as it was written, in waltz time, or in a very slow ballad tempo. And, instead of that supreme Sinatra confidence, it sounds wistful and tentative.

Pretty much all Howard's compositions did in those days. His other great flying line comes in another cabaret song called "Walk Up", a recollection of love in a cheap flat up the stairs on the fourth floor: "We'd fly up every night." It's an intimate, rueful lyric, but a little too special, too particular. Howard's cabaret songs from the Fifties seem so specific to that world, and a little exclusive of everybody else's. He wasn't wealthy and nor were his friends, but even a fourth-floor walk-up had a kind of romance to a boy from Burlington, Iowa. "He was the epitome of a certain kind of New York elegance that people that came to New York aspired to," said Jim Gavin, author of *Intimate Nights: The Golden Age Of New York Cabaret*. Howard was homosexual, and that was easier in the city, too.

He started out at 16, playing piano in a dance band through the Depression. Like Bob Hope, he worked with the Siamese twins Violet and Daisy Hilton, accompanying them at the piano through their lively three-legged tap routines. Howard moved on to accompany the drag act Ray Bourbon, and eventually to New York, the Rainbow Room, and the life he'd wanted all along. It's a small, in-the-know world, and "In Other Words" is tailored for it, at least in its suggestion that big, bellowed professions of love are not what really matters.

In 1953, he finished up "In Other Words", and took it to a publisher, who loved everything about it except that first line of the chorus. "Fly me to the moon"? Nobody said "fly me"; it didn't sound right. How about switching it to "Take me to the moon"? Howard resisted, which was just as well. There were over a hundred recordings in the next few years, and the song never did take flight. Then the Sixties came along, and the space race got going, and so did bossa nova, and a chi-chi ballad for the cognoscenti suddenly seemed in tune with the times. Peggy Lee suggested re-naming it "Fly Me To The Moon", and her conductor, Jose Harnell, had an instrumental bossa hit with it.

Basie and Sinatra enlarged the song, opened it up for the world beyond 52nd Street. It's literal now: it flies to the moon, a love song for the space age, a wild ride with a well-stocked wet-bar. In the Nineties, Sinatra did a couple of faux "duet" CDs, in which he recorded his songs solo and Phil Ramone then scrambled around to find supposedly young, supposedly hot acts who could be pasted in to the tracks. For "Fly Me To The Moon", they asked the country singer George Strait, and the strained hipster patter of the intro – George's banter with an absent Frank, a Frank who left the studio months earlier, a Frank who's never even heard of George Strait – sums up, in a desperate wannabe-cool kind of way, the transformation of Bart Howard's little cabaret ballad:

Hey, Francis, I don't know 'bout you but I could use a break...
Maybe a trip or somethin'...

Fly Me To The Moon...

By this time "Fly Me To The Moon" was such a Vegas uber-swinger, the overwrought cabaret songstresses defiantly reclaimed the song, putting it back in three-quarter or ballad time. The critic Will Friedwald says the fast and slow versions are really two separate numbers, respectively "Fly Me To The Moon" and "In Other Words". So Bart Howard achieved a rare distinction: the only one-hit songwriter to get two standards out of his one hit.

It was enough. After the Sinatra recording, he retired on the song, and dabbled in interior decorating for most of the rest of his life: a modest, dapper man who'd written a tune about not flying to the moon that somehow wound up there. Had any other nation beaten Nasa to it, they'd have marked the occasion with the "Ode To Joy" or *Also Sprach Zarathustra*, something grand and formal. But there's something very American about Buzz Aldrin standing on the surface of the moon with his cassette machine: Sinatra "cocksure" in 4/4, with Count Basie and Quincy Jones. The sound of the American century as it broke the bounds of the planet: a Bart Howard song finally playing among the stars.

The Atlantic Monthly

Beam movie star

JAMES DOOHAN
MARCH 3RD 1920 ~ JULY 20TH 2005

SOME MEN ARE born great, some achieve greatness, and some have great catchphrases said to them. James Doohan is an honorary member of that last category. He was the guy who spent four decades on the receiving end of the request to "Beam me up, Scotty" – if not on TV, where no character on *Star Trek* ever actually uttered the words, at least in real life, where fans would cheerfully bark the injunction across crowded airport concourses in distant lands, and rush-hour freeway drivers would lurch across four lanes of traffic to yell it out the window at him. Elvis is said to have greeted him with the phrase, and Groucho, too. There are novels with the title, and cocktails. On Highway 375 to Roswell, New Mexico, you can stop at the Little A-Le-Inn and wash down your Alien Burger with a Beam Me Up, Scotty (Jim Beam, 7 Up and Scotch).

It wasn't supposed to be the catchphrase from the show: that honor was reserved for Gene Roddenberry's portentous sonorous orotund grandiosity – the space-the-final-frontier-boldly-going-where-no-man's-gone-before stuff. The beaming was neither here nor there: it was a colloquialism for matter-energy transit, or teleportation – or, more to the point, a way of getting from the inside of the space ship to the set of the planet without having to do a lot of expensive exterior shots in which you've got to show the USS Enterprise landing and Kirk, Spock et al disembarking. Instead, the crew positioned themselves in what looked vaguely like a top-of-the-line shower, ordered Scotty to make with the beaming, and next thing you know they were standing next to some polystyrene rocks in front of a backcloth whose colors were the only way of telling this week's planet from last week's. "Beaming" was *the* special effect – the one that saved *Star Trek* from having to have any others.

Like all authentic pop-culture moments, it was a happy accident. In September 1966, in the first broadcast episode, they beamed without benefit of Scotty. He showed up in the third, beaming up a destroyed star ship's "space recorder" – ie, a trash can on legs. Would a beam by any other name – Bud, Nigel, Paddy, Miguel - have smelt as sweet? James Doohan was a Canadian of Irish stock, and, as an old CBC radio actor, had a score of accents on tap. Which, he asked Gene Roddenberry, would they like? They left it to him and, because the character was an engineer and the Scots were the great engineers of the British Empire and certainly of Canada, he chose to make his character Scottish and gave it his own middle name – Montgomery Scott. And a minor character somehow evolved into the de facto Number Three on the Enterprise's crew and, as the man responsible for nursing the space ship through whatever cockamamie scheme Captain Kirk was minded to put into action, Scotty over time became the guardian and spirit of the Enterprise itself. "I cannae change the laws of physics for you!" he would protest, before gamely giving it a go.

Star Trek has famously devoted fans – Trekkies or Trekkers: if memory serves, the latter is the preferred term, though the former is the title of Roger Nygaard's full-length documentary on the phenomenon. But "Beam me up" long ago beamed itself off the Enterprise and into the wider world. As great unspoken screen dialogue goes, it's rivaled only by "Play it again, Sam" – and even then "Play it again" has never demonstrated quite the versatility of its rival. In *Every Man's Battle: Winning The War On Sexual Temptation One Victory At A Time*, Stephen Arterburn suggests the phrase as a useful way to keep male appetites in check: if your wife were suddenly "beamed up" into your motel room, would she approve of what you're up to? Something to ponder before you buy the gal in the lobby bar that second margarita, or even press the "order" button on the adult video channel.

On the other hand, Howard Markman, PhD, head of the Center for Marital and Family Studies at the University of Denver, uses "Beam me up, Scotty" as shorthand for a classically uncommunicative male attitude to spousal conflict. Weary of his wife's incessant nagging, the husband rolls his eyes heavenward, murmurs "Get me outta here, somebody", etc. The "beam me up" approach will only make the wife even more enraged.

So "Beam me up, Scotty" can help your marriage or destroy it. You could wind up celebrating your anniversary dancing with your beloved to "Beam Me Up, Scotty" by Tom Rush or nursing the blues in that bar outside Roswell staring into the bottom of your fifth Beam Me Up, Scotty. "This phrase works in almost any situation," writes Dave Marinaccio in *All I Really Need To Know I Learned From Star Trek*. "For example: You've forgotten your spouse's anniversary. At the moment your spouse discovers your blunder, you simply say, 'Beam me up, Scotty'... 'Beam me up, Scotty' is just a way of saying the world is beyond my control." Marinaccio argues it's the pithier version of "God grant me the serenity to accept the things I cannot change..." and the less vulgar and stupid version of "Sh*t happens" – though this suggests a degree of fatalistic acceptance one would not associate with, say, expelled Representative James Traficant's frequent Congressional deployments of the term:

> *Mr Speaker, today Congress will debate two bills. The first bill is partial birth abortions. The second bill is wildlife and sport fish restoration. Unbelievable. Kill the babies but save the trout and the tit mouse. Beam me up. In fact, beam me up, Scotty.*

Or:

> *Think about it. While 60 percent of taxpayer calls to the IRS go unanswered, the IRS agents were watching Marilyn Chambers do the Rotary International. Beam me up here. It is time to pass a flat 15 percent sales tax and abolish this gambling, porno-watching IRS completely.*

BEAM MOVIE STAR

With the Congressional Record awash in "Beam me up, Scottys", eventually somebody decided it was time for *Star Trek* to put the famous words belatedly in Captain Kirk's mouth. So, after the best part of quarter of a century, he finally delivered them to his engineer in the fourth *Trek* movie. By then, Scotty felt about Kirk the way Jim Traficant felt about the IRS porn junkies. Jim Doohan never cared for William Shatner, the ranking Canadian on the bridge of the Enterprise, and would gladly have beamed him out for good. He was unable to flip Shatner the finger because his middle digit had been shot off on D-Day, but he metaphorically gave him it at every opportunity. At fan conventions, Shatner would be backstage bemoaning the obsessiveness of the Trekkies/Trekkers, while Jimmy would be out on stage cheerfully doing shtick at Shatner's expense: he'd attempt to beam Kirk up but only his toupee would materialize, etc. Doohan aged better than most of the crew: in the Nineties, avuncular, moustachioed, burly and bleary, he looked more like a Scotty than he had in the Sixties. Unlike many of his colleagues, he was at ease with the very precise niche celebrity *Star Trek* had brought him. It was a life, though not as he'd once known it.

Conceived in Ireland and born in Vancouver, Doohan spent his childhood in Sarnia, Ontario, where his father was a dentist and veterinarian, and an abusive drunk. After high school, Jimmy enlisted in the Royal Canadian Artillery and on D-Day scrambled ashore Juno Beach. He took eight bullets that day – four in the leg, three in the hand which cost him his finger, and one in the chest where it was stopped by a silver cigarette case – after which he spent the rest of the war with the Royal Canadian Air Force. As a result of D-Day, they had to get a body double in for finger close-ups in *Star Trek*, but then again it was a Scots officer who first gave him prolonged exposure to the accent that would make his fortune.

So an Irishman who fought with the Canadians against the Germans became a Scotsman who fought with the Americans against the Klingons. Doohan helped invent the Klingon language and he got more credit for it than most kilted purists were willing to give him for

299

his Scottyisms – "Have a bonny trip!", "That'll put the haggis in the fire" and other innovations yet to pass the lips of any pure-blooded haggis-eater. But the obvious criticism of *Star Trek* is that its intergalactic lingo was *too* unchanged: in the episode in which Scotty makes his debut, another crew member lies in the sick bay and complains that Kirk's making him read all this "longhair" stuff. It seemed unlikely even then that "longhair" would survive the centuries as a synonym for "intellectual" and Scotty's innovative neologisms have at least the merit of being potentially spoken in the distant future.

Come to think of it, they're being spoken now. Last year a fellow in Florida sent me an e-mail about Iran's nuclear program with the subject header "That'll put the haggis in the fire." Indeed, as the years went by, James Montgomery Doohan's fake Scots engineer became more real than most Scots and most engineers could ever hope to be. Awarded an honorary doctorate by the Milwaukee School of Engineering, he was amazed to discover that in a poll of the students many claimed to have been drawn to the field by Scotty's TV adventures.

Meanwhile, in memory of Doohan, West Lothian Council wants to put up a plaque in Scotty's hometown of Linlithgow – the first time a memorial to someone's birthplace has been put up 217 years before he was born. If, indeed, he was born in Linlithgow. Aberdeen councilor Pamela MacDonald claims he was born in her town, on Constitution Street, and Elgin councilor Keith Sands and Lesley Hinds, Lord Provost of Edinburgh, have staked claims on behalf of their own municipalities. While Doohan's ashes are to be fired into space and scattered among the stars, poor Scotty remains unbeamed and ensnared by the surly bonds of earthbound jurisdictions.

A beamer by nature as well as by trade, James Doohan was an easygoing working thesp content to be known as the all-time great beam-movie actor. There's a "Star Trek" convention somewhere or other every weekend, which means we'll be hearing "Beam me up, Scotty" on earth for some decades yet. And as radio waves go on eternally bouncing around in space, hither and yon, right now in some distant galaxy some 1967 crew member is demanding "Mr Scott" (Captain Kirk's preferred formulation) beam him up, to the bemusement of any aliens in earshot. It's just a phrase, no author crafted it, but it growed like Topsy and the man to whom it's addressed will be beaming forever in reruns and among the stars: Play it again, Scotty.

The Atlantic Monthly

Truth and consequences

HIS HOLINESS POPE JOHN PAUL II
MAY 18TH 1920 ~ APRIL 2ND 2005

"HOW MANY DIVISIONS has the Pope?" sneered Stalin of Pius XII. Uncle Joe's successors lived long enough to find out. John Paul II's divisions were the Poles who filled the streets to cheer him on his return as pontiff to his homeland in the summer of 1979, and the brave men who founded the Solidarity union 18 months later, and began the chain of events that within a decade swept the Communists from power in Central and Eastern Europe and finally Mother Russia itself. One day we will know the precise combination of Bulgarian Secret Service, East German Stasi and Soviet KGB that lay behind the 1981 assassination attempt on the Holy Father. But you can see why they'd be willing to do it. By then the sclerotic Warsaw Pact understood just how many divisions this Pope had.

Twenty-six years ago, one young physics student summed up the hopes he and his compatriots had invested in that Papal visit in this simple declaration: "What I want to do is to live without being a liar." The Soviet Union and its vassals were an empire of lies, and, while you can mitigate (as many Poles and Russians did) the gulf between the official version and grim reality with bleak jokes, living an epic lie day in day out is corrosive of human dignity. That Polish physics student had identified instinctively what would be the great over-arching theme of John Paul II's papacy: to quote the title of his later encyclical, *Veritatis Splendor* – the splendor of truth.

Der Spiegel this week published a selection from the creepy suck-up letters Gerhard Schröder sent to the East German totalitarian leadership when he was a West German pol on the make back in the Eighties. As he wrote to Erich Honecker's deputy Egon Krenz, "I will certainly need the endurance you have wished me in this busy election year. But you will certainly also need great strength and good health for your People's Chamber election." The only difference being that on one side of the border the election result was not in doubt.

When a free man enjoying the blessings of a free society promotes an equivalence between real democracy and a sham, he's colluding in the great lie being perpetrated by the prison state. Too many western politicians of a generation ago – Schmidt, Mitterand, Trudeau – failed to see what John Paul saw so clearly. It requires tremendous will to cling to the splendor of truth when the default mode of the era is to blur and evade. And, when it came to *veritatis splendor* in the western world, the Pope had a tougher sell. If I were pontiff – and no, don't worry, I'm not planning a mid-life career change – but, if I were, I'd be a little irked at the secular media's inability to discuss religion except through the prism of its moral relativism. In an hilarious self-parody of the progressivist cocoon, on Saturday afternoon the *New York Times* website posted its obituary of John Paul II as follows:

> *Even as his own voice faded away, his views on the sanctity of all human life echoed unambiguously among Catholics and Christian evangelicals in the United States on issues from abortion to the end of life.*

NEED SOME QUOTE FROM SUPPORTER

> *John Paul II's admirers were as passionate as his detractors, for whom his long illness served as a symbol for what they said was a decrepit, tradition-bound papacy in need of rejuvenation and a bolder connection with modern life.*
>
> *"The situation in the Catholic church is serious," Hans Kung, the eminent Swiss theologian, who was barred from teaching in Catholic schools because of his liberal views...*

Etc, etc, etc, detracting away all the way to the foot of the page. Given that the press had been dying for John Paul to die for days, to the point where many papers were running the Pope's-life-in-pictures specials while he was still alive, you'd think by the weekend the *Times* would have had the basics covered. But no. The pontiff's many "detractors" were all lined up and ready to go, but, despite over a billion Catholics in the world and millions of evangelical Protestants throughout America who also admire him, the paper somehow failed to notice till the last minute that they'd overlooked something - "NEED SOME QUOTE FROM SUPPORTER". That's as memorable a line as *The New York Times* will publish this year: they should nominate it for a Pulitzer. (Since they probably won't, the eagle-eyed chaps at the Powerline website who spotted it have preserved it for posterity.)

As for the "passion" of the Holy Father's "detractors", that had the soothing drone of *bien pensant* autopilot:

> *Among liberal Catholics, he was criticized for his strong opposition to abortion, homosexuality and contraception...*

Shocking: a Pope who's opposed to abortion, homosexuality and contraception; what's the world coming to? *The Guardian's* assertion that Karol Wojtyla was "a doctrinaire, authoritarian pontiff" at least suggests the inflexible authoritarian derived his inflexibility from some ancient operating manual – he was doctrinaire about his doctrine, dogmatic about his dogma – unlike the *Times* and *The Washington Post*, which came close to implying that John Paul II had taken against abortion and gay marriage off the top of his head, principally to irk "liberal Catholics". But, either way, the assumption is always that there's some middle ground a less "doctrinaire" pope might have staked out: he might have supported abortion in the first trimester, say, or reciprocal partner benefits for gays in committed relationships.

The root of the Pope's thinking – that there are eternal truths no-one can change even if he wanted to – is completely incomprehensible to the progressivist mindset. There are no absolute truths, everything's in play, and by "consensus" all we're really arguing is the rate of concession to the inevitable: abortion's here to stay, gay marriage will be here any day now – it's all gonna happen anyway, man, so why be the last squaresville daddy-o on the block? We live in a present-tense culture where novelty is its own virtue: *The Guardian*, for example, has already been touting the Nigerian Francis Arinze as "candidate for first black pope". This would be news to Pope St Victor, an African and pontiff from 189 to 199 AD. Among his legacies: the celebration of Easter on a Sunday.

That's not what *The Guardian* had in mind, of course: they meant "the first black pope since the death of Elvis" – or however far back our societal memory now goes. Yet, if you hold an office first held by St Peter, you can say "been there, done that" about pretty much everything *The Guardian* throws your way. If your papacy is founded on *veritatis splendor*, all you can do when you seek consensus between truth and lies is tarnish that splendor. But to the modern secular sensibility truth has no splendor: certainly there is no eternal truth; instead, it's eternally up for grabs. Once upon a time we weren't cool about abortion: now we are. Soon we'll be cool about gay marriage. And a year or two down the line we'll be cool about something else that's currently verboten.

When Governor Jim McGreevey announced last year he was stepping down, he told the people of New Jersey: "My truth is that I am a gay American." That's a very contemporary formulation: "my" truth. To John Paul II, there was only "the" truth. To the moral relativists, everyone's entitled to his own – or, as the Governor continued, "one has to look deeply into the mirror of one's soul and decide one's unique truth in the world." That sappy narcissism is what the *New York Times* boilerplate boils down to: "abortion, homosexuality and contraception" is an alternative Holy Trinity for the church of the self. Whatever one feels about any of those topics, they seem a bizarre prism through which to judge the most consequential Pope of the modern era, a man who unlike Pius XII was not swept along by the times but instead shaped them decisively. Given that "abortion, homosexuality and contraception" boil down to the prioritizing of sex as self-expression over everything else in the world, even as a criticism of Karol Wojtyla's papacy the charge is shriveled and reductive, reflecting mostly the parochialism of western secularism.

When the Holy Father created new cardinals in 2003, he held one name back, keeping it secret or *in pectore* – "in the heart", the words used for a cardinal in a state where the church is persecuted. Which country is it? Some say China, the great growth area for Christianity. Think of that: a Chinese cardinal providing one of the 118 votes for John Paul's successor. Among liberal "Catholics" in Manhattan and Boston, the pontiff may be a reactionary misogynist homophobe condom-banner but, beyond those stunted horizons, he was a man fully engaged with the modern world and shrewder at reconciling it with the splendor of the eternal truth than most politicians. Western liberals claim the Pope's condom hang-ups have had tragic consequences in Aids-riddled Africa. The Dark Continent gets darker every year: millions are dying, male life expectancy is collapsing, and such civil infrastructure as there is seems likely to follow. But the most effective weapon against the disease has not been the Aids lobby's 20-year promotion of condom culture in Africa but Uganda's campaign to change behaviour and to emphasise abstinence and fidelity – ie, the Pope's position. You don't have to be a Catholic or a "homophobe" to think that the spread of Aids is telling us something basic – that nature is not sympathetic to sexual promiscuity. If it weren't Aids, it would be something else, as it has been for most of human history. What should be the Christian response? To accept that we're merely the captives of our appetites, like a dog in heat? Or to ask us to rise to the rank God gave us – "a little lower than the angels" but above "the beasts of the field"? In *The Gospel Of Life*, the Pope wrote:

> *Sexuality too is depersonalized and exploited: …it increasingly becomes the occasion and instrument for self-assertion and the selfish satisfaction of personal desires and instincts. Thus the original import of human sexuality is distorted and falsified, and the two meanings, unitive and procreative, inherent in the very nature of the conjugal act, are artificially separated…*

Had the Pope signed on to condom distribution in Africa, he would have done nothing to reduce the spread of Aids, but he would have done a lot to advance the further artificial separation of sex, in Africa and beyond. Indeed, if you look at *The New York Times*' list of complaints against the Pope they all boil down to what he called sex as self-assertion.

Thoughtful atheists ought to be able to recognize that, whatever one's tastes in these areas, the Pope is on to something – that abortion et al, in separating the "two meanings" of sex and leaving us free to indulge in one while ignoring the other, have severed us almost entirely and possibly irreparably from traditional impulses, like societal survival.

Karol Wojtyla was the third longest-serving pontiff of all time, after Pius IX, Pope from 1846 to 1878, and the first Pope, St Peter, whose papacy lasted from AD 30 to the mid-60s. When you hold an office held by St Peter, you're not operating on media time. If the progressivists' assumption is that gay marriage, like abortion, is inevitable so the Pope might as well sign on, why bother with religion at all? The difference between the modern west's Church of the Self and John Paul's church is that the latter believes in the purpose of life. The Church of the Flavoured Condom, by contrast, believes that man is no more than the accumulation of his appetites, and so you might as well license them. Given what Aids has done to African mortality rates and what abortion has done to European demographics, John Paul II's eternal truths look a lot more rational than those of the hyperrationalists at *The New York Times*. John Paul II championed the "splendor of truth" not because he was rigid and inflexible, but because he understood the alternative was a dead end in every sense. To Karol Wojtyla, truth was not just splendid but immutable: he proved his point in the struggle against Communism; one day the west will recognize that he got it right closer to home, too.

The Irish Times/The Daily Telegraph

Twentieth-century Darwin

FRANCIS CRICK

JUNE 8TH 1916 ~ JULY 28TH 2004

FRANCIS CRICK is dead and gone. He has certainly not "passed on" - and, if he has, he'll be extremely annoyed about it. As a 12-year old English schoolboy, he decided he was an atheist, and for much of the rest of his life worked hard to disprove the existence of the soul.

In between, he "discovered the secret of life", as he crowed to the barmaids and regulars at the Eagle, his Cambridge pub, on a triumphant night in 1953. The opening sentence of his paper, written with his colleague Jim Watson, for *Nature* on April 25th that year put it more modestly:

We wish to suggest a structure for the salt of deoxyribose nucleic acid.

That's DNA to you and me. And it's thanks to Crick and Watson that we know the acronym and that it's passed into the language as the contemporary shorthand for our core identity. Your career choice? "She says being a part of academia seemed to be hard-wired into her DNA because her father was a professor at the University of Virginia." (*The Chicago Tribune*) Socio-economic inequality? "Income distribution appears to be hard-wired into the DNA of a nation." (*The Washington Post*) New trends in rock video? "Staying cool is hard-wired into the DNA of MTV." (*The Los Angeles Times*)

Francis Crick was the most important biologist of the 20th century. Like Darwin, he changed the way we think of ourselves. First, with Watson, he came up with one of the few scientific blueprints known to the general public – the double-helix structure of DNA (though he left it to Mrs Crick, usually a painter of nudes, to create the model). Later, with Sydney Brenner, he unraveled the universal genetic code. Today, Crick's legacy includes all the thorniest questions of our time - genetic fingerprinting, stem-cell research, pre-screening for hereditary diseases, the "gay gene" and all the other "genes of the week"... In Britain, they're arguing about a national DNA database; on the Continent, anti-globalists are protesting genetically modified crops; in America, it was traces of, um, DNA on Monica's blue dress that obliged Bill Clinton to change his story. If you're really determined, you can still just about ignore DNA – the OJ jury did – but, increasingly, it's the currency of the age. Crick called his home in Cambridge the Golden Helix, and it truly was golden – not so much for him personally but for the biotechnology industry, something of a contradiction in terms half-a-century ago but now a 30-bil-a-year bonanza.

"We were lucky with DNA," he said. "Like America, it was just waiting to be discovered." But Crick was an unlikely Columbus. The son of a boot factory owner, he grew up in the English Midlands, dabbling in the usual scientific experiments of small boys – blowing up bottles, etc – but never really progressing beyond. Indeed, as a scientist, he wasn't one for conducting experiments. What he did was think, and even then it took him a while to think out what he ought to be thinking about. His studies were interrupted by the war, which he spent developing mines at the British Admiralty's research laboratory. Afterwards, already 30 and at a loose end, he mulled over what he wanted to do and decided his main interests were the "big picture" questions, the ones arising from his rejection of God, the ones that seemed beyond the power of science. Crick reckoned that the "mystery of life" could be easily understood if you just cleared away all the mysticism we've chosen to surround it with.

That's the difference between Darwin and Crick. Evolution, whatever offence it gives, by definition emphasizes how far man has come from his tree-swinging forebears. DNA, by contrast, seems reductive. Man and chimp share 98.5 per cent of their genetic code, which would be no surprise to Darwin. But we also share 75 per cent of our genetic make-up with the pumpkin. The pumpkin is just a big ridged orange lump lying on the ground all day, like a fat retiree on the beach in Florida. But other than that he has no discernible human characteristics until your kid carves them into him.

Yet the point of DNA is not just to prove that the pumpkin is our kin but to pump him for useful information. According to Monise Durrani, a BBC science correspondent, the genetic blueprint of the humble earthworm is proving useful in the study of Alzheimer's. Do worms get Alzheimer's? And, if they do, what difference does it make? As Ms Durrani says, "Although we like to think we are special, our genes bring us down to Earth... We all evolved from the same soup of chemicals." It turns out there *is* a fly in my soup, and a chimp and a worm and a pumpkin.

Having found "the secret of life", what do you do for an encore? Crick disliked celebrity, and had a standard reply card printed to fend off his fellow man: "Dr. Crick thanks you for your letter but regrets that he is unable to accept your kind invitation to..." There then followed a checklist of options with a tick by the relevant item: send an autograph, provide a photograph, appear on your radio or TV show, cure your disease, etc. This is a view of man as 75 per cent pumpkin but capable of crude, predictable, repetitive patterns of imposition on more advanced forms of life. Dr Crick also turned down automatically honorary degrees and disdained the feudal honors offered by the British state. Presumably the hyper-rationalist in him consigned monarchical mumbo-jumbo to the same trash can of history as religion, though he eventually relented and accepted an invitation by the Queen to join her most elite Order of Merit. Religion he never let up on. The university at which he practiced his science is filled with ancient college chapels, whose presence so irked Crick that, when the new Churchill College invited him to become a Fellow, he agreed to do so only on condition that no chapel was built on the grounds. In 1963, when a benefactor offered to fund a chapel and Crick's fellow Fellows voted to accept the money, he refused to accept the argument that many at the college would appreciate a place of worship and that those who didn't were not obliged to enter it. He offered to fund a brothel on the same basis, and, when that was rejected, he resigned.

His militant atheism was good-humored but fierce, and it drove him away from molecular biology. As the key to the mystery of life, DNA seems a small answer to the big picture, so Crick pushed on, advancing the theory of "Directed Panspermia", which is not a Clinton DNA joke but his and his colleague Leslie Orgel's explanation for how life began. Concerned by the narrow time frame – to those of a non-creationist bent - between the cooling of the earth and the rapid emergence of the planet's first life forms, Crick determined to provide another explanation for the origin of life. As he put it, bouncing along a tenuous chain of probabilities, "The first self-replicating system is believed to have arisen spontaneously in the 'soup,' the weak solution of organic chemicals formed in the oceans, seas, and lakes by the action of sunlight and electric storms. Exactly how it started we do not know...

> The universe began much earlier. Its exact age is uncertain but a figure of 10 to 15 billion years is not too far out...
>
> Although we do not know for certain, we suspect that there are in the galaxy many stars with planets suitable for life...
>
> Could life have first started much earlier on the planet of some distant star, perhaps eight to 10 billion years ago? If so, a higher civilization, similar to ours, might have developed from it at about the time that the Earth was formed... Would they have had the urge and the technology to spread life through the wastes of space and seed these sterile planets, including our own?..
>
> For such a job, bacteria are ideal. Since they are small, many of them can be sent. They can be stored almost indefinitely at

very low temperatures, and the chances are they would multiply easily in the 'soup' of the primitive ocean...

"We do not know... uncertain... not too far out... we do not know for certain... we suspect... chances are..." And thus the Nobel prize winner embraces the theory that space aliens sent rocketships to seed the earth. The man of science who confidently dismissed God at Mill Hill School half a century earlier appears not to have noticed that he'd merely substituted for his culturally inherited monotheism a weary variant on Greco-Roman-Norse pantheism – the gods in the skies who fertilize the earth and then retreat to the heavens beyond our reach. To be sure, he leaves them as anonymous aliens showering seed rather than Zeus adopting the form of a swan, but nevertheless Dr Crick's hyper-rationalism took 50 years to lead him round to embracing a belief in a celestial creator of human life, indeed a *deus ex machina*.

He didn't see it that way, of course. His last major work, *The Astonishing Hypothesis*, was a full-scale assault on human feeling. "The Astonishing Hypothesis," trumpeted Crick, "is that 'You,' your joys and your sorrows, your memories and your ambitions, your sense of personal identity and free will, are in fact no more than the behavior of a vast assembly of nerve cells and their associated molecules. As Lewis Carroll's Alice might have phrased it: 'You're nothing but a pack of neurons.'"

It's not a new idea. Round about the time Dr Crick was working on his double-helix, Cole Porter wrote a song for a surly Soviet lass fending off the attentions of an amorous American:

> *When the electromagnetic of the he-male*
> *Meets the electromagnetic of the female*
> *If right away she should say this is* the *male*
> *It's A Chemical Reaction, That's All.*

Of course, in the film of *Silk Stockings*, Cyd Charisse eventually succumbs to Fred Astaire and comes to understand her thesis is not the final word. Even if the Astonishing Hypothesis – that there's no "You", no thoughts, no feelings, no falling in love, no free will - is true, it's so all-encompassing as to be useless except to the most sinister eugenicists. And in the end Francis Crick's own life seems to disprove it: He was never a dry or pompous scientist, he liked jokes and costume parties, he was an undistinguished man pushing 40 with one great obsession. Perhaps the combination of human quirks and sparks that drove him to chase his double-helix are merely a chemical formula no different in principle from that which determines variations in the pumpkin patch. But, even if Francis Crick is 75 per cent the same as a pumpkin, the degree of difference between him and even the savviest Hubbard squash suggests that as a unit of measurement it doesn't quite suffice.

It is too late to retreat now. Francis Crick set us on the path to a biotechnological era that may yet be only an intermediate stage to a post-human future. But, just as a joke that's explained is no longer funny, so in his final astonishing hypothesis Dr Crick eventually arrived at the logical end: you can only unmask the mystery of humanity by denying our humanity.

The Atlantic Monthly

RECESSIONAL

One for the road

BILL MILLER
FEBRUARY 3RD 1915 ~ JULY 11TH 2006

FRANK SINATRA called himself a "saloon singer", because that's where he used to sing, way back when in Jersey juke joints and road houses. Not for long. He was too good, even then. But for a while, if you headed up to the Rustic Cabin on Route 9W in the Garden State, they had this pianist pushing a little half-piano from table to table and the waiter would sing with him and they had a tip jar on the lid and you couldn't help noticing the kid sang awful good for a waiter, and pretty soon the singing was earning him, as he figured it, "about 15 clams a week".

Thirty, 40, 50 years later, week in, week out, the same singing waiter with full supporting orchestra was barreling through a set at some grim rock stadium on the edge of a strip mall in some nondescript suburb. And, midway through, the lights would dim and Frank Sinatra would announce that he would now sing a "saloon song" and proceed to shrink whichever sterile aircraft hangar he'd been booked into down to the size of those poky smoky New Jersey saloons of his youth. There were the old props – the tumbler, the cigarette – and the scene-setting grew ever more ornate over the years, expanding into an almighty pile-up of retro hipsterisms as Frank prepared us for the tale of some emblematic long-lost loser whose "chick split, flew the coop, cleaned out his stash and left him cryin' into a gallon of Muscatel". And under the spiel a tinkly tipsy barroom piano intro would begin, and Sinatra would invite us to "assume the position of the bartender" and listen to the old, old story:

> *It's quarter to three*
> *There's no-one in the place*

Except you and me
So set 'em up, Joe
I got a little story
You oughtta know...

We all knew the story. But the strange thing is, through the Sixties, Seventies, Eighties and into the Nineties, no matter how flip the speaking part got, by the time Frank started to sing that first line the semi-parodic grooviness was all gone, and you were in for the most intense four minutes in the show, intimate and universal, bleak but weirdly exhilarating. The man playing the piano was Bill Miller, and that intro to "One For My Baby (And One More For The Road)" is his invention. It's a marvelous thing that works at so many levels: it evokes the tinny sound of a saloon piano, and it meanders a little woozily like a fellow who's drunk a skinful heading back to the bar for one more, and it also has a kind of bleak weary acceptance about it, as if both storyteller and barman know that in the end the one buttonholing the other will change nothing; it's self-aware about its self-pity, it understands that, in everything that matters, it's already past closing time. And it's also an acting performance, in that Miller is playing not just the piano accompaniment to the song but also the role of the barroom pianist in the story the singer's telling. Miller matches the paradox of the vocal performance with one of his own: just as Sinatra gives what Robert Cushman called "a perfectly controlled performance of a man who's falling apart", so the pianist under the cover of a rinky-dink saloon piano provides an amazing harmonic intensity.

That's a hell of a lot to cram into a few bars. I once tried to say all the above to Bill Miller, and he said:

Yeah.

Oh, well. That's what he said back in 1951 when he was playing at the Desert Inn in Vegas and Sinatra came by to ask if he'd like to work with him:

318

Yeah.

He stayed for the best part of half a century, and played Sinatra songs to the very end, dying in Montreal, after a hip operation and a heart attack while in town for a month of shows with Frank Sinatra Jr. He was 91, and had to be helped from his wheelchair to the piano stool. But the fingers still worked. A few months after Sinatra's death in 1998, Miller returned to the stage for a concert by Frank Jr. The lights were dimmed, the pianist took his seat in the dark, unannounced, and began to play "One For My Baby". "The audience let out a gasp," remembered Junior. "They were all Sinatra fans and they recognized Bill immediately."

Miller wasn't exactly unsung. *Au contraire*, on stage, seven-eighths into "Mack The Knife", Frank liked to take a chorus to introduce the musicians:

> *We got Bill Miller playin' the piano*
> *And this great big band bringin' up the rear*
> *All these bad cats in this band now*
> *Make the greatest sounds you ever gonna hear...*

But that was pretty much it in the way of public acclaim, aside from on-stage references to his ghostly pallor ("Our pianist is a man we call Suntan Charlie..."). Yet Miller and a handful of other guys who made up the Sinatra rhythm section up there with him night after night in Vegas and Atlantic City and London and Rome and Rio and Tokyo belong to a very exclusive club. Bill outlasted Ava and Marilyn and Mia and the other dames, and Dino and Sammy and most of the pallies, too. And the musicians got the best snaps for the scrapbook – not the tuxedoed bonhomie and Friars' Club kibitzing you see in the pics of Frank and Bob Hope and John Wayne, not the pasta joint mug shots of Frank and lesser buddies, but Frank at work, *with you!* There's a great photo of Miller half a century ago, doodling at the keyboard, tie loosened, bleary eyed, cigarette hanging from his lower lip, and Frank leaning on the piano, tanned and open shirted, hand in pocket, looking over the sheet music - and beaming with delight. Miller's running through a number for him, and Sinatra's liking what he hears, and maybe it's going to be the next "I Get A Kick Out Of You" or "You Make Me Feel So Young". In other words, Miller is in the act of helping make Sinatra Sinatra – which is, in the end, the only reason we're remotely interested in what broads he's nailing.

He was born across the water from Frank, in Brooklyn a few months earlier. At 16, he was billing himself as "Bill Miller, The Ace Of Jazz". At 18, he was pianist for Larry Funk And His Band Of A Thousand Melodies, and then came Red Norvo and Charlie Barnet. Heading home from a gig at the 1940 World's Fair, he and the gal he was dating had the car radio on. "Hey, listen," she said. "Doesn't that sound good? That's Dick Haymes." Miller said, "No, it's not Dick Haymes. Dick Haymes doesn't sing that good." He had to wait till the end, and the disc-jockey's announcement: "All Or Nothing At All" by Harry James and his orchestra, vocal refrain by Frank Sinatra.

A decade later, Frank had had it all and was on his way back down to nothing. Miller was the man at the keyboard as Sinatra rebuilt his career. I'm ashamed to say that the first time I was in a room with him and I asked who he was and someone said, "Frank's accompanist, Bill Miller", I couldn't have been less impressed. I mean, when you've got Sinatra singing, how hard can it be to play along? I came to understand that, in fact, it makes all the difference. Miller was famous for the saloon songs – "One For My Baby", "Drinking Again", "Empty Tables", a trio of Johnny Mercer three-in-the-morning numbers. Or check out the beautiful ethereal celesta on "If I Had You". It was recorded in June 1962 at the CTS studio in Bayswater, London, and the only reason Miller was playing the celesta was because the piano was a dud. "Somebody forgot to tune the goddamn thing," said Miller, and, while they were all standing around wondering if the session was a washout, Frank said, "Hey, is there a celesta anywhere?" If you listen to the track now, it's hard to imagine it with anything else.

But Miller was also indispensable to the other side of the singer – the swingin' Sinatra you hear on his up-tempo "Way You Look Tonight". The bassist Chuck Berghoffer once asked him, "How do you swing so hard? What do you think about?" "I just get a cuckoo rhythm section," said Frank, "and stay out of the way."

Not exactly. He rode on top of it, like a surfer coming in on the perfect wave. Miller was always the heart of that side of Frank, the rhythmic piano intros that kick-start "The Lady Is A Tramp", or "Lonesome Road", or even "Ol' MacDonald". Yes, that "Ol' MacDonald", the nursery rhyme:

> *Ol' MacDonald had a farm*
> *Ee-i-ee-i-o*
> *And on that farm he had a chick...*

You can pretty much guess how things go from there. Plenty of Sinatra scholars loathe that record: Why would a guy who can sing Rodgers and Hart record "Ol' MacDonald"? As the detractors see it, because he can; it's a power trip, a way of saying "Screw you" to the world. Say what you like about gangsta rap, but even Snoop Dogg isn't arrogant enough to give us "Ol' MacDonald had a farm/And on that farm he had a ho..." But I love that "Ol' MacDonald". It builds wonderfully, and Alan and Marilyn Bergman's lyrics, despite boxing themselves into the nursery rhyme's with-a-little-this-here-and-a-little-this-there structure manage to top each verse with the next:

> *...with a promenade here and a promenade there*
> *At a square dance, boy, this chick was no square...*

That said, with the best will in the world, "Ol' MacDonald" isn't exactly an interesting tune, and that's where Miller comes in. His piano helps make it such a wild ride. He's like the mechanical hare at the greyhound track, if a mechanical hare could swing: he sets off, and Sinatra takes off, too.

In 1964, the pianist's home in Burbank was washed away in a mudslide. The Millers were swept away with it: their teenage daughter Meredith made it to the top of a hill, and Bill was rescued hanging from a car, but his wife Aimee was only found the following night. Sinatra identified the body and then went to see Miller in hospital. "If it's any consolation," said Frank, "there wasn't a mark on her."

As the laconic Miller told friends: "It wasn't any consolation."

But Frank paid the medical expenses and got Bill a new place. And, when they inevitably bust up in the late Seventies, Sinatra hired other pianists but stayed away from "One For My Baby" altogether. Anyone can conduct "My Way" (as Miller did on the hit recording) but Sinatra understood that the truly definitive Sinatra song depended on the presence of another man. In 1985 Miller returned for "One For My Baby" and one more decade for the road.

The song had been around 15 years before Bill and Frank claimed it definitively in the late Fifties. But, until their version, it had never really broken out to top-rank standard. Fred Astaire introduced it in *The Sky's The Limit* , a sluggish 1943 movie in which the star plays a Flying Tigers air ace in love with Joan Leslie. Things aren't going well by the time he sings "Baby", in the inevitable barroom setting but with various maudlin flashbacks to happier times. And then, when the bartender refuses to top up the glass and walks out of the room with the bottle, Astaire goes into one of the most frenzied tap dances of his career: no grace, no wit, no playfulness, just driven energy, like a rage you're trying to purge. And the bartender re-enters, ready to head home, and Astaire shrugs off the frenzied dance with a casual, "Well, that's how it goes...

And, Joe, I know you're getting anxious to close...

And Astaire wants him to know he's fine for the road:

> *Don't let it be said*
> *Little Fred-*
> *-die can't carry his load...*

It's not the greatest Astaire routine, but it's the best thing in the picture. So naturally a theater owner in San Francisco wanted the scene cut because such "wanton description" of alcoholic imbibing during wartime was "extremely distasteful if not unpatriotic".

Oh, well. Harold Arlen's tune is what he called one of his tapeworms – not 32 bars, but 58: it has a kind of tipsily meandering unhurried quality just right for the situation. "One For My Baby" is one of those songs everybody thinks is all about the words. And it is a great lyric, with a lovely conversational opening: "It's quarter to three…" But it sounds great because Arlen's deceptively simple piano and the intense chromatic writing show off the words to their very best.

The text is Johnny Mercer, of course. But did you know he wrote it about Judy Garland? They'd been having one of those affairs that are born doomed. And, just as Mercer had finally decided to ask his wife Ginger for a divorce, Walter Winchell came on the radio and announced that Judy had eloped to Vegas with the composer and bandleader David Rose. You don't need to know that to appreciate the song – the point of popular music is, as Goethe said, to take the specific and make it universal. But Mercer's affair colors his approach to the lyric. Garland's rising star would have been badly dented by revelations of an affair with an older married man, so Mercer was unable to talk about his great lost love - even in a song about getting a load off your chest. Instead, he wrote a song about talking about a lost love that never does actually talk about it:

So set 'em up, Joe
I got a little story
You oughtta know…

But the song never does tell us the "little story". That's its genius. It's all images – a suggestion of emotional cataclysm rather than an attempt to explain the details:

I got the routine
Drop another nickel
In the machine
I'm feeling so bad
Won't you make the music
Dreamy and sad...

There's a really good basic rule for pop lyrics that songwriters today ignore way too often: eschew self-pity. A singer comes out and says, God, I'm feelin' miserable, my gal left me, I wanna shoot myself. Who cares? Yet Mercer took the classic self-pitier – the maudlin drunk, last barfly in the joint, head down in the beer nuts, hectoring the poor weary sap behind the counter to hear one last story before closing up - and he managed to inject some authentic feeling into it. All it needed now was the right singer.

Sinatra got to it in 1947, and it's ...okay. You can tell he likes the song, but it's like a lot of other stuff he was trying out in that period: he knows something's in there, but he hasn't found the key to the door. He knows it's a story about a guy, a vignette, a little noir drama. Axel Stordahl gives him some rinky-dink saloon piano, and Frank whistles into the distance as the number ends. But he hasn't cracked the code.

A decade later, he did. By then, he'd hooked up with Miller, and they were, musically, inseparable. For *Only The Lonely* , there were two "One For My Baby"s. On the first night, the band repaired to some little joint and asked Joe to set 'em up, and Bill and Frank stayed behind in the studio and blocked out a terrific intense take of the song. It's not just Miller's sensitivity to Sinatra's phrasing, but the strong harmonic support he provides. The next night they redid it with the Nelson Riddle arrangement – a gossamer hint of strings plus Gus Bivona's alto. That's the take they put on the album. But the solo with Miller was the version insiders talked about, and over three decades later Capitol finally released it.

ONE FOR THE ROAD

The closest relationship of Sinatra's life was not with any composer or arranger or (for Kitty Kelley fans) mob bosses or First Ladies but with the man he called "my partner at the piano". And when Bill Miller returned in the mid-Eighties, and Frank took "One For My Baby" out of the trunk, there was one last classic recording, too. The final track on Sinatra's 1993 *Duets* isn't a duet at all – or at least not a celebrity duet. For "Baby", Phil Ramone, the producer, had approached Carly Simon, which gives you some idea of how awry this project went. But Carly nixed the idea on the grounds that the song gave the impression of encouraging alcoholic beverages as a prelude to motor vehicle operation and, being at the time a spokesperson for Mothers Against Drunk Driving, she felt she couldn't be seen to endorse such a thing. For once, hallelujah for political correctness! Thanks to Miss Simon, Frank got the vocal to himself, albeit introduced by an atrocious bit of Lite FM instrumental slurping. But never mind that. Take a chisel to the CD and remove Kenny G's syrupy drooling of "All The Way" on the front of the track and then sit back as the strings recede, and Bill Miller begins his bar-room piano noodling. It's the best duet on the album – just Frank and Bill – and the latter doesn't even get a credit on the outer sleeve, just a tiny namecheck deep in the interior of the small print as "Mr Sinatra's pianist". The voice is rough, its vulnerability deliberately exposed, especially on the last line's long goodbye. But, harrowing as it is, it's a final Sinatra masterpiece. The piano dies away and the last saloon singer lays down his burden: one for us and one for that long, long road.

> *Well, that's how it goes*
> *And, Joe, I know you're getting anxious to close*
> *So thanks for the cheer*
> *I hope you didn't mind my bending your ear...*

No, we didn't. Five years later, Miller played it at Sinatra's funeral. The familiar introduction, but no voice came in, no "It's quarter to three..." In all the years Bill Miller had accompanied the familiar words, for the first time ever, there was no-one in the place except him.

ACKNOWLEDGMENTS

"All Bout U" (1996) by Lawrence Black, Cordozar Broadus, Yafeu Fula, Nathaniel Hale, Johnny Lee Jackson, Thomas Jenkins, Tupac Shakur and Bruce Washington © Black Hispanic Music/Universal Music/Yaki Kadafi

"Ambitionz Az A Ridah" (1996) by Tupac Shakur and Delmar Arnaud © Suge Publishing/Universal Music/Warner Bros Music

"Begin The Beguine" (1935) by Cole Porter © Warner Chappell Music

"Can't We Be Friends?" (1929) by Kay Swift and Paul James © Warner Chappell Music

"Danke Schoen" (1963) by Bert Kaempfert, Kurt Schwabach and Milt Gabler © Screen Gems-EMI Music

"Fly Me To The Moon" (1954) by Bart Howard © Hampshire House Publishing

"I Want To Be Happy" (1924) by Vincent Youmans and Irving Caesar © Irving Caesar Music/Warner Chappell Music

"I'm A Little Bit Fonder Of You" (1930) by Irving Caesar © Irving Caesar Music

"It's A Chemical Reaction, That's All" (1955) by Cole Porter © Warner Chappell Music

"It's Not Where You Start (It's Where You Finish)" (1973) by Cy Coleman and Dorothy Fields © Aldi Music/Notable Music

"Ol' MacDonald" (1960) by Lew Spence and Alan and Marilyn Bergman © Lew Spence Music/Threesome Music

"One For My Baby (And One More For The Road)" (1943) by Harold Arlen and Johnny Mercer © Harwin Music

"The Riviera" (1953) by Cy Coleman and Joseph McCarthy © Notable Music/Sony-ATV Tunes

"Swanee" (1919) by George Gershwin and Irving Caesar © Irving Caesar Music/New World Music

"Tea For Two" (1924) by Vincent Youmans and Irving Caesar © Irving Caesar Music/Warner Chappell Music

"Thanks For The Memory" (1938) by Ralph Rainger and Leo Robin © Paramount Music

"This Ole House" (1954) by Stuart Hamblen © Hamblen Music

"The Very Thought Of You" (1934) by Ray Noble © Quartet Music/Range Road Music

"What'd I Say" (1959) by Ray Charles © Unichappell Music

"Witchcraft" (1957) by Cy Coleman and Carolyn Leigh © Morley Music/Notable Music

"Why Must The Show Go On?" (1935) by Noel Coward © Warner Chappell Music

Cover (clockwise from top left): Bob Hope (NBC), Idi Amin (PTI), Jack Slipper, Diana Mosley (Getty), Pope John Paul II, Jack Paar, John F Kennedy Jr (AP), Vilgot Sjöman, Queen Elizabeth the Queen Mother (BBC), Stuart Hamblen, Paula Yates, Prince Rainier (AFP), Arthur Miller (AP), Diana, Princess of Wales (MGN), Strom Thurmond, Ray Charles (Dig), Rose Mary Woods (AP), Alistair Cooke (WGBH), Cy Coleman, Leopoldo Galtieri (AP), John Profumo (AP), Madame Chiang Kai-shek (Wesleyan College), Ronald Reagan, Eugene McCarthy (AP), Tupac Shakur, and Princess Margaret

AND DON'T FORGET...

Mark Steyn

From Head

To Toe

AN ANATOMICAL ANTHOLOGY

In this collection from Mark's body of work, Steyn takes a tour round some delightful parts – from the Liberian President's ears and John Kerry's hair to Al Gore's calves and the Duchess of York's toe. Plus the right to bear arms, Mrs Thatcher gets the elbow, economic muscle, John McCain's rib tickler, and all the naughty bits, including Bill Clinton's executive branch and *The New York Times*' Adam Clymer. This book is a great introduction to the broad range of Mark's writing, as he takes on US drinking habits, the Nepalese monarchy, the art of the cigarette song, conservative cool, Canada's socialized health care, Bush, Blair, Saddam, Michelle Pfeiffer's torso, Dr Christian Barnaard's heart and much more. And don't miss his great appendix!

UNITED STATES	CANADA	UNITED KINGDOM
$19.95	$29.95	£12.50

MARK STEYN RETURNS…

…in this Sunday's Chicago Sun-Times *and* Orange County Register;

…in Monday's New York Sun *and* Washington Times;

…in Tuesday's Jerusalem Post;

…in Thursday's Maclean's;

…in Saturday's Hawke's Bay Today;

…in the next National Review, Western Standard, Atlantic Monthly, Investigate *and* New Criterion;

…and at SteynOnline.com